Sex and Manners

Theory, Culture & Society

Theory, Culture & Society caters for the resurgence of interest in culture within contemporary social science and the humanities. Building on the heritage of classical social theory, the book series examines ways in which this tradition has been reshaped by a new generation of theorists. It also publishes theoretically informed analyses of everyday life, popular culture, and new intellectual movements.

EDITOR: Mike Featherstone, *Nottingham Trent University*

SERIES EDITORIAL BOARD
Roy Boyne, *University of Durham*
Mike Hepworth, *University of Aberdeen*
Scott Lash, *Goldsmiths College, University of London*
Roland Robertson, *University of Aberdeen*
Bryan S. Turner, *University of Cambridge*

THE TCS CENTRE
The *Theory, Culture & Society* book series, the journals *Theory, Culture & Society* and *Body & Society*, and related conference, seminar and postgraduate programmes operate from the TCS Centre at Nottingham Trent University. For further details of the TCS Centre's activities please contact:

Centre Administrator
The TCS Centre, Room 175
Faculty of Humanities
Nottingham Trent University
Clifton Lane, Nottingham, NG11 8NS, UK
e-mail: tcs@ntu.ac.uk
web: http://tcs.ntu.ac.uk

Recent volumes include:

Liberal Democracy 3.0
Stephen P. Turner

French Social Theory
Mike Gane

Thorsten Veblen on Culture and Society
Stjepan Mestrovic

Five Bodies: Re-figuring Relationships
John O'Neill

Sex and Manners

Female Emancipation in the West, 1890–2000

Cas Wouters

SAGE Publications
London ● Thousand Oaks ● New Delhi

First published 2004
Reprinted 2005

Published in association with Theory, Culture & Society, Nottingham Trent University

SAGE Publications Ltd
1 Oliver's Yard
55 City Road
London EC1Y 1SP

SAGE Publications Inc
2455 Teller Road
Thousand Oaks, California 91320

SAGE Publications India Pvt Ltd
B-42 Panchsheel Enclave
Post Box 4109
New Delhi – 100 017

British Library Cataloguing in Publication data

A catalogue record for this book is available from the British Library

ISBN 0 8039 8369 7

Library of Congress Control Number Available

Printed and bound in Great Britain by Athenaeum Press, Gateshead

Contents

Preface   vii

1 Introduction   1

  1.1 Perspective and Contents: An Overview   1
  1.2 On Regimes of Manners and Emotions   8
  1.3 Manners and the Modelling Function of Good
      Societies   10

2 Confined to the Drawing Room   14

3 Dancing Fury   19

4 To Pay or Be Paid For?   24
  4.1 England   25
  4.2 Germany   27
  4.3 The Netherlands   28
  4.4 The USA   30

5 Going to Work: Manners at Work   33
  5.1 The USA   34
  5.2 England   40
  5.3 Germany   43
  5.4 The Netherlands   44

6 Developments in Courting Regimes   47
  6.1 Introduction   47
  6.2 Chaperonage and the Courting Regime in England   50
  6.3 Chaperonage and the Courting Regime in Germany   57
  6.4 Chaperonage and the Courting Regime in the
      Netherlands   64
  6.5 Chaperonage in the USA   75
  6.6 Chaperonage Compared: Some National
      Differences and General Trends   83
  6.7 The American Dating Regime   85
  6.7a The Stag Line, Cutting In, Getting Stuck   95
  6.7b The Line   96

6.7c Dating, Necking and Petting in the 1930s and
early 1940s   98
6.7d Dating Codes After the Second World War   103
6.7e In and Out of Circulation   105
6.7f The Sexual Revolution in the USA   111
6.7g The 1980s and 1990s   115
6.8 Courting Regimes Compared: Some National
Differences and General Trends   119

7 The Lust- Balance of Sex and Love Since the Sexual
Revolution: Fuck Romance!   124
7.1 Introduction   124
7.2 The Sexual Revolution   126
7.3 From 'Sexual Liberation' to 'Sexual Oppression'   128
7.3a The Anti-Pornography Movement   130
7.3b What is the Price of Sex?   133
7.4 Revival of Lust   135
7.5 A Lust and Love Revival   137

8 International Comparisons, Theoretical Interpretations,
and Regularities in Processes of Emancipation and Integration 140
8.1 From a Comparative Perspective: Developments in
Europe and in the USA   140
8.2 Balancing: The Lust-Balance and the Balance
of Power, the Balance of Controls,and the We–I Balance 148
8.3 Regularities in Processes of Emancipation and
Integration   153
8.3a Lust Anxiety: Social and Sexual Fear of 'Heights'
and 'Depths'   153
8.3b Three Types: Trend-followers, Radicals and Moderates   155
8.3c Phases in Processes of Emancipation, Accommodation
and Integration   157
8.3d Intensified Tugs-of-War and Ambivalence   159

Notes   162
References   165
Manners Books   171

Name Index   177
Subject Index   181

Preface

This book is the result of a larger research project consisting of a study of changes in English, Dutch, German, and American manners books from the end of the nineteenth to the end of the twentieth century. The research design of historical and international comparison focuses on changes and differences in the codes and ideals of manners and emotion management regulating the relationships between people of different rank and different gender. This book focuses on the latter; it presents, compares and interprets national differences and changes pertaining to the relationships between women and men. Special attention is paid to changes and differences in courting and dating. From the perspective of the research project as a whole, many developments presented in this book appear to be specific examples of more general trends and overall processes. In all four countries under study, general trends in all relationships – including those between women and men – have been an informalization of manners, a diminishing social and psychic distance between people, expanding social integration and mutual identification, and an 'emancipation of emotions' implying rising demands on emotion management and self-regulation. Of course, overall processes such as rising social constraints towards self-restraints such as reflection, presence of mind, consideration, role-taking, and the ability to bear and control conflicts, allow for many differences in pace and place. The historical and international comparison in the research project and in this book focuses on these differences as well as on general trends.

My interest in manners and manners books began in the late 1960s. It originated from being impressed by the enormous changes in all kinds of manners taking place at that time, as well as by reading Norbert Elias's The Civilizing Process ([1939] 2000), for which his study of manners books provided a significant empirical basis. In the late 1980s, I expanded my study of Dutch manners books and headed for a systematic international comparative study. I started out to make myself acquainted with the manners books of the three other countries by developing an overview of the literature with the help of existing bibliographies, bringing them up to date where necessary. In the 1990s, I gathered and studied a large selection of etiquette books in several libraries, an important criterion being whether a book had gained wider recognition, that is, whether and how many times it was reprinted. From these and other books, for instance, the large numbers of manners books for sale in the main bookshops in Berlin, London and Washington at the time of my visits, I extracted whatever seemed interesting from the perspective of the general research questions. It meant being alert and open to anything that seemed typical for a country or a time, anything that would reveal something about the relationships between people of different rank (or class) and sex, and anything that would imply a change in demands on emotion management or, more generally, self-regulation. In addition, I always compared (changes in) the formal and the informal, the public and the private, in such matters as introductions, the use of personal pronouns, 'social' kissing, dancing, dating, visiting hours, etc. Besides all this, I made myself familiar with the body of literature on manners books. The earlier reports of my research project that have been used to write this book are Wouters 1987, 1995, 1998b, 1999c, 2001a, and 2001b.

In the process of getting acquainted with the manners books of the three countries other than the Netherlands, I have profited from a bibliography and a number of excerpts from nineteenth- and twentieth-century English etiquette books compiled by Stephen Mennell, who very kindly supplied me with copies. In order to find my way into the world of German manners books, the (1984) study by Horst-Volker Krumrey has been a great help. It reports changes in German etiquette books between 1870 and 1970. When my research took me to Berlin, I also benefited from discussions with him. An introduction to the history of American manners was found in a book on this subject by Arthur M. Schlesinger (1946). On the American etiquette books of the twentieth century, Deborah Robertson Hodges has published an annotated bibliography (1989). Both that book and conversations with its author have been helpful in studying the American sources. The same goes for an interview with Judith Martin, better known as Miss Manners. In order to understand the development of courting manners in the USA, I have further profited from studies such as those by Bailey (1988), Baltzell (1964), Caldwell (1999), Fass (1977), Gorer (1948), Mead (1950), Rothman (1984), and Waller (1937).

With regard to the period immediately preceding the period covered in my research, the nineteenth century, in addition to a considerable number of manners books from this century that I have studied, I have drawn on many other studies of these sources, among them the studies of English manners books by Michael Curtin (1987), Leonore Davidoff (1973), and Cecile Porter (1972), and the studies of American ones by John Kasson (1990), Karen Halttunen (1982) and Dallett Hemphill (1996, 1999).

My research project and this book owe a debt to Norbert Elias's work in many ways, but in particular for using his theoretical perspective on manners as explained in his *The Civilizing Process*. Elias presented a large number of excerpts from manners books in chronological order, thus revealing an overall directional trend in codes of manners and emotion management. By studying these sources, he uncovered evidence of long-term changes in these codes as well as in people's psychic make-up. Elias made connections between the changes in personality structure and changes in the social structure of European societies and offered explanations why this happened. With Elias, I understand changes in the code of manners and feeling to illuminate changes in relationships *between* individuals and groups (nation-states, social classes, sexes, and generations) as well as psychic processes *within* people, in how individuals manage their emotions and 'relate to themselves'. This theoretical perspective will be outlined in the introduction that follows, but it will avoid polemics. Instead, I have preferred to apply this perspective in a diachronical and systematical study of original sources from four countries over a period of more than a century. In contrast to the bulk of studies on the history of relationships between the sexes and their sexuality, Foucault's work included, this study is primarily based upon original sources and upon the work of others who use original sources. This book will provide many quotations from manners books. The authentic sound and the eloquence of these various voices in the choir of history function as empirical evidence. I have tried to orchestrate these voices according to current issues or themes, nationality, and historical sequence. As this sequence is not always indicated before each quotation, the reader is advised to keep an eye on the publication date in the reference following it.

Acknowledgements

My research project and I owe a lot to Michael Schröter, Berlin, Jonathan Fletcher and Lisa Driver-Davidson, Cambridge, and Irwin and Verda Deutscher, Washington. Not only as hosts when I came to study and collect manners books, but also as partners in discussing problems and data they have been most helpful, particularly Michael Schröter. At some stages of the writing process, I have received comments from Rineke van Daalen, Eric Dunning, Jon Fletcher, Tom Inglis, Richard Kilminster, Stephen Mennell, Jakob Pastoetter, Michael Schröter, Peter Stearns, Bram van Stolk, and Luuk Wouters. I am grateful for their support and valuable comments. My language, including my translations from German and Dutch sources, has been corrected by Eric Dunning and Stephen Mennell. Thanks a lot Stephen! Thanks a lot Eric!

Of course, my work owes a lot to the support of my intimates and friends of whom I would like to mention Truus, Julia, Roos, Sam, and Joost. And it pleases me enormously to dedicate this book to my grandson, Sam Voerman.

Cas Wouters
Amsterdam, November 2002

1

Introduction

1.1 Perspective and Contents: An Overview

This book reports on a larger comparative study of changes in American, Dutch, English and German manners books from the end of the nineteenth century to the end of the twentieth century. It focuses on changes in the codes of manners and emotions regarding the relationships between women and men, particularly on changes in courting regimes, that is, in the socially organized opportunities for and limitations on courting. From such changes in manners books as disappearing rules for chaperonage and the appearance of new rules for new situations such as public transport, public dances, dates, and the workplace, it will be shown that (and how) women's sources of power and identity have changed and expanded. At the start of the period of research, the last decade of the nineteenth century, these sources were restricted to the home and 'good society', that is, the circles of social acquaintance among people of families who belong to the centres of power, to the establishments (or their functional equivalent down the social ladder). Within the hierarchically layered networks of families that constitute good society, it was women who organized social gatherings such as dinners, visits and parties (they usually still do), thus forming the channels in which reputations are made and broken. In the twentieth century, increasingly large groups of middle-class and working-class women came to be represented in the dominant code of manners and emotions, and came to turn their attention to it. This expansion demonstrates a change in the balance of power between the sexes in favour of women. It is part of more general processes of women's emancipation and social integration.

These trends have not been restricted to the relationships between the sexes: emancipation and integration have apparently involved both the sexes and the classes, and both are characterized by similar part processes: research data show a diminishing social and psychic distance between the sexes and between the classes. Direct references to large differences in power and respect have faded from these sources as well as the more extreme forms of expressing social and psychic distance. Over the whole period covered in the research, manners in general, and manners between women and men in particular, have become more informal, more differentiated and varied for a wider and more eclectic public. An increasing variety of behavioural and emotional alternatives came to be socially accepted. This is one aspect of what I call the twentieth-century process of informalization. At the same time, as the spectrum of accepted emotional and behavioural alternatives expanded, an acceptable and respectable usage of these alternatives implied a continued increase in the demands on emotion management. A major reason is that the ways in which individuals made their selection of behavioural alternatives became increasingly important as a criterion for status attribution or ranking, for gaining respect and self-respect. Another reason is because the code of manners and emotion management demanded increasingly strict control of displays of superiority and inferiority. Therefore, informalization processes also involve rising social constraints towards such self-restraints as reflection, presence of mind, consideration, role taking, and the ability to bear and control conflicts.

Particularly in the 1960s, the process of informalization spread to increasing numbers of people to include most layers of society: 'emancipation' (of the working classes, of women, of homosexuals, etc.), 'equality', 'permissiveness' and the 'permissive society' became hot topics in public debates. The study of changes in manners books shows that, from the end of the nineteenth century onwards in all four countries under study, there has been a long-term process of informalization, proceeding in a number of consecutive short-term waves or spurts. These occurred in the *fin de siècle* (around 1900), in the 'Roaring Twenties', and in the 1960s and 1970s. Particularly in these short-term phases, the social and psychic distance between people of different social status (including the sexes) reduced significantly while their mutual identification increased. In subsequent (short-term) waves of (re)formalization, the codes of manners returned to greater formality. On the whole, however, the codes continued to allow for greater variation and to attest to a larger spectrum of socially accepted alternatives. To some extent, manners that in the preceding short-term phases of informalization had become more informal, were incorporated into the dominant code. In the twentieth century, short-term phases of informalization have been decisive in determining the direction of the process as a whole. There has been a spiral process of informalization.

The overall dynamic momentum of these directional processes derives from 'the increasing division of functions under the pressure of competition' (Elias, 2000: 433), tending to integrate growing numbers of people in expanding and increasingly dense networks of interdependence. In the period covered by my research, the twin processes of differentiation and integration of social functions have also exhibited a spiral movement. Continued differentiation of functions allowed for diminishing power inequalities and eventually for the collective emancipation of whole social groups. The latter has been characteristic of each short-term phase of informalization. In the other phase, co-ordination and integration of social functions and institutions became dominant (power inequalities stabilized or increased), which limited the emancipation opportunities of individuals and spurred accommodation, a stronger identification with the established and their codes, more open displays of distinction, and (re)formalization. Thus, the transition from one phase to the other was directly connected to the presence or absence of collective emancipation opportunities (see Wouters, 1986, forthcoming).

The changes in popular dances can serve as a visual illustration of the short-term phases of informalization and (re)formalization in a spiral movement. At the beginning of the twentieth century, the popular waltz visualized the prevalent ideal of relationships of harmonious inequality between the sexes: the man led, the woman followed, and together they created harmonious figures. Each movement on his part presupposed one on her part and vice versa. In the 1920s, the waltz came to be seen as a manifestation of an old-fashioned and more inhibited way of dancing. But, at the start of the century, the waltz still represented a break from earlier group dances such as the popular cotillion. Accordingly, as a dance for two, the waltz was a clear step in the direction of individualization. Actually, the waltz was a prelude to the individualized dancing of the 1920s. At that time, however, the waltz was scorned and new dances (among which the Charleston is best remembered) were welcomed as 'the liberation from the constraints of earlier dance figures ... in one word: one dances individually' (Viroflay-Montrecourt, 192–, II: 68). From the end of the 1920s onwards, the waltz and other such dances regained popularity and they prevailed until somewhere in the 1960s when individualized dancing again became popular and even dominant. In individualized dancing, each individual tries to adjust his or her movements to the music as well as to those of the partner. The dancers follow less of a set pattern; their movements are more informal and more varied. It is less easy to see who is leading and who is following, and it is less predictable. Different shades and gradations of leading and following are possible. If the two partners are well matched, there can very well be moments when all the separate, loose movements nevertheless seem to flow together into joint harmonious figures. This would seem to be the lofty ideal of individualized dancing. In the 1980s and 1990s, there was a revival of the older type of dance styles, and popular style dances like salsa fit the description of the waltz again. Many other dances involved sticking to the style of individualized dancing, and thus the whole twentieth–century trend in dancing runs parallel to the spiral movements in the process of informalization: more variation, enlarged choice of acceptable alternatives.

This example is one of many showing how processes of emancipation and social integration are connected to the process of individualization or, more precisely, to a spiral movement in the 'We–I balance' of individuals in the direction of the I, that is, the I-identity of most individuals took on a stronger emotive charge as compared to their we-identities (the groups people refer to as we) (Elias, 1991; Wouters, 2002). At the beginning of the twentieth century, the I-identity of individuals was highly subordinated to their we-identity, but throughout the century there was a zigzag spiral movement in the direction of emphasizing personal identity rather than group identity. At the same time, the balance of controls shifted from an emphasis on external social controls to an emphasis on self-control. In terms of the example of dancing: the fixed steps, dance-cards, dancing programmes and dance masters that used to regulate and control manners and activities in the ballroom and on the dance floor have disappeared; in dancing as elsewhere, people have come to navigate predominantly under their own steam, that is, they have come to rely on their own and each other's self-control. Dancing masters, so to speak, have become internalized.

These changes in the balance of controls, in the We–I balance and in the spiral process of informalization can be understood as manifestations of overall processes of social integration. The latter were carried by the successive ascent of larger and larger groups, their increasing status and power relative to other groups, their representation in good society and in the dominant codes and ideals of behaviour and feeling, in an overall style of emotion management, in *social habitus*. As more and more groups and strata became further emancipated and came to be represented in the various centres of power and their good societies, their members came to orientate themselves to the same codes of manners and feeling, and they came to experience all others who did so as belonging to their we-group or nation. This expanding group-feeling or widening identification somewhat weakened the boundaries of class, ethnicity, sex, age and religion, and provided a basis for a rising societal level of mutual trust or mutually expected self-restraints and, correspondingly, a declining level of anxiety, mutual suspicion and hatred.

A quite simple illustration of this ongoing process of social integration consists of the fact that, in the course of the twentieth century, the public of readers of manners books expanded. Authors of manners books in the four societies under study increasingly came to direct themselves to wider middle-class and 'respectable' working-class circles, and thus, manners books came to represent growing numbers of people from more layers of society. This expansion was more or less running in tandem with the social emancipation of these people, and also, of course, with the growth of wealth over broader social layers. The same movement characterized other advice literature: 'the articles in the early decades [of the twentieth century] are aimed at a much more affluent group of women than in later decades, and we would expect the subculture of these affluent women to be less traditional than that of average women' (Cancian and Gordon, 1988: 329). The widening of the circles of the readers of manners books implied a widening of the circles directing themselves to the dominant code, which, therefore, in the course of the century increasingly became the *national* code.

Advice on such topics as courtship, dancing, dating, engagement and marriage reveals the processes of the social emancipation of women and the accommodation of men, together with the inherent pressure to control feelings of inferiority (women) and superiority (men). In my study, I have taken feelings and gestures of superiority and inferiority into special consideration. During the whole period covered in my research, direct references to large differences in power and respect have continued to fade from manners books and other advisory texts. Discussing differences of rank and power, particularly the connected feelings of superiority and inferiority became increasingly embarrassing and taboo. In the 1980s, this stimulated the emergence of 'political correctness' (see Hinz, 2002: 163–5). The trend of increasing social controls towards restricting and avoiding expression of feelings of superiority and inferiority, whether pertaining to manners between people of different social class, age or gender, can be traced back to earlier ages. And it was continued in the twentieth century. As noted, according to Elias, the dynamic momentum of this directional process derives from 'the increasing division of functions under the pressure of competition.' It comprises 'the tendency to more equal dependence of all on all, which in the long run allows no group greater social power than others and nullifies hereditary privileges' (2000: 433). The dynamics of co-operation and competition tended to integrate increasing numbers of people in expanding and increasingly dense networks of interdependence. Elias showed how these changes in interdependency networks (or figurations) are connected to changes in the sources of power and identity, in the competition for status and a meaningful life, and also to changes in the ways in which people of different class, sex or age demanded and showed respect or feared the loss of it. By the end of the nineteenth century, social superiors and inferiors (in classes and sexes) had become interdependent to the extent that expressing social and psychic distance had to be done in relatively cautious and concealed ways.

Based on the evidence from these sources and from this (Eliasian) perspective, in this book I sketch the expansion of upper-class and middle-class women's sources of power and identity – traditionally restricted to the home and good society (or its functional equivalent in other social strata). In Chapter 2 a sketch of this confinement to the drawing room forms the point of departure from which my study jumps into the stream of history. Indeed, much of the emancipation of women in the twentieth century can be described as women increasingly succeeding in escaping from being confined to their home and good society. I have used this escape as an organizing principle in this book: Chapters 3–6 will focus upon four major ways of escaping from this confinement. One of these ways is that women had to get rid of chaperones; they had to become their own chaperone and to do their own courting (Chapter 6). They also had to gain the right to pay for themselves (Chapter 4), and the right to earn, to have a job and go to work (Chapter 5). In all these respects, transitional phases are observed and presented according to both nationality and historical sequence. At work, for instance, the transition shows changing mixtures of traditional drawing-room manners and business or office manners. The data also show national varieties, either a development in the direction of a synthesis between the two codes or one in the direction of segregation: one code for work settings and another for dates and other social occasions.

Two other ways of escaping home have been going out to take part in sport and going out to dance. From scattered remarks in manners books, it appears that sport as a way to escape parental control and to meet contemporaries of the opposite sex has been quite significant. And it did raise many eyebrows, of course, regarding female participation in 'masculine' sports (see Dunning, 1999; Elias and Dunning, 1986), but not as many as going out to dance did, at least not in manners books.[1] Public dance halls were places of great excitement because of the novelty of erotic steps to 'wild' music in addition to the lack of parental control over these places where the young could become partners and hold and touch each other for the duration of a dance. To some extent, the brief report of some of these changes in Chapter 3 may be read as a prelude to the changes that get most attention: those in chaperonage and courting. These will be dealt with in Chapter 6 entitled 'Developments in Courting Regimes'. These developments coincide with an emancipation of sexuality. This emancipation consisted of an increasing erotic and sexual presence of mind, more latitude in sexual activity, and a spread of (awareness of) the erotic and sexual aspects of relationships. This emancipation of sexuality depended upon the emancipation of women, that is, upon women becoming more equal erotic and sexual partners in relation to men: a change from being mainly sexual objects towards becoming more equal sexual subjects. The empirical question is: how did these courting regimes change? More specifically: what changes can be found in manners books (and also dating advisories) regarding the socially organized opportunities for and limitations on courting possibilities such as those for being alone together and going somewhere alone together? And what changes can be traced in the manners and ideals regarding meeting when young people are eventually enabled to find and choose a partner and make the transition from parental to marital home?

A leading focus in this study of changing courting regimes is on changes in the codes of manners (ideals and practices) regarding the relationship between the longing for sexual gratification and the longing for enduring intimacy. This balance of sex and love is conceptualized as the 'lust-balance'. Throughout the century, the traditional lust-balance of a lust-dominated sexuality for men and a complementary (romantic) love- or relationship-dominated sexuality for women has been shifting in the direction of a 'sexualization of love' and an 'eroticization of sex', provoking new and more varied answers to the lust-balance question: when or within what kinds of relationship(s) are (what kinds of) eroticism and sexuality allowed and desired? This focus is further discussed in the introductions to Chapters 6 and 7.

Until the 1920s, in all four countries under study, advice concerning courting and chaperonage shows a similar overall development. From the 1920s onwards, however, advice on dating, petting and necking only appeared in American manners books, signifying the development of the dating system in the USA. An attempt is made to describe and explain the rise and fall of the American dating system, and also of its successor, 'going steady', or rather, going 'in and out of circulation' (6.7). In this attempt to understand, interpret and explain the rise of this first western youth culture – which was restricted to the USA in contrast to the second youth culture, that of the 1960s, which was a western international one – attention is paid to the peculiarities of the dating system such as the competitiveness involved and practices such as 'rating', 'necking', 'petting', the 'line', the 'stag line', 'cutting in', and 'getting stuck'. The dating regime was the first social institution which substituted for and succeeded the previous regime of rather strict parental and family control of courting possibilities. The escape of young people from under the parental wing and the formation of a relatively autonomous courting regime of their own, were a novelty in the history of the relationship between the sexes. Its significance has provided a motive not only for focusing extensively on developments in the American courting regime, but also for concentrating on changes in financial (in)dependence. This is based on a (hypo)thesis developed during this study, namely that the relatively early rise of greater freedom for both sexes in the dating system partly explains the relatively late acceptance of the right of women to pay for themselves and also the development of a double standard of manners, one regulating the relationships between the sexes at work and another one for dating and relating outside work situations. In the 1980s and 1990s, these two codes and ideals still appeared to govern the relationships between women and men. This led to the assumption that this continuity is a social legacy of the dating regime as it developed in the 1920s and 1930s. In addition, this continuity appears to be related to the relatively lower level of social integration in the USA. The structure of this book partly derives from these hypotheses; following them demanded, for instance, presentation of the data on changes in financial (in)dependence first, before those on chaperonage and courting.

My initial comparison of national differences between, and general trends in, courting regimes (6.8) is restricted to the period up to the Sexual Revolution and focuses on developments in the USA and in the three European countries under study. Before the development of the dating system, in all four countries under study young people first had to commit themselves to an engagement before they were allowed to touch and hold and kiss. Up to World War II, trends went in the same direction of an emancipation of the younger generations and their sexuality, and both courting relationships and engagements increasingly came to be charged with sexuality. In the European countries, however, this emancipation was relatively limited. After that war, when it became socially accepted that young people in the European countries would also practise some form of 'dating' and 'going steady', trends in all four countries more or less converged.

Only since the Sexual Revolution have women themselves actively taken part in public discussions about their carnal desires and the achievement of a more satisfactory lust-balance. From then on, increasingly large groups of people have been experimenting between the extremes of desexualized love (sexual longing subordinated to the continuation of a relationship) and depersonalized sexual contact. In an attempt to capture the developments which have taken place since the Sexual Revolution more fully, in Chapter 7 I use data obtained from sociological and sexological research, and draw additional empirical evidence from sexual advice books and from a study of (changes in) the most popular Dutch feminist monthly magazine. The latter source implies (and allows for) a focus on women, the women's movement, the emancipation of women, and, by implication, on the emancipation of female sexuality. In Chapter 7 I focus mainly on general trends.

In the final chapter, I first discuss a few national differences. These largely pertain to a continued discussion of the dating regime and its vicissitudes. I further propose the hypothesis that the relative early rise of greater freedom for both sexes in the dating system is connected in explanatory ways to the relatively late acceptance of the right of women to pay for themselves and, more generally, to a relative lagging behind in the trend towards a more equal balance of power between the sexes (Section 8.1). Sections 8.2 and 8.3 are focused on theoretical connections and conclusions. The changes in courting regimes, and their prevailing lust-balances, clearly indicate how the trend towards a more equal balance of power between the sexes has been connected with changes in the balance of controls (of external social controls or constraints and self-restraint or self-control), more specifically to a rise of the socially demanded self-regulation of individuals. Section 8.2 contains a further specification of these connections between changes in the lust-balance, in the balance of power, the balance of controls, and in We–I balances. The book concludes with an attempt to interpret and explain the changes in these four balances (lust-balance, power balance, balance of controls, We–I balance) by presenting them as regularities in all processes of emancipation and social integration (8.3). Four such regularities are distinguished.

In the next two sections I will first focus on manners books as a source of empirical evidence.

1.2   On Regimes of Manners and Emotions

Changes in manners provide indications of changes in behaviour as well as in the sensibilities and norms regulating what range of behaviour is allowed, what is prescribed, and what is forbidden. Seen from a long-term perspective, some changes in this range have become formalized as good manners, others as laws. The code of manners and the judicial code supplement and reinforce each other; both provide motives and criteria for punishment and reward. Transgressions against the code of manners are punished in a variety of ways, ranging from assigning blame by means of gossip to excommunication, all involving a loss of face, respect, or status. Manners provide important criteria for social ranking.

Within the relationships in which they grow up, all individuals face demands for self-regulation according to the regimes of manners and emotions prevalent in their particular group and society. Any code of manners functions as a regime, that is, as a form of social control demanding the exercise of self-control. It functions as a regime of manners and emotions. All people develop emotional impulses and counter-impulses that are more or less attuned to these regimes. Regardless of the specific way and direction in which they develop, all their life people remain emotional beings; they can never be *not* emotional. Nor is it possible for them not to behave. What varies is the intensity and complexity of emotions as well as the degree and pattern of individual and social control over them. The latter are displayed in their manners of behaviour. This is why the study of any regime of manners can reveal a corresponding regime of emotion management or self-regulation, and why the history of manners offers empirical evidence for developments in the relations *between* individuals and groups (social classes, sexes, and generations) as well as *within* individuals, in their patterns of self-regulation, personality structure and habitus.

The history of manners in Europe and the USA until the end of the nineteenth century, which is the period preceding my period of research, can be interpreted as a long-term process of the formalizing of manners and disciplining of people. In this process the codes of manners became increasingly strict and detailed, while a particular type of self-regulation, a type of personality with a particular, rather rigid conscience formation, developed, spread, and became dominant. In contrast to the long-term process of formalizing manners and disciplining people, the twentieth century witnessed a long-term process of informalizing of manners and a controlled decontrolling of emotion management: manners became more lenient, more differentiated and varied for a wider public; an increasing variety of behavioural and emotional alternatives came to be socially accepted.

As bonds of co-operation and competition between individuals and their groups change, so do the regimes of manners and emotions, and the emotional make-up of the individuals concerned. Precisely these connections make the study of collective changes in manners and emotion management important and promising.

However, manners as a serious object of study have faced a major obstacle in strong social pressures of status competition and status fears. No matter what social definition of 'good manners' may prevail, if these 'good manners' do not appear to come 'naturally', that is, more or less automatically, the effect is ruined. Only manners springing from the inner sensitivity of 'second nature' may impress as 'natural'. Otherwise, the taint of status longings and status anxieties attach to an individual, provoking embarrassment and repulsion. Thus, status competition and inherent status fears have exerted pressure to associate the entire topic of manners with lower classes and lower 'instincts'. That is, the subject of manners was limited to spheres and circles in which good ones were taken to be absent. Throughout the period from the 1920s to the 1960s, manners were discussed mainly in the context of the behavioural 'problems' of the lower classes, of children having to learn such things as table manners, as well as of social climbers and *nouveaux riches* who were usually seen as being too loud and too conspicuous. Status fears have thus functioned as a barrier to developing the level of reflexivity needed for serious interest in the history of manners. This is why the historian Michael Curtin opens his outstanding dissertation on Victorian English manners by presenting and solving the following paradox in his short, three-page Preface. On the one hand, as the first sentence of his preface, he writes: 'Etiquette is a subject which interests only a few.' On the same first page, the statement is contradicted by a convincing argument that 'etiquette is all around us' and that it is 'important because it is so pervasive'. On the next page he offers the following explanation of the contradiction between interest and importance:

> [I]t is only in the twentieth century, after at least six hundred years of lively and public interest and concern, that the cause of good manners has gone underground. While the Victorians had already dethroned manners from the high position they reached in Georgian times, they lacked the twentieth century's shame and penchant for euphemism, when dealing with matters of etiquette. (1987)

It was shame, Curtin argues, that prevented well-mannered persons from admitting that they were following explicit rules, and which made them believe and/or pretend 'to obey some inner light or to express one's individuality or creativity' (1987: i–iii). This shame consists of status fears, that is, the fear to admit, even to oneself, that one is orientated oneself to the example of social superiors and is driven by status motives. This orientation and motivation, especially in this combination, have become taboo on account of their direct connection with feelings and displays of superiority and inferiority, to status triumphs and status defeats. Thus, these shame fears have stopped people from perceiving their own manners as the outcome of social and psychic processes.

1.3 Manners and the Modelling Function of Good Societies

The codes expressed in manners books may reveal a mixture of actual and ideal behaviour, but these ideals are *real*, that is, they are not constructed by social scientists. Manners books provide evidence of changes in the way all kinds of relationships are ideally fashioned among the established who form the good society of every society. The concept of a good society was used in nineteenth- and twentieth-century manners books and it was introduced to sociology by Norbert Elias:

> 'Good societies' are a specific type of social formation. They form everywhere as correlates of establishments which are capable of maintaining their monopoly position longer than a single generation, as circles of social acquaintance among people of families who belong to these establishments ... In Britain there is a 'high society' with a long tradition, where, until recently, the court was the pinnacle of the hierarchy and at the same time the centre-piece which integrated it ... When the integration of a country is incomplete or belated, as was the case in Germany, many local 'good societies' develop; none, however, gains undisputed precedence over all the others and becomes the authoritative source for the behavioural code or the criteria of membership for all the others. (1996: 49)

As the authors of manners books take their cue from good society and the manners that prevail there, their books reflect changes in the manners and ideals of the 'minority of the best' (Elias and Scotson, 1994). It is here, in the centres of power and their good societies, that the dominant social definition of proper ways to establish and maintain relationships is constructed and/or confirmed. Authors of manners books try to capture the sensibilities and practices that reflect these relationships, and to sell this knowledge to insecure social climbers. These authors are not backed up by any profession, in academia or anywhere else, and they neither possess nor produce any expert knowledge other than that based upon participant observation in good society. This knowledge can only become profitably exploited (published and sold) if they know how to address people who aspire to acceptance in higher social circles but are insecure about how to achieve this. Every author of a manners book has to deal somehow with the difficulty of presenting the manners that include to the excluded, the higher-class manners to lower-class people, without ever making this (too) explicit. For these books to be sold, the readers had to be lifted up, not put down.[2]

The first extensive study of the modelling function of good society was by the French sociologist Gabriel Tarde. In his *Laws of Imitation*, published in 1890, Tarde captured his view on the modelling function through the metaphor of a water tower: 'Invention can start from the lower ranks of the people, but its extension depends upon the existence of some lofty social elevation, a kind of social water-tower, whence a continuous waterfall of imitation may descend' (1903: 221).

The modelling function of a good society operates only partly as a rational individual choice because differences in manners and rank become ingrained in the personality of individuals – their habitus – as they grow up. Identification with established groups is in most cases almost automatic, particularly at times when their superior position is hardly or not contested. As there is no I-identity without a we-identity, the identification with the established is a we–identification that develops as part of any developing We–I balance of individuals. It includes the more or less automatic adoption of their definitions of 'a good life', and of what it takes to pass for 'a man of the world' or 'a woman of the world'.

Authors of manners books have also shown themselves to be well aware of the modelling function of good societies. For instance, Emily Post, author of America's most famous twentieth-century etiquette book, first published in 1922, describes and explains the process by relating it to growing prosperity: 'What was once considered the tradition of gracious living of the few has in these times of plenty rightly become the heritage of us all' (1960: xxvii).[3] Authors also state repeatedly that prosperity may be a necessary condition, but that it is not sufficient in itself. As an American author put it, 'the rich seek the culture and the courtesy of good society, because of the finish and the éclat thus given to their wealth and their homes' (Houghton et al., 1882: 16). And in nineteenth-century England it was aristocratic rather than middle-class manners that were taught in etiquette books: 'Aristocratic manners did not appear to contradict economic success but rather to crown it with a diadem of high culture' (Curtin, 1985: 413).

Good manners are usually seen as trickling down the social ladder, and if seen solely from the perspective of individual social ascent, they do indeed trickle down. In times of large-scale social mobility, however, as one or more entire social groups ascend by becoming represented in the established power centres, some of their manners will rise up the social ladder with them. On the whole, indeed, the social mixing of people tends to coincide with some mixing of their codes and ideals. In contrast to *individual* social ascent, the ascent of an entire social group involves a change in the whole shape and volume of the social water tower, to use Tarde's metaphor. It involves some form of mixing of people and their manners. The sediments of this mixing process can be seen in longer-term changes in etiquette books: the patterns of self-regulation of increasingly wider social groups are reflected in the codes of manners.

Most popular views only contain a vague and flat image of 'the socio-economic elite' or good society. They do not consider changes in the social composition of the centres of power and of good society. These centres do not only change in composition but also in representation. For example, the former Dutch Queen, Juliana, had already compared her function as a queen to that of a social worker, but her daughter, Queen Beatrix, clearly presents herself, and is to a large extent perceived, as a woman with a job. Moreover, she strongly claims her right to have a private life. Both, a job and a private life, were unthinkable in court societies, and they are clearly examples of an upward movement along class lines, for work used to be an attribute of the lower classes.

This example of Queen Beatrix also serves to illustrate a related trend in the modelling function of good societies. By presenting herself as a woman with a job, the queen also came to represent all women with a job. In a similar way, the social code of good society came to represent increasing layers of society as these layers became emancipated and were integrated into society. In order to avoid social conflict and to maintain their elevated position, the people in the centres of power and in good society increasingly had to take the socially and politically rising groups into account. As part of this, they had to show more respect for their ideals, sentiments, morals and manners. Thus the dominant code of good manners, modelled after the example of good society, has come to reflect *and* represent the power balance between all groups and strata integrated in society at large.

Some changes in manners are symptomatic of changing power balances *between* states. As France became the dominant power in Europe, French court manners increasingly took over the modelling function previously fulfilled by Italian court manners. In the nineteenth century, with the rising power of England, the manners of English good society came to serve as a major example in many other countries. At the beginning of the period of my research, around the turn of the nineteenth to the twentieth century, according to many German and Dutch etiquette books, English manners had become the main model all over Europe. In 1890, a German author wrote that nothing could be worse than to be taken for a barbarian by an

Englishman (Franken, 1890: 16, quoted in Wander, 1976: 8–9). And in another German book, of which a translation was also published in the Netherlands, one reads: 'At present, one gives preference more often to the English customs; these are also adopted by the French themselves' (Bruck-Auffenberg, 1897: 3).

After World War II, when the USA became a dominant superpower, American manners served more easily as a model. Before the war, the modelling function of these manners had already been rising, in particular because of the relatively early development of a youth culture in the USA, and, in close connection with that, of an appealing entertainment industry, summarized and symbolized as Hollywood.

2

Confined to the Drawing Room

The historian Michael Curtin distinguishes between the English eighteenth-century courtesy-book genre and the nineteenth-century etiquette-book genre. Authors of courtesy books, like Chesterfield and Knigge, were aristocrats and thus familiar with courts and the lifestyle cultivated and appreciated within them. The transition from the one genre to the other is centrally characterized by the declining importance of the aristocracy, the gentry and patricians and their centres of power, that is, courts. Whereas the courtesy genre was dominated by men, the whole etiquette genre was (and is) dominated by women, both as authors and, most probably, as readers. This reflects the widening sphere of opportunities that women came to enjoy in the nineteenth century: the opportunities to pursue a career of largely independent sociability associated with the opportunities of the drawing room, not those of the wider society. 'It was in the sociability of the "lady" – that is, the woman who toiled neither in the home nor the marketplace – that the etiquette book found its characteristic, though not exclusive, subject matter' (Curtin, 1985: 419).

These changes in the social position of women were connected with the rise of the entrepreneurial bourgeoisie, their representation in the centres of power, and their increasing incorporation into good society. The whole social existence of these entrepreneurs depended heavily upon contracts regulating the conditions of such activities as buying, producing, selling and transporting. In turn, the making of these contracts as well as the conditions stipulated in them depended upon an individual's reputation as being financially solvent and morally solid. To a large extent this reputation was formed in the gossip channels of good society (or its functional equivalent among other social strata). In developing the level of trust and respect in a relationship necessary for signing a contract, an invitation into the social world was an appreciated strategy. Men could demonstrate and prove their respectability and trustworthiness in social life, in their relationships with women in general and with their own wife in particular. They could show this to potential clients or business partners by inviting them into their home and into the rest of their secluded social world. To be introduced, accepted and entertained in the drawing rooms and parlours of the respectable or, to put it in a different way, to be successful in the social world, was (and is) an important and sometimes even necessary condition for success in business or, for that matter, in politics.

The reputation for moral solidity referred to the self-discipline involved in orderliness, thrift, and responsibility, qualities needed for a firm grip on the proceedings of business transactions. Moral solidity also included the social and sexual spheres, and it seemed inconceivable how any bourgeois man could possibly create the solid impression of being able to live up to the terms of his contracts if he couldn't even keep his wife under control and his family in order. Therefore, bourgeois means of controlling potentially dangerous social and sexual competition depended to a substantial degree on the support of wives for their husbands. Her support and social charm could make a crucial difference, as is implied in the opinion of a manners book author that 'nothing makes a man look more ridiculous in the eyes of the world than a socially helpless wife' (Klickman, 1902: 25).

At the same time, these pressures offered specific opportunities to women. As the social weight of the bourgeoisie increased, middle-class women enjoyed a widening sphere of opportunities. Although confined to the domain of their home and good society, in the nineteenth century upper- and middle-class women more or less came to run and organize the social sphere. The workings of good society took place in large part in women's private drawing rooms. To a large extent, women came to function as the gate-keepers of this social figuration, as arbiters of social acceptance or rejection. This function became a major source of power and identity. Leonore Davidoff, too, has pointed to this connection between the rising middle classes, the growing importance of social circulation in good society, and rising opportunities for women:

> Society in the nineteenth century, especially in England, did become formalised. One way of formalising a social institution is to use specialised personnel to carry out its functions. In nineteenth-century England upper- and middle-class women were used to maintain the fabric of Society, as semi-official leaders but also as arbiters of social acceptance or rejection. (1973: 16)

Until the second half of the twentieth century, it was more or less taken for granted that women would devote a great deal of their time and efforts to advancing their (and their husband's) social position in good society, or its social equivalent. For example, in 1922 Mrs Post gave the following advice to a woman who comes to live in a new town:

> The husband at least makes business acquaintances, but the wife is left alone. The only thing for her to do is join the church of her denomination, and become interested in some activity ... Her social position is usually gained at a snail's pace ... it is fatal to be pushing or presuming. (1922: 69)

Manners books occasionally state quite explicitly why manners are important to upward mobility for women and why their husbands are in turn dependent upon the upward mobility of their wife:

> it is their duty to keep well in touch with the more ceremonious side of life *for the sake of their husbands*. And this last is one of the most important reasons why a woman should pay all heed to the subject of etiquette. It is well known that the average man can only advance so far as his wife allows him. If her horizon is cramped and petty, he will find himself practically chained down to it, no matter how he may chafe against it ... Society will fraternise with the millionaire and ignore his misplaced *h's* and his absence of good

breeding, while they drink his wines and assist him in various ways to spend his money; but the wives and daughters of these men will not visit his wife and daughters, nor receive them into their houses, if they lack refinement and culture ... [M]any a selfish, indolent, or ignorant woman has spoilt her husband's prospects in life, and ruined every chance of his realizing the great ambitions that at one time or another possess the soul of every true man, by neglecting this side of her wifely duties; just as many another has practically made her husband famous by unselfishly devoting her life to his interests. (Klickman, 1902: 4–5)

Thus, the importance of manners and acceptance into good society were central to the upward mobility of both women and men. The people who maintained contacts via the social gatherings of good society not only had social interests in common but also commercial and political ones. These social gatherings provided opportunities for pursuing these interests, of course. A suitable moment for business talk and subtle negotiations began after dinner, when the ladies had left the table and the men enjoyed a good glass and a cigar. Here is an evocation of such a scene in nineteenth-century USA, described from the viewpoint of women: 'The time between leaving the dinner table and being joined by the gentlemen is generally a very easy and social one with the ladies ... Presently, coffee is handed out, and then the gentlemen come dropping in, the young ones first and the politicians last' (quoted in Hemphill, 1999: 184). To raise their commercial or political interests, men have often suggested that their wives should organize some social gathering like a dinner. And women of this class took the task for granted, as did the authors of manners books. A retrospect of the 1950s said:

Dinner-giving was once the most important of all social observances. Now, owing to the difficulties of finding adequate domestic staff, comparatively few people can cope with a formal dinner party in their own homes, and they choose to entertain at restaurants, hotels, and at their clubs. For the benefit of the few, however, the following guidance is offered on the giving of formal dinner parties.

An invitation to dinner conveys a greater mark of esteem, or friendship and cordiality, towards the guest, than is conveyed by an invitation to any other social gathering, it being the highest social compliment that is offered. Dinner-giving is in itself not only a test of one's social position but it is also a direct road to obtaining a recognised place in society, and a means of enlarging a limited acquaintance. A reputation for giving good dinners is in itself a passport to fashionable society. (*Manners and Rule*, 1955: 50)

In the USA, at a time of 'conspicuous consumption', a male etiquette writer, referring to 'the tyranny in large cities of what is known as the "fashionable set" formed of people 'willing to spend money', claimed that 'this circle lives by snubbing' (Hanson, 1896: 39). His choice of words may have been gender-related, for it was women who organized and to a large extent controlled the functioning of good society, one of their instruments being a constant stream of praise gossip and blame gossip (Elias and Scotson, 1994). Indeed, in a paragraph on *the gentle art of snubbing*, the English Mrs Humphry wrote in 1897:

Tact is both innate and acquired. The root of the thing must be born with the possessor, or the soil will prove uncongenial. Years of mingling in good society are necessary to its full development, and though a delicate sense of what is due to others is of the very essence of tact, it is never quite perfect without a knowledge of the gentle art of snubbing. This is an accomplishment which some women never acquire. They cannot firmly repress the unduly officious or the over-eager without adopting harsh measures or losing their temper. Where they should simply ignore, they administer the cut direct. ... the woman who cannot snub, on occasion, may be pronounced almost incapable of giving good dinners. Her visiting list, instead of being kept carefully weeded, will certainly run to seed in a way that will militate against the harmonious selection of her guests. (1897: 72)[1]

However important their functioning in good society was for them as a source of power and identity, 'respectable' women and young girls were at the same time confined to the domain of their home and good society: 'The only "safe" contacts they would have outside the home were with a few selected other girls, clergymen, or in the context of small-scale charity work, particularly teaching in Sunday schools' (Davidoff, 1973: 51).

In nineteenth-century good society, manners were not only decisive in making friends, and, through friends, in gaining influence and recognition; they also functioned as a means of winning a desirable spouse. At the start of the period covered in my research, in all four countries under study the overture to marriage – courting – was practised in ways that largely resembled each other. It was done mainly by the young man calling at her parents' house. Young people were able to get acquainted at particular social gatherings such as dinners, parties and balls, most of them given in the drawing rooms of their parents or those of friends or relatives of their parents. A young man could court a young woman by expressing a special interest in her. If he did, she could ask him to visit her at home, that is, to call at her parents' home. If she refused, she was either not attracted to him and his courting behaviour or unable to secure her parents' consent to the invitation. When he called, he was received in the drawing room, parlour or, in the USA, on the porch. In each case, someone else would be present or within hearing distance. The young man could be invited to call again, or not, and he could, of course, decline the invitation. But if his calling was continued, these visits were expected to culminate in his proposal of marriage: 'If after a reasonable time no proposal of marriage is made, it would be well to let the friendship pass with the melting of the winter snows or the falling of the autumn leaves, according to the season' (Wade, 1924: 116). If a proposal did follow and she and her parents accepted it, the couple would first become 'engaged' to be married. Sexual experimenting was explicitly excluded from this 'engagement'. However, it was generally expected that most couples would 'fall' and give in to temptation if/when given the opportunity. Therefore, even when engaged, the respectable couple would not be left alone very much; that would damage their reputation. This was the prevailing courting regime in all four countries under study. Its main location was the drawing room. Then, from the end of the nineteenth century onwards, '[a]lternative models of femininity – the university woman or even the suffragette – offered "careers" that competed with some success against fashionable Society' (Curtin, 1987: 243–4).

> In all of social life, in fact there was beginning to be provision for respectable women to meet in public places outside their own homes. Cafés, the growth of tea rooms, the use of buses, even the provision of public lavatories for women, were as important in freeing middle-class women from strict social ritual as the slow erosion of chaperonage. Contact by telephone and the later mobility that came with cars began to undermine the most formal parts of etiquette. (Davidoff, 1973: 67)

The historian Porter adds the importance of 'the coming of the bicycle and women taking up more sports' (1972: 81). Dancing and dance halls also played their part in the process of female emancipation. In the next chapter, I shall investigate that part.

3
Dancing Fury

Going out to public dance halls signified a breakthrough in the relationship of young people with their parents because, in comparison to private ball-rooms, parents had hardly any control over their public counterparts. It also involved a small revolution in the relationship between the sexes. The movements of the dances to the new 'wild' music were experienced as erot-ically and seductively liberating. They symbolized a new freedom of move-ment that was also inherent in the free and easy access to dance halls and to the opposite sex: almost anyone, including those who would not be invited to a private dance, could get in and at least look at unknown women or men. They could even become dancing partners and hold each other for the dura-tion of the dance. These dramatic novelties were dealt with in manners books. Early in the twentieth century, in a Dutch book in which several dances were presented and discussed, the main distinction made was between ballroom dances and dances practised in public dance halls (only). At the end of their book, the authors discussed the 'cake walk', a craze that came in from Paris, and they declared themselves to be strongly against the dance:

> It is not suitable for the Dutch Ballroom, for these intensely fatiguing and ridiculous jumping movements and bestial positions cannot get the approval of our distinguished dancing public. To us it seems that one must have lost full consciousness in order to carry out these uncomfortable grimaces in the face of others ... The future will probably prove our opinion correct, and the 'Cake Walk' will be practised only at public dances. (Polak and Polak, 1903: 100)

Early in the century, a few authors wrote that it seemed that private balls were no longer as fashionable as they once had been, and sports were men-tioned as a likely cause (ECvdM, 1911: 98). Sports provided less formal opportunities for meetings between the sexes and they were also less char-acterized by class-ridden rules like: 'Never forget to wear gloves, because dancing with bare hands is simply not permitted in our class' (ECvdM, 1912: 227). At the same time, gloves may be taken to have symbolized the wall of social distance between the sexes: holding a woman (of their own class) was exceptional and therefore the intensity of the exciting experience needed to be toned down by a token of formality and restraint: gloves. This formality ended in the late 1910s with the enormous rise in popularity of new dances and new rhythms. Moreover, ladies and young girls from good families began to go out to dance in public places! In 1919, a Dutch author wrote the following words as an addition to earlier editions of her manners book:

> Fifteen years ago it would have been completely unnecessary to say anything about dancing in public. Ladies and young girls from good families did not dream of exhibiting their talents anywhere but at invitation balls. Public dance halls were for soldiers and servant-girls. In recent years, there have been enormous changes. Evening and afternoon dances are held in the tearoom, dining room and hall of restaurants of high standing, a fashion that came to us having spread from abroad. (Viroflay, 1919: 54–5)

During the 1920s, this way of escaping from being confined to the segregated women's world boomed. Many commentators, usually a bit worried, spoke of a 'dance fury' in this connection:

> One was no longer satisfied with the 'queen of dances', the waltz, initially giving her other names, Hesitation or Boston, but soon having her pushed aside by twosteps and foxtrots, by tangos, furlanas, jazzes, shimmies, cakewalks, très moutardes, rag-times, charlestons, blackbottoms, heebie-jeebies and whatever else the future may bring!
>   Everywhere, in all modern establishments, she finds the facility to gratify her dancing lust. She dances at a fashion show, she dances at exhibitions, she dances summer and winter, at all hours of the day! ...
>   What is there against the young girl amusing herself? Nothing, of course. And those who oppose it may be reminded of the fact that fulminating against the 'dance fury' has happened at all times; the waltz, nowadays so tame, was also once sneered at for being frivolous, even indecent. (Kloos-Reyneke van Stuwe, 1927: 158–60)

The Dutch social arbiter who first discussed this novelty tried to raise sympathy for the 'new fashion' by branding as 'old-fashioned' all mothers who objected to their daughters' presence 'on a dance floor that is open to everyone'. She added: 'The only rule one can urge to be rigorously maintained is: do not dance with a stranger' (Viroflay, 1919: 55). In a later book, the same author first reported that the older generation mourned the disappearance of all grace and elegance from dancing, and lamented that youth was no longer showing any sense of decency. She herself, however, obviously appreciated these 'rhythms vibrating through the limbs', and she welcomed 'the liberation from the constraints of earlier dance figures, dancing to the nuances of each melody according to personal taste; in a word, one dances individually' (Viroflay-Montrecourt, 192–: II, 68). In a description of some of the male movements, she added: 'he has to take care that he dances in such a way that his positions do not become indecent – which is very difficult considering the fact that most of these modern dances stem from places where they were intended to be indecent, even very indecent!' (Viroflay-Montrecourt, 192–: II, 69). Remarks like these clearly suggest a connection between the emancipation of the lower and supposedly 'indecent' classes and the lower and supposedly 'indecent' emotions. The same suggestion was put forward retrospectively in the 1950s: 'One was of the opinion that a girl in silk stockings could only walk towards her ruin. Yet she wore them to the cinema to see Pola Negri and Rudolf Valentino,' and also to 'the threatening sounds of the enticing rhythms of the Charleston and the "Black Bottom", which could only be danced to by very common females in very vulgar places' (Bruyn, 1957: 5–6).

At the time of these dances, the reproach of vulgarity was loudly present even in the words of authors who wrote in favour of dancing them and against the puritanical critique. One American author, for instance, wrote that the modern dances are reported as being 'criticized because of the objectionable method of holding the partner, and also because of the "shaking and wiggling" motions of the bodies of the dancers'. The author then continued: 'however this may be, these dances have now won acceptance if not approval, and it has been demonstrated that they can be performed gracefully and without giving offence to the most squeamish chaperon' (Holt, 1920: 179). Only in the American sources did chaperones appear as an argument in this discussion, a finding which seems to contradict the reputedly greater freedom of people in the USA. It is also strange in light of the fact that these dances originated mostly in this self-same country. In Chapter 6, particularly in sections 6.5 and 6.6, I deal with these contradictions.

The following quotation from an American manners book refers to 'vigorous crusades' and to 'anti-immorality dancing committees', but not to the chaperone. It was written in a paragraph headed *A Plea For Dancing*:

> Lately there has been a great deal of unfavourable criticism directed against the modern dances. There have been newspaper articles condemning the 'latest dance fads' as immoral and degrading. There have been speeches and lectures against 'shaking and twisting of the body into weird, outlandish contortions.' There have been vigorous crusades against dance halls ... Dancing, even the shoulder-shaking, oscillating dancing of to-day, is really not intended to be vulgar or immoral at all, despite the crusade of anti-immorality dancing committees! (Eichler, 1923: II, 104–5)

'Low', 'common', 'vulgar', these were a few of the favourite words of opponents of the new dances and dancing places. Usually these opponents consisted of clerical and local authorities. In the Netherlands, a study of documents from these sources shows that they 'mainly focus on the possibility – and the danger – of meeting and relating freely with someone of the opposite sex'. Obviously, it was taken for granted that this freedom would be abused. Moreover, the 'periodically recurring brochures, pastoral letters and sermons were full of verbal violence, showing no hesitation whatsoever in fully disclosing the identity of the persons who had danced' (Derks, 1991: 391–6). Later in the decade, even the Dutch government was sufficiently worried by the new freedom of dances and dancers to establish a government committee whose task it was to investigate the 'problem of dancing'. Some local authorities took austere measures. One reported proudly: 'The authorities now know at any time, where, when, and who is dancing' (*Rapport*, 1931: 60). Apparently, the emancipation of 'lower' layers of emotion triggered the social authorities to consider and enact social regulations. From the perspective of individuals, authorities included, the process also involved their self-regulation for it became increasingly difficult simply to ward off or avoid these emotions (see Wouters, 1998b). The new freedom therefore also entailed new demands on behaviour and emotion management: to give free rein to the emotions involved but without losing control over them. These are demands on self-regulation that are inherent in all processes of informalization, and they usually present a typical emancipation problem: a specific ambivalence between old and new sources of power and identity. In the mid-1920s, this was expressed clearly by two English authors:

> Yet the limited outlook instinct seems to have been ground into women so thoroughly in the Ages, that they are unable to escape from it even in their new freedom. Thousands of girls think of nothing but dance, dance, dance! A doctor friend suggested to me that the 'one partner' idea was probably a subconscious attempt on the part of women to get away from wide possibilities, and get back to the old ingrained safety of the narrow outlook ... In the old days the girl or woman saw nothing but husband and family in the ordinary way, so the varying partner at a dance came as a distinct relief. Now in her wider life, women come upon so much unexpected variety that they turn instinctively to the one man limitation to which, as a sex, they have been so long accustomed. The 'one partner' craze was a bad one, from every point of view, especially when it came to women paying a particular man to dance with her, or, as was often done, hiring a stranger from some enterprising firm. When we reached that stage, dancing was no longer an amusement, but an obsession, and a dangerous one too. After all, there is really much more enjoyment in the change of partners, if we can only bring ourselves to admit it, and it is pleasant to see that it is coming into its own once more. (Terry, 1925: 69–70)

In another etiquette book, also published in 1925, a chapter on dancing opens as follows:

> The last few years have seen not only a change in the actual style of ballroom dancing but also a tremendous expansion of the opportunities for indulging in this pastime, and all classes of society have taken to dancing practically anywhere and everywhere, on every possible occasion ... Many of the restrictions with which Mrs Grundy once fettered the dance-loving maiden were gaily cast aside at much the same time as when old favourites, such as square dances, stately minuets, graceful cotillions and waltzes were succeeded by the one-step and fox-trot, while chaperons faded away like dim ghosts of the past during the war and programmes became unnecessary as a means of recording dances promised, as the fashion came in for a couple to become recognised 'dancing partners,' who would dance together throughout the evening, probably during the London season, accompanying each other to two or three dances in the same evening, or early hours of the next day. Now the pendulum is in some respects swinging back again. Gradually the chaperon is reappearing, though not often do we find her the formidable, lynx-eyed dragoness of former days, who kept her young charge strictly to her side between dances – the modern maid's independent temperament would not submit to that – and the chaperon of today is often as keen upon dancing and having a good time as are the younger folks. Many hostesses, too, now clearly intimate their dislike of the one-partner practice, so that it is again usual for a lady to distribute her favours among a number of gentlemen during the evening. This

is certainly a more sociable practice. The one-partner vogue was carried to selfish and sometimes most discourteous extremes. (Burleigh, 1925: 108–10)

This one-partner craze was discussed only in English manners books, but in the USA the existence of the same 'vogue' or 'craze' was at least suggested in remarks like 'It is always permissible to ask a hostess if you may "bring" a dancing man who is a stranger to her. It is rather difficult to ask for an invitation for an extra girl' (Post, 1922: 253). The same suggestion is found in a Belgian manners book written in Dutch: 'It is becoming increasingly fashionable nowadays, that young girls bring their regular dancing partners, with their parents' consent, of course. That makes it easier for hosts, because it exempts them from the obligation to invite twice as many young men as young women' (Paeuw, 1934: 187).

In Germany, the author of a 1919 manners book depicted dancing as a disease: 'A new flu has arrived ... and it is called the foxtrot – the new dancing craze' (Koebner, 1919: 95). On the whole, however, I have found only a few traces of the dancing fury in German etiquette books. In Germany, more than anywhere else, the dance euphoria of the 'Golden Twenties' ran in tandem with widespread social misery, rising crime and suicide rates. The authorities had other worries, and a conservative politician explicitly preferred 'the people to amuse themselves with music and dance instead of organizing demonstrations' (quoted in Klein, 1994: 168). In 1935, the Nazis declared a 'war against swing' and banned 'Nigger-Jazz' from the air. According to sociologist Gabriele Klein, 'the revolt of the senses' had in fact come to an abrupt end in the year of the Depression. The jazz dances and "black" dances, being gender neutral, egalitarian, and involving seemingly unbridled physicality had already provoked a body-hostile reaction. When the anxiety of the Depression was added, jazz turned all at once into a penniless art (1994: 169–77). Not entirely, however, as is documented in detail by the Dutch historian Kees Wouters who has written a fascinating study on this war against 'unwanted music' – as he entitled his study, focusing both on Germany and the Netherlands (Wouters, K., 1999): throughout their entire time in power, the Nazis systematically continued their 'war against swing' by arresting people who performed or listened to this music (see also Zwerin, 2000).

4

To Pay or Be Paid For?

Women's chaperones not only watched over their charges but also paid their bills. As women tried to do away with chaperones and to replace them with gentlemen-escorts, the question of whether the women should be allowed to pay for themselves became an issue of greater concern. And it certainly created an important problem. Michael Curtin has summarized it thus:

> Money was a real asset not merely a ceremonial gesture ... Some ladies wished to make clear that the relations between themselves and their escorts were of a public and egalitarian nature, not romantic as between lovers or dependent as between father and daughter. Chivalric deference was not well suited to comradely relations ... In addition, those who paid the servants, waiters, cabmen, and other lackeys who surrounded the rich and who knew their secrets owned their allegiance ... To transfer this power from husbands and fathers, whose intentions were supposed to be benevolent, to outsiders was obviously dangerous. (1987: 272–3)

Apparently, women who wanted to 'escape' from the imprisonment of the 'home' and to get rid of the system of chaperonage, had to put up with this interpretation of a transfer of power over women to outsiders. Going somewhere with relative strangers without the protection of a chaperone was considered dangerous enough in itself, but being financially dependent upon this 'outsider' enlarged the danger considerably. 'In her intercourse with men a woman should take care to avoid all pecuniary obligations ... We repeat that a woman cannot be too particular in placing herself under obligations to a man' (*Etiquette for Ladies*, 1900: 95–6). Whenever her way was paid for by such a person, her father or husband was advised to send him a postal money order immediately (Humphry, 1902: 174). This interpretation of a transfer of power may have waned, but it has not disappeared. The danger can be recognized in the warnings of most authors of American etiquette books in their paragraphs on dating: girls should not 'feel compelled to "pay" for every date. There's no law that says you must kiss your escort at parting!' (Sweeney, 1948: 27). The danger is discussed in a German manners book from the 1950s through a reference to those 'contemptible male figures who only invite and treat a woman generously in order to oblige them'. When the time of collecting dues has come, either the friendship ends or the woman pays (Meissner, 1951: 260). And in the 1980s, the dangers of the 'power transfer' are recognizable from an English etiquette book which held that:

> The person who issues the invitation pays. Usually he pays for her. His payment is for the pleasure of her company – nothing more ... If he is courting her he should pay. One day she will become pregnant or give up work

temporarily to look after their under-fives and she needs to know that he is able and willing to pay for two – even three. (Lansbury, 1985: 77)

In the phrase 'His payment is for the pleasure of her company – nothing more', the danger of the 'power transfer' is still recognizably present. If he thinks his payment is for more, or 'worth more', this may even end in what was later to become called a 'date-rape'. On their way towards gaining greater control over the dangers connected with this view of a 'power transfer', women had to establish the right to pay for themselves.

4.1   England

The payment issue was first dealt with in English etiquette books in the early twentieth century. For example, a social arbiter wrote in 1902 that:

> It is the man's place to pay for what refreshments are had, if the ladies do not insist on paying their share; and if he invites the ladies with him to go in somewhere and have some, then the case is simple enough. But if the lady expresses a wish to pay, and means it, – and there is but little difficulty in knowing when she does mean it, – it is only polite and kind on the part of the man to let her do so, and whatever his feelings may be he must give in. (*Etiquette for Women*, 1902: 59)

In the 1920s, Lady Troubridge, whose etiquette book was popular from the mid-1920s through the 1930s, explicitly connected a woman paying for herself as a means of avoiding 'obligations':

> Sometimes, at the end of an evening, a lady will say to a man who has accompanied her in trains or taxis, 'How much do I owe you for fares?' If she insists on paying, it is good manners to accept, as her insistence shows that she does not wish to feel under any obligation. (1926: 81; 1931: 320)

Lady Troubridge also wrote that 'the only place where formal introductions are not necessary is at sea. Life on shipboard is more or less free from conventionality', but probably precisely for that very reason she warns: 'The young lady who is alone should be careful that she does not make haphazard acquaintances among the men on board ... She must never allow a man whose acquaintance she has made only on board ship to pay any of her expenses' (1931: 358–9). In the 1930s, the issue of women paying for men came up for discussion but was rejected, although only half-heartedly. This emerges from the mocking tone adopted by Lady Troubridge in her explanation why:

> Etiquette is against your paying them [men] back in their own coin – i.e. by asking them to dine with you tête-à-tête, as your guest. The reason for this ruling ... is simply that such an invitation would clash with the male pride, and with their code, which is definitely against being 'stood' an evening's entertainment by a girl. (1939: 167)

By the 1950s, the number of women of independent means had multiplied, and the rule that 'if she insists on paying, it is good manners to accept' had trickled down the social ladder. The transition had reached a remarkable stage:

> The going has never been so good for a bachelor woman who has a paid job. She not only gets her pay packet and her independence but she is still able to enjoy the remnants of masculine gallantry. In many fields she is paid a salary that compares with a man's and she can still graciously lie low when it comes to standing her round of drinks when men are about. The new problem is not whether she should go out to work, but how far she should carry the new equality into her social relationship with men, when she should assert her independence and when she should fall back on her femininity, when to take charge with businesslike efficiency and pay the bill, and when to sparkle sweetly over the pink champagne, while he foots the bill. (Edwards and Beyfus, 1956: 135)

To have a choice between coexisting codes, an old and a new one, is characteristic of a period of transition. By 1969, when a new edition of Edwards' and Beyfus's book was published, this particular choice had not disappeared altogether: the first part of the above quotation was kept, and only the last part of the sentence – 'when men are about' – was deleted. The other sentences had been changed into:

> The position is now that in her relationship with men at work she counts as one of them, but on private social occasions she has the option of falling back on her femininity – or asserting her independence and taking charge with natural efficiency. With the men at work she is at least expected to offer to pay a round of drinks. (Edwards and Beyfus, 1969: 117)

The references to whether she should go out to work and sparkle sweetly over the pink champagne had been removed, and the 'new problem' has become a 'position'. It was admitted that 'the girl has a greater sense of freedom if she pays her way. She is under no obligations and so has greater choice in the ways in which the relationship can develop, and in the way the evening is spent.' Moreover, it had become more obvious that 'it is no longer accepted for a girl to go out with someone three or four times without sincerely offering to pay her way, or at least returning hospitality' (Debrett, 1981: 275). At the time, some ambivalence was still to be heard: 'The modern girl, especially if she is earning, usually prefers paying her share or contributing. A happy arrangement. One wonders, if, when the idea of sex equality in everything was first mooted, the ladies realised they might have to pay for it!' (Lady Penelope, 1982: 113). This ambivalence, however, was transitional. By 1992 it had even become 'difficult to credit that there was a stage when men did not wish to be seen in public being paid for by a woman' (Beyfus, 1992: 16).

On the whole, the range of possibilities was expanding rather than declining. An English manners book from 1989 may serve as an example of the increase of socially accepted behavioural and emotional alternatives

– a characteristic of an informalization process. The author first mentions the old rule 'that if a man asked a woman out, he paid', and than writes that: 'some still do, but women can't dine endlessly without offering a crust in return'. Some women:

- expect to pay alternate meals – with the payer choosing the restaurant,
- insist on always going Dutch,
- pay only if a man earns no more than they do,
- never pay but do entertain the man at home,
- pay for themselves only when they want to keep sex out of the friendship.

> The whole subject is tied up with attitudes to sex as well as money. Women who pay say it frees them from the obligation to sleep with a man. But those who don't pay say they feel no such obligation. They like the romance of being taken out, and enjoy entertaining a man in return. Couples should do what suits them ... But no meal buyer should feel that sex is owed and the other person shouldn't feel bought. Even an extravagant meal costs less than a good prostitute and no one should be set cheaper than a professional. (Bremner, 1989: 25)

This author uses the expression of 'going Dutch' in an original and telling way when writing on the question whether or not to ring (or to send flowers or champagne to) the other the next day after having spent the night together. 'It's stylish and charming to do so,' she writes, but 'not doing so isn't a breach of good manners' for they may 'feel they've simply "gone Dutch" on a pleasure – so there is no one to thank' (Bremner, 1989: 27–8).

4.2   Germany

In the German etiquette books, the issue of women paying for themselves began to be dealt with much later than in England: approximately around 1930. In 1933, for instance, Meister wrote: 'Until a few years ago, it was still taken for granted that a man paid the bill. Today, a young lady has achieved independence and often earns as much as a man' (quoted in Krumrey, 1984: 399). Up until the 1950s, it was repeated that he should pay but she might pay her share in advance or later. In a section entitled *Does a Gentleman Pay for a Lady?*, the author of a best-selling German manners book after World War II started out by describing how this war had changed the position of women from helplessly weak creatures into strong and decisive women:

> And when we came home, they spoke a masculine, sometimes even a raw language. In this language, they demanded complete equality, and got it. We men, we won comrades in them and we lost our toy. The women won our admiring respect and lost our courtesy ... Therefore, ... in the company of a man, she pays whatever a man in her place would have paid in similar circumstances. (Meissner, 1951: 256–7)

The 1951 edition of von Franken's popular manners book also said: 'In former times, it was taken for granted that a man paid the bill. Today, a woman wishes to be independent of men in this respect, too' (von Franken, 1951: 200). In the 1950s, many German authors praised independence, particularly financial independence. According to one author, many relationships between young men and young women had lost harmony, innocence and security,

> because one partner gave up financial independence. In general, the principle of 'separate purses' has come to be taken for granted among young people when they go out together or on a trip or holiday. In most cases they both earn their own money, and therefore they should each take care of themselves ... Being treated, easily leads to losing independence. (Oheim, 1955: 127–8)

For some time, disputes over this issue continued but, by the 1970s, all social arbiters came to join this stance and approved of a woman's right to pay the bill whenever she wished to.

4.3   The Netherlands

The most popular Dutch manners book of the early twentieth century contained the following advice: 'A gentleman always pays all expenses when taking charge of a lady, unless she is personally opposed. And in our present age when women are independent, they much prefer to pay for themselves. Of course, a gentleman is obliged to respect such a preference' (ECvdM, 1911: 50). Paying was also discussed in the context of young people going on skating trips. When they stopped to have lunch somewhere, the young ladies were advised to pay for themselves 'as no one feels good about constantly being treated by the gentlemen' (ECvdM, 1912: 175). In the same context, another author positively mentioned

> the habit of country girls in the province of Zealand of depositing their silver purse with their cavalier, tacitly permitting him to use it in contributing towards expenses. Maybe young ladies could learn from this and discretely give their purse to their escort before the waiter brings the bill. For if others always pay for them, young ladies will eventually have qualms and feel driven to excuse themselves, even though they would actually love to come. (Margaretha, 1921: 216)

Also at clubs, paying for herself was recommended, for 'in these times of independence, a girl really is able to take care of herself' (ECvdM, 1920: 104).

In the 1930s, the voices on this topic became more mixed. On the one hand, the praise of independence remained: 'Ever since a woman has made herself more independent, she no longer wants to depend on a man so absolutely; and as their relationship has become more comradely, money is discussed more openly and honestly' (Alsen, 1936: 58). And: 'Paying is a man's job, of course, even though the costs of the outing may be shared. Today, it is no longer considered unseemly for a woman to pay her own expenses, but even then it is better if he pays the waiter and settles up with her later' (Haluschka, 1939: 95). But other voices on the subject did not like women to be so free. Good friends could agree to pay for their own ticket to the theatre or the cinema, but 'it isn't the best cavaliers who nowadays propagate the idea that the girls they are going out with can pay their own share. In this way, every single trace of chivalry disappears' (Haeften, 1936: 139).

To the 1942 edition of her popular manners book, Amy Groskampten Have added the possibility of women buying tickets in advance, thus avoiding 'the always embarrassing situation of settling up' (1942: 53), but all 12 editions (in between 1939 and 1957) contain the following rejection of women paying for themselves:

> There is no objection against a couple going out together regularly to arrange to do so on separate accounts, but it does not offer evidence of good taste when a girl, after she has been taken out by a young man a few times, places her purse on the table saying 'I will pay for myself'. Among the young people of today, there are those who tacitly accept it if a woman pays for herself and sometimes for her escort as well, but a well-bred gentleman will not tolerate this. (1939: 51)

It was not until the edition of 1966 that the part after the last comma was left out (Groskampten Have, 1966: 50). Judging from this authoritative book, it is only for a few decades that the Dutch have been 'going Dutch'. The possibility of women paying for themselves was mentioned positively (again) from the 1950s onward.

The completely rewritten fifteenth edition of Amy Groskampten Have's book which appeared in 1983 says that the old custom that men always paid for women was, by that time, definitely a thing of the past: 'Today, it depends upon many different considerations whether he pays or she, or both, or this time he, next time she, or whether they have yet some other arrangement' (1983: 54). In this edition, a woman who does not pay her share by buying her round of drinks in a pub is even called a sponger:

> It is more frequently possible for a woman to be and to remain relatively independent. If she has a job herself, then – assuming she doesn't prefer to sponge on someone else – she will like being able to pay her own bills so that she is free in her relations with others. (Groskampten Have, 1983: 54)

When rounds of drinks are ordered in a pub, no one is exempt from the obligation to take turns in footing the bill: 'That has nothing to do with being a man or being a woman, but with sponging' (Grosfeld, 1984: 171). The word sponging presupposes a process of social equalization in which partners share both the right and the obligation to pay.

4.4   The USA

In the USA, the tradition of men paying for women lingered on for a longer time. It was not until the 1970s that the connection between (in)dependence and paying appeared in manners books. In her fascinating study of the American dating system, Beth Bailey emphasizes exactly this connection by concluding that 'the centrality of men's money in dating conferred power – and control of the date – upon men. When women paid their own way on dates, men lost that extra power. They were no longer the provider, no longer in control' (1988: 110). Thus, the danger of the 'power transfer' was clearly recognized, although only in retrospect.

In 1937, Emily Post complained about the persistence of the tradition of men paying for women:

> In this modern day, when women are competing with men in politics, in busi-
> ness and in every profession, it is really senseless to cling to that one obsolete
> convention – no matter what the circumstances – that the man must buy the
> tickets, pay the check, pay the taxi, or else be branded a gigolo or parasite. The
> modern point of view has changed in every particular save this one! (1937: 365)

This may sound modern but Emily Post's solution to the problem reads like an anti-climax. She only allows for one exception: 'On occasion, when agreed beforehand, girls as well as men pay their own checks' (1937: 369), and for the rest she advises: don't let him pay more than he can afford, an advice that is repeated throughout the decades. Boys, on their part, are advised to be careful in suggesting a date: 'It's not so much what you suggest as *that* you suggest. If it's a "Let's go out. Where'll we go?" kind of invitation, a man has more or less given a woman carte blanche on his wallet' (Ostrander, 1967: 52). In the 1930s, even co-eds were advised against going Dutch: 'Dutch treats have not worked. Too much independence on a girl's part subtracts from a man's feeling of importance if he takes her out and can do nothing for her' (Eldridge, 1936: 216). Another pressure in the same direction stemmed from the fact that in the dating system, 'a "belle" is rated by the amount of money spent on her'. Accordingly, 'the date starts as an invitation from a young man to a girl for an evening's public entertainment, typically at his expense, though since the depression girls occasionally pay their share' (Gorer, 1948: 114).

> In the 1950s and 1960s the practice of 'going Dutch' seemed to decline
> in the USA: The Purdue Opinion Panel 1957 Poll of 10,000 high school stu-
> dents finds that the popularity of 'going Dutch' is declining among teen-agers.
> In 1948, 37 per cent thought that boys and girls sharing expenses 'fifty-fifty'
> was a good idea. By 1957, only 25 per cent favored the practice. Boys now
> have more money than they did in 1948, and in most cases they like to pay
> their full dating costs. (Duvall, 1958: 138–9)

A book from 1960 discusses 'Dutch Dates' as the exception to the rule, and the rule is authoritative: 'Though it may not be entirely fair, it *is* the way of the world for a fellow to pay a girl's expenses on a date.' Accordingly, 'Dutch-Treat dates shouldn't get to be a habit with you *or* the fellow' (Unger, 1960: 104–7) Around 1960 women were allowed, in exceptional cases, to invite a man to dine with them – 'A situation that caused great embarrassment some years ago but is taken casually today' – but her paying for the dinner had to be hidden: 'If she has no charge account and has to pay the check before her guest, this will be embarrassing' (Post, 1960: 62). Amy Vanderbilt left the following sentences unchanged in the 1952, 1963 and 1972 editions of her book:

> Dating, for boys, does bring with it increased financial responsibilities. While a certain amount of Dutch treating goes on, especially in group entertainment, a boy usually does pay for the entertainment of his special date. If his allowance is not adequate for his participation in the social activities of his high school group and if his parents cannot comfortably increase it, then after-school jobs must provide the difference. (1963: 558; 1972: 705)

Until well into the 1970s, it was still taken for granted that the male should pay, and although the possibility of 'going Dutch' had been mentioned earlier, it was only from the 1970s onwards that it was mentioned sympathetically. In this decade, new advice concerning the situation of businesswomen 'on the road' being approached by strange men again shows how important, even decisive, is 'the right to pay':

> If you are travelling and someone presentable begins to speak to you in a nice way and asks if he may join you (and you would like to talk to someone), say, 'Yes, please join me.' Make it clear you will put your own drink on your own bill, however. If he insists on paying for that cocktail and you decide to have one more with him, say firmly, but again with a smile, 'I would like another one, but this time both drinks go on *my* bill.' He will understand you are not letting him pick you up. (Vanderbilt, 1978: 451)

Obviously, her 'right to pay' protected her against the 'power transfer', that is, against being perceived as a sexual conquest and treated as a 'pick-up girl'.

In the 1980s, this old question *Should you offer to pay your own way or some of the expenses on a date?* is answered in a variety of ways, but also very negatively:

> Certainly not! Unless you know the man very well, love him, and want to help him over a hard time in his life. If a man asks you out, he expects to pay for the whole evening. Any decent man would be insulted if you even suggested paying for yourself' (Cartland, 1984: 5).[1]

At the same time, however, the problems and dangers of the 'power transfer' remained acute, as appears from attacks on personifications of Mr. Danger: 'He should know that it is a lady's prerogative to say no. They should both know that sexual attentions should never be demanded or given out of the disgusting notion that they are a return to the person who pays the entertainment bills' (Martin, 1983: 277).

In the 1990s, some advisors still firmly reprimanded a woman for paying on a date: 'Equality and Dutch treat are fine in the workplace, but not in the romantic playing field' (Fein and Schneider, 1995: 38). And others continued to consider the issue of who should pay a difficult item. Under the heading *Who Pays for What on a Date and When and How*, Laetitia Baldridge, who was Amy Vanderbilt's successor after the latter had died (both authored million-selling manners books), wrote, for instance: 'Today, with women's equality and with women owning their own money, the cost of a date is often split.' The simplicity of this statement turns out to be deceptive, because 'The question of who pays for what on a date is as complicated and potentially embarrassing as the confusion among the parents of the bride and groom over who will pay for what in the wedding when the groom's family is assisting the bride with the financial responsibility' (1990: 172). Even at the beginning of the twenty-first century, 'going Dutch' is still not considered 'normal'. If she does not suggest it, in most cases he is still expected to pay for both of them. Here the Americans lagged behind.

5
Going to Work
Manners at Work

Of course, gaining 'the right to pay' was only a small step on the way towards overcoming the danger of 'transferring power over women from husbands and fathers to outsiders'. A more important step was 'the right to earn', to enter the labour market and aim at financial independence. Going out to work in offices, libraries, hospitals, schools, etc. was another aspect of the development of women 'escaping' from homes where they were 'kept' by fathers and mothers and husbands, and entering the wider society.

Towards the end of the nineteenth century, a Dutch author recommending young women to become economically independent wrote: 'No-one will perceive the independent, keenly operating woman as the very picture of a frustrated lover' (A, 1894: 49). Indeed, that very picture was one of the images against which working women had to fight. American books contained similar suggestions: 'Ladies who are engaged in business (like school-teachers, artists, dressmakers, physicians, music teachers, or in other self-supporting occupations), are released from the necessity of having a chaperon' (Bradley, 1889: 321), And: 'In the old-fashioned conception of a woman who worked outside her home, it used to be taken for granted that she must be denied social consideration and must give up her share of fun in the world' (Harland and Water, 1905: 445). From this point of view, the chaperone was a sexy attribute.

Daughters from families which circulated in 'Society' had to overcome still other status barriers on the way to gaining the right to work:

> Retail trade was once supposed to mark the limitations that society permitted to its members. The higher finance, large wholesale dealings were quite in accord with dignity and rank. Then the line began to be stretched, and the director's position in a bid manufacturing concern or in the distribution of popular commodities, was not only tolerated but coveted. The very last barriers of this kind have been swept away. Titled women open shops for the sale of millinery or flowers, and embark upon the dressmaker's trade, personally attending to their customers, and advising them as to design and colours. Young ladies work in teashops in order to learn the business, hoping to start similar establishments of their own. (Cassell's, 1921: 7)

In 1926, Lady Troubridge connected a retrospect to a prospect and a cause when she wrote:

> There was a time not very long ago when women's interests were confined chiefly to the home. For a woman to be actively engaged in some business or profession meant one of two things, either she was an old maid or she was 'queer', but to-day woman is a citizen and may use her talents and capabilities in any way in which she chooses ... It may take many years before she is

regarded as the equal of man in business and professional life and politics, and until that time arrives it behoves every woman ... to do her share in building up the right attitude towards sex equality. (1926: 375)

For a long time, women at work were strongly confronted with the problems related to the interpretation of a 'power transfer' and were trying to cope with them. At work, both men and women were, so to speak, put to the test: both had to unlearn their habitual out-of-business 'social' expectations of each other. These centred on sexuality and marriage. At work, both women and men had to learn how to relate to each other more or less regardless of sexual attraction and gender expectations. For each of the sexes, these learning processes were quite different: men had to put up with women competing for the same job and, at work, they had to adjust their manners and minds to pragmatic business relations with the 'new women' as they were often called. For women, the learning process implied the need to unlearn their old good-society roles and attitudes. In other words, finding a paid job and gaining financial independence demanded the price of having to give up much of their traditional sources of power and identity derived from their functioning at home and in good society, grouping around femininity and marriage, sex and socks. Quite often, and especially around the turn of the nineteenth to the twentieth century, women could only derive little power and identity from their functioning in society outside good society. Therefore, many women must have experienced a tug-of-war between their old nineteenth-century sources of power and identity and their newly gained, twentieth-century sources. This meant that, at some times and in some respects, they will have stuck to traditional resources. Many criticized women for this ambivalence. An example is the American author who wrote: 'Let the new woman prate as much as she please about her independence of man, but she is the first, nevertheless, to rise up in indignation if any of the same old chivalry is omitted' (Hanson, 1896: 362). In manners books, the change in the balance between the two coexisting social codes and in the connected tug-of-war or ambivalence can be followed throughout the twentieth century.

5.1   The USA

As early as 1905, at a time when women's attempt to escape from the confines of the home was still highly controversial, a principal argument against what was later called the 'second shift' (Hochschild, 1989) was formulated:

They expect from her a double duty and this is manifestly unfair ... Men are treated far more considerately in this regard than women. Nothing is allowed to interfere with the average businessman's arrangements. To facilitate these everything possible is done by his family. This may be because men are more insistent, because they have a way of *demanding* their rights. It would be well for women in business, well also for their families, that they should 'look sharp' and pursue the same policy. (Harland and Water, 1905: 451–2)

Today, this kind of view of the consequences of having a job for women's tasks at home may seem a truism. At that time, however, this kind of argument was exceptional. It was not repeated, for instance, by Emily Post, whose first edition of her million-copy-selling etiquette book was published in 1922. Here is a rather graphic example from the 1940s of an attempt to merge elements of the private sphere into the public sphere, and thus to combine new and traditional sources of power and identity:

> A successful business woman I know has an adoring husband. People have wondered how such an aggressive, efficient woman can keep her fine he-man interested. And here is the secret. She's afraid of mice! She mustn't be left alone in their apartment for a minute without his protection ...
>
> How can a brisk, bright, efficient woman appeal to the chivalry of men and keep their business respect at the same time? By getting the men around her to do things for her! She should not impose upon them and make a nuisance of herself. But at least once a month, she should ask the boss to do something for her, if nothing more than to move her desk a quarter of an inch. (Wilson, 1942: 230)

Of course, one might point to many other barriers to women's emancipation, but without taking this tug-of-war or ambivalence into account, it will be hard fully to understand or explain why women's struggle against having to work a 'second shift' has been so weak for so long. Illustrative is the fact that in the 1952, 1963 and 1972 editions of Vanderbilt's million-copy-selling manners book, the following observation, written in an acquiescent tone, is left unchanged:

> A woman must be superlatively good at her job to give her employer full value while working as well as a head of a family. Her personal problems must be kept carefully in the background, and she must necessarily work more efficiently on her two or more jobs than does the man by her side, who traditionally is always protected against personal encroachments upon his business or professional life. (1952: 206)

In the genre of manners books, the problems confronting women who want to go to work and their struggle against having to work a 'second shift' remain underexposed to this day.

The ambivalence between old and new sources of power and identity was clearly recognized early in the twentieth century:

> The prejudice which so long existed among men against women in business relations was partly caused by the thought that they could never forget they were women, could never discuss work or business relations on impersonal and rational grounds. The first lesson a woman must learn in making her own way financially is to appreciate that ... her place of employment is no place for superfluous courtesies. The cultivation of a cool, matter-of-fact, unsentimental way of looking at the work in hand is the only path to honourable achievement. (Harland and Water, 1905: 447)

At that time, the novelty was not this kind of advice but rather the increasing number of women going out to work. Similar advice had been presented already throughout a large part of the nineteenth century, for instance, in Eliza Wade Farrer's popular nineteenth-century American manners book, first printed in 1837 and reprinted as late as 1880:

> Mrs. Farrar was particularly stern about the business lady. She should, it was said, avoid like the plague 'the pretty little arts and graces, the charming ways which are so delightful in a parlour, but which are so utterly out of place, have even been dangerous, in the arena of daily struggle for bread and butter.' (quoted in Miller, 1967: xiii)

In the 1920s upper- and middle-class women who entered the labour force, and therefore had to unlearn their old good-society roles and attitudes, were warned against office romances and 'office wolves'. Authors strongly emphasized that women should behave 'impersonally' in offices. This is how Mrs Post put it: 'At the very top of the list of women's business shortcomings is the inability of most of them to achieve impersonality. Mood, temper, jealousy, especially when induced by a "crush on" her employer, is the chief flaw of the woman in business' (1922: 551). However, she should not try to become 'one of the boys' – that would be classed as going over the top. Instead, a woman should try to see herself as one member of the corporation, and see to it that she was treated as such.

Another author offered similar advice from which it also appears that a 'crush on her employer' was characteristic of a period of transition and its confusion between the two coexisting codes:

> the modern tendency to ignore the line between employer and employee is not as complimentary to the latter as at first appears. This is particularly true as regards the young woman of the business and professional world who loses much more than she gains in accepting an invitation to dine, to take tea, or to dance with her employer ... unfortunately it is considered a favor to be invited to dance by one's boss – which puts the relation of partners out of joint from the start ... Hence, except for the community dances, or a special civic occasion, the girl employee does well to decline all social attentions from her employer. She will also do well, in accepting any attention from her fellow employees, to establish her own personal standards entirely apart from her business life. In this way, those seeking her acquaintance or friendship will be paying her a personal compliment rather than accepting her as part of the day's work. (Wade, 1924: 333–6)

A similar kind of advice was given in the 1930s, for instance by Mrs Post, who wrote 'sex is one thing that has no place in business' and concludes: 'The ideal business woman is accurate, orderly, quick and impersonal.' This advice leaves such a woman nothing of the femininity that blossomed in good society. However, the pendulum was swinging even further to the extreme of rigorous and harsh advice: 'The perfect secretary should forget that she is a human being, and be the most efficient machine that she can possibly make of herself – in business hours' (Post, 1931: 549–50).

Obviously, the hardness and rigour of an impersonal machine were perceived as necessary for learning the business code and unlearning the woman-in-good-society code – but only during business hours. A manners book of 1936 also says: 'In business you have to be *impersonal* in your relations with others', but by this time, the expected 'shock' of such a tough statement was followed by an attempt to soften the reader up:

> Being impersonal does not mean being indifferent or wooden. On the contrary, you must be intensely alert and interested in order to succeed in any position. But you must leave personal feelings out ... It takes personal quality, and qualities, of a high order to be impersonal. You need to possess and exercise qualities such as self-control, dignity, and good humour in order to behave in an impersonal manner when you can't help feeling very personal. (Landers, 1936: 221–3)

In 1942, in the eleventh edition of a popular advice book for women, an influence from the business sphere to the private sphere is observed: women in business transferred their newly acquired business-world habitus to their social-world habitus: 'With the greater acceptance of the business woman in the national pattern, the woman is lifted out of her exaggerated femaleness. War lifts her out of it still further' (Wilson, 1942: 230). After the war, women were on the one hand lifted out of 'exaggerated femaleness' in the social world, and on the other, they were liberated from impersonal, rigid and machine-like behaviour in the office. At this point in time, an attempt at a synthesis of good-society femininity (thesis) and impersonal office machine (antithesis) stated that:

> [she]doesn't need to be any less feminine and charming in her office than outside of it. In fact feminine charm is one of her major personal assets, and she is careful not to lose or destroy it. But there's a difference in being gracious and charming to all people, in all situations – and deliberately using one's charms for personal gain. The well-bred woman in business does not make a practice of resorting to feminine wiles or coquetry to achieve her aims. (Eichler Watson, 1948: 497)

In a chapter on women in business, Amy Vanderbilt supported the same ideal synthesis by offering a variation upon the old distinction between the woman with a job and the lady in the domain of home and good society: 'Every woman who refuses to become "one of the boys" in business and who insists she be treated as a lady in the human rather than in the drawing-room sense does her share toward a better understanding between the sexes' (1952: 206). Some advice nevertheless remained ambivalent: 'Your office life should be impersonal. If you have a romantic involvement with another employee, it should not be common knowledge.' Anyway, 'your personal life should not affect office life' (Ostrander, 1967: 86).

In 1975, Emily Post's daughter Elisabeth copied the sentence containing the word impersonal, but she followed the trend towards a perspective on women as equal human beings by writing subsequently:

In spite of all this, a woman should not try to hide or downgrade her femininity. There has always been and always will be a difference between the two sexes – and '*Vive la différence!*' Women who think that they can compete better with men by trying to be masculine are totally mixed up. While a career woman has no business trying to gain an advantage by using her sex, she should not disregard the *natural* advantages it gives her, either. Men have far more respect and admiration for a *feminine* woman who handles a job well than one who does the job but looks and acts like a misplaced male. (1975: 749–50)

In this 1975 edition, Elisabeth Post reflected the 'spirit of the times', the times of the Sexual Revolution, by writing: 'a little mild flirting, an occasional "mixed" lunch, preferably not as a two-some, help to lighten the inevitable boredom of day-to-day business' (Post, 1975: 749). That spirit, however, had been formulated more potently in *The Cosmo Girl's Guide to the New Etiquette*, edited by Helen Gurley Brown. The quotation that follows is from a section on 'Office Romance':

A ton of impressive words have been written about the pitfalls of intraoffice romance ... *what a bore!* ... With a measure of good sense, good manners, and old-fashioned consideration you can sidestep the booby traps and soften the potential for trauma that may exist in office romance. For as sure as gender (and what could be surer) you *are* going to flirt with the men you meet professionally. (1971: 120)

Other authors of the period contradicted this daring attitude: 'Business frowns upon any outward manifestation of attraction between the sexes ... Though there may be subsurface ripplings, men and women must work together almost as if unconscious of each other's sex' (Whitcomb and Lang, 1971: 383). And yet these authors also strongly reflected the era of the Sexual Revolution:

Conducting an intraoffice romance requires great skill and delicacy ... In an office in this day and age a girl can't go Victorian and declare her virtue slandered by the cad who tells her a slightly off-colour joke or puts his arm around her shoulders. But expressing displeasure at this stage (either by a feigned look of alarm or by coolly and quietly moving away) will probably discourage further advances. Act naturally, change the subject, and ignore it. (1971: 384–5)

This rather acquiescent stance became much more militant in the 1980s. The issue of sexual harassment arose, especially at work, and clearly outdated this earlier stance, particularly the remark about 'his arm around her shoulders'. And it led to Elisabeth Post's remark on 'a little mild flirting' being branded 'politically incorrect'. In Post's 1984 edition, the swing of the pendulum had gone in the other direction again, although not all the way back to the 'impersonal machine'. Now, she shunned the sexual suggestiveness of a décolleté and of a dress 'slit to the thigh'. Their place was taken by glamour and style:

> Business entertaining in the evening is common these days, and women have the task of dressing attractively while still appearing businesslike. Décolleté cocktail and evening dresses are out, along with those slit to the thigh. Night time sex appeal may easily dim a woman's daytime professionalism. Colours and fabrics can give even conservative clothing the glamour and style women desire without suggestiveness. (Post, 1984: 497)

Avoiding 'office wolves' was still considered good advice, but no longer enough. Moral indignation entered the tone. Indeed, Post's renewed 1992 edition did contain a paragraph on sexual harassment, while one headed 'Sex in the Workplace' was written entirely in the tone of 'Neither sex nor sexual attraction belong in the office' (1992: 229–30).

In the same year, in a personal communication, America's Miss Manners (Judith Martin) expressed herself to be against using first names at work because greater formality and larger social and psychic distance would provide women with additional protection.

In one of the above quotations, businesswomen and their business manners were observed to have influenced manners in the sociability sides of life. The same logic would lead one to suppose that increasing numbers of women entering business and reaching executive status would turn 'going Dutch' into an increasingly accepted and expanding practice. Rising numbers of women earned enough money to do so. Moreover, female executives occasionally had to pay entertainment or other bills for male clients or to take their share of cheques when lunching with male business associates. The data cited in Chapter 4, however, indicate that the effect of business manners on dating manners, particularly on 'going Dutch', was small, if not entirely absent. These data suggest that this contradiction between business manners and courting or dating manners was maintained, that the two coexisting codes were solidified and kept apart as a 'double standard', rather than that some kind of synthesis developed. This outcome can be traced in the history of advice on women executives paying for men. Here is a quotation from the early 1950s:

> In all cases (for the sake of the man) a woman tries to avoid a public display of her financial arrangements. Onlookers cannot know the circumstances, and men are easily embarrassed by a career woman's usurpation of their traditional role. Even if she is lunching a junior executive, it is courteous to allow him the dignity of seeming to pay the bill. The arrangements for the preservation of male pride can be made in several ways. (Vanderbilt, 1952: 208)

All the ways she mentions serve to preserve male pride by hiding the fact that he does not pay. Apparently, this procedure persisted, for a quarter of a century later, in the 1978 edition of this book, Amy Vanderbilt, the author of this million-selling manners book, takes the stance that, in relation to a woman outside job hours, a man should pay. From her lines emerges the man in private as the 'real' or the 'whole' man, not merely that part of him in business. Already in the introduction, a double standard is reported to have evolved 'quite logically':

> Women in positions of authority in the business world have greatly multiplied. Never before have men and women competed so avidly with each other in the business and professional worlds. A double standard has quite logically evolved. Men and women are free to treat each other in the traditional male-female patterns in their social lives outside the office, but in the office ... the successful woman executive treats the male executive like a colleague to whom every consideration should be shown. Additionally, she shows by her friendly but no nonsense manner that she can hang up her own coat, push in her own chair, and, in general, take care of herself! (1978: xi)

In accordance with the reported double standard, Vanderbilt states explicitly that 'when a woman lunches or dines with a man on business, they are not on a date'. An earlier manners book also emphasized this through the heading: 'When a date is not a date', and although the authors start this section with the sentence 'In offices where a young crowd works together, the boys may treat some of the girls as part of the gang,' they turn against this practice among colleagues: 'If one check is presented for a mixed group the girls as well as the men will each put enough money to cover the meal and tip in the center of the table' (Whitcomb and Lang, 1971: 368).

Although in the 1978 Vanderbilt edition women were advised, for good commercial reasons, of course, to give way to men who still found it hard to 'be treated' to a business lunch, there was less resignation in the way this advice was formulated: 'If the man she has invited to lunch is really uncomfortable about her paying (and a woman should sense this immediately when she is making arrangements with him beforehand), then it is better to settle the bill with the head waiter away from the table' (Vanderbilt, 1978: 448–9). In this chapter, the office is called the 'equal world' in which 'whoever happens to be in the lead opens the door and holds it for the other. Whoever first sees the taxi hails it,' etc. (Vanderbilt, 1978: 436). The implication of calling the office an 'equal world', however, is an 'unequal social-life world'.

5.2   England

In England, the code of manners for women at work seems to have developed along lines comparable to those in the USA. One similarity is an initially extreme swing of the pendulum towards a strict ban in business on the manners of sociability in good society. This extreme was reflected in an accusing remark on

> the numerous class of women engaged nowadays in businesses and professions who ... make themselves as hard, aggressive and generally unattractive and disagreeable as possible ... Everyone will know the type of woman referred to, usually distinguished by a high-pitched 'head' voice, ultra-precise speech and a self-assured manner. (Scott, 1930: 18–19)

However, this advice is also significantly different from American advice and even contrary to it, for it was directed explicitly against women in business trying to mould their manners according to some antipode of the traditional ideal of a good-society woman. Lady Troubridge, writing at about the same time, advised in a matter of fact way that:

> A girl who goes into the world to make a career needs, like any other girl, amusement and indulgence in feminine pastimes, but she must learn to keep her business life and her private life separate. She will do well especially to keep her love affairs to herself, and not indulge in affairs of the heart with men with whom she is connected in her business concerns. (1931: 381)

In 1956 and in the context of this warning, a keen observation was made by the authors of a best-selling manners book: 'now that class distinctions in speech, dress and behaviour are disappearing ... it is much more likely today that she will catch the boss's eye' (Edwards and Beyfus, 1956: 137). Indeed, in processes of social integration, people of different classes increasingly direct themselves to the same code of manners and emotion management, and as the social and psychic distance between them thus decreases, sensitivity for the erotic and sexual aspects of their relations increases. The same authors also articulated some of the difficulties that this intensified awareness of sexual attraction presented for women regarding the necessity to develop a new code of manners at work: 'One of the dilemmas of being a career girl is that she can never be sure whether the man's interest in her is professional or not.' And: 'True, some girls may get ahead faster in a tight mauve sweater, but the safest rule for office dressing is Sex after Six' (1956: 138 and 124). These sentences were deleted from the 1969 edition of this book. They reflected a perspective on women at work as still being highly interested in the erotic and sexual aspects of their relationships in that context. By the end of the 1960s, this perspective had become outdated. By then, it had come to count as not emancipated enough. It was too strongly and singularly based upon traditional good-society sources of power and identity. The new outlook, representing a new phase in female emancipation, preferably disregarded sex and sexuality. Thus, in a new section entitled 'Going after an Office Job', all advice was directed equally at men and women. Only once was the new outlook made explicit: 'If the boss is a man, how far should you behave as you do on a social occasion, and how far should you maintain a strict employee relationship? You can't go wrong by being formal ... and the same goes if the boss is a woman' (Edwards and Beyfuss, 1969: 140–4). But in a rapidly informalizing world, the meaning of being formal or keeping a distance was in constant flux.

In the early 1980s, the difference between the two codes as well as the similarity between developments in the USA and England, came out in observations such as: 'There are still men who are seriously embarrassed to be entertained at a restaurant by a woman, even for a business lunch' (Debrett, 1981: 268). However, the statement that 'a man who, in a social context, would always rise when a woman enters the room, and always opens the door for her to leave, is not expected to leap up and down each time his secretary walks in and out of his office', was now contrasted by the following firm and unambiguous expectation of women: 'Professional and managerial women prefer to be treated with no less, but equally no more, courtesy than their male colleagues.' The conclusion: 'People in business are people, not men and women' (Debrett, 1981: 250, 256). This formulation of the ideal code for people in business is similar to a formulation of the ideal code for all other relationships (as was formulated in defence of male courtesies against feminists who had rejected them in the 1980s): 'Good modern manners dictate that courtesies are extended by *everyone* to anyone who might welcome them, regardless of sex' (Bremner, 1989: 23). Apparently, the two codes, the one for business and the other for other social occasions, were tending towards a synthesis.

From the early 1980s onwards, problems arising from the co-existence of the two codes were attributed increasingly to men: men were attacked for making passes at work. At first, in England just as in the USA, avoiding 'office wolves' and using humour were mentioned as major ways to 'nip the problem in the bud', but in the 1990s, these tactics no longer sufficed. More active strategies and policies, like appointing well-trained personnel officers, were advised (Rees, 1992: 335). The observation that 'many women who prefer to debar gender-based courtesies in the workplace are perfectly happy to accept them in personal relationships' sums up a discussion focused on women (Beyfus, 1992: 10). In contrast, men were depicted as part of the problem:

> In a work context many men appear to feel the lack of guidelines on how to behave politely with women both as equals and as chiefs. The complicating factor here is the traditional precepts of etiquette, which are based on a protective attitude towards women, conflicting with a situation in which the so-called weaker sex are equals or have the whip hand. (Beyfus, 1992: 286)

On the same grounds another author complained: 'The basic trouble is that men are not sure how to deal with women they encounter at work. They may only be used to dealing with women as friends or sexual partners and they have no frame of reference for this other type' (Rees, 1992: 335).

Apparently, the gap between business manners and non-work manners was most problematic at office parties. Indeed, at these parties, being a mixture of a business situation and a non-work social occasion, the two corresponding codes tended to get mixed up. From the 1960s onward, advisors warned against office parties, because 'heavy flirtatiousness ... is embarrassing the next morning' (Edwards and Beyfus, 1969: 51–2), or because 'People tend to drink too much, let their hair down too far' (Debrett, 1981: 269). And the two codes were continuing to cause trouble in the 1990s, for this is how a section on this topic opens: '*The office party*. Or licensed sexual harassment' (Rees, 1992: 336).

5.3   Germany

In the German manners books of the second half of the century, office parties were also mentioned regularly, but not for flirtations or sexual harassment. Here, discussions of office parties always went hand in hand with warnings against offering the 'Du', that is, against offering to use the familiar form instead of sticking to the formal pronoun 'Sie'. It was taken for granted that this will be regretted the next day at the office. Apparently the transition from the formal 'Sie' to the informal 'Du', marked in Germany by a special *rite de passage*, has a special social meaning. It is related to a much stronger sensitivity regarding the public—private distinction (see my forthcoming book). Accordingly, German manners books focused more strongly on home than on work, that is, they dealt with such questions as whether women should be allowed to go to work and what the consequences would be for their husbands, their families and themselves. Early in the century, it was from this perspective that female employees, 'whose number by the mid-twenties had reached one and a half million, three times as many as in 1907' (Klein, 1994: 159), were hotly debated. The same goes for the 'new woman' who rejected prudery and narrow-minded, stiff and overbearing Prussian ways of behaving. By the mid-1920s, the relational difficulties of women in leading positions came in for discussion: 'this is the sharpest reef a woman in an executive position has to skirt around: it is the difficult task of turning the ruling man into a serving member without being able or permitted to utilize the weapons a women as a sexual being has at her disposal' (Schidlof, 1926: 270, 275). The main recommendation was to utilize her motherly talents instead. The ban on utilizing sexual attributes and talents was repeated throughout the following decades, although with less rigour than in the USA. In the 1930s and 1940s, the new editions of a manners book that was first published in 1916, warned female employees not to flirt with their boss:

> To flirt is a private activity, not appropriate at the office. Meanwhile, many young couples have nevertheless come to know and fallen in love with each other at work. If only they keep in mind that business should not suffer from feelings, then working comrades may even love each other and get engaged. It should happen more often. (Weißenfeld, 1941: 111)

In the 1950s, these warnings still contained the same half-heartedness. The secretary, an author argued, should persuade everyone to see her as a colleague only and 'to forget that she is attractive, *if* she is attractive' (Meissner, 1951: 82). A warning against 'more than comradely bonds' in the office was followed by a reference to the USA, where 'whole books have been written on the ideal secretary'. In them, it was reported, the relationship to her employer was dealt with extensively, and among the instructions was the rule 'only to accept his private invitation if his wife or another respect-commanding lady is present'. The comparison to the USA was concluded by stating: 'To what extent such rigorous rules can be implemented in the not so simple German practice is, of course, an open question.' All the same, readers were advised 'strictly to separate their professional life from their private life, so that even special friendships and ties between male and female colleagues will not stand out, do not even come out' (Meissner, 1951: 85–6). Apparently, the strict separation was for appearances' sake. When she went to an interview, 'Even if she has nice legs, and is well-versed in flirting, she will, provided she is tactful, not bring them conspicuously as weapons to the meeting' (Oheim, 1955: 378). She is not advised to hide them, though. The emphasis was on being inconspicuous.

Throughout the whole period, most German manners books kept giving positive advice on courtesy towards women at work. An example from the 1990s: 'Equal rights did not liberate men from being as courteous to female colleagues as to any other female: give precedence, hold doors open, fetch or offer coffee, present a chair.' Yet, in a sentence added to this discussion, the double standard surfaced: 'A woman who wants to do without this obligingness should not be rashly ridiculed' (Schönfeldt, 1987: 272). An author on business manners summarized the position of most working women by pointing to a contradiction that women executives were confronted with:

> they are expected to present themselves as women, and yet accommodate to demands that still are geared to men, as working hours exemplify ... On the one hand, they must bring their female capacities to work and they should not want to imitate men. On the other hand, they should, of course, also demonstrate that they have all the male capacities and qualities for management. (Wrede-Grischkat, 1992: 185–6)

Advice on how women were expected to meet these contradictory demands centred on self-assurance, on developing an all-round composure and confidence in manners, expertise, clothing, posture and voice (make it sound low!). Motherly qualities were no longer mentioned but still recognizable in specifically female leadership qualities such as the softening skills that women are supposed to possess and that could possibly make up for hard and one-sidedly male working conditions. A study of changes in German advice literature by Stefanie Ernst (1999) provides further details on the 'double role expectation' women were confronted with.

5.4   The Netherlands

The history of women in the Netherlands going to work is different. For many decades their numbers lagged behind. Dutch women, particularly married women, were kept at home more often and for much longer than in the other countries under study. At the end of the nineteenth century, young Dutch women were advised to develop their talents, to get some qualification or diploma in education, for that will 'protect them from colourless, nerve-racking boredom. Labour *is* a blessing' (A, 1894: 49). However, because Dutch cultural patterns were not interrupted either by

World War I or by a revolutionary labour movement, in some respects the nineteenth century lasted longer in the Netherlands than elsewhere in Europe. The feminist Johanna Naber complained that:

> one of the most fatal consequences of the World War was most certainly that women were defeated completely in their struggle for economic freedom, that what had been gained in the last quarter of a century was largely lost again ... Even from occupational sectors in which, before the war, women had made themselves at ease, men started forcefully to push them aside. (1923: 139–41)

In 1924, a measure allowing the dismissal of female civil servants upon marriage came into effect. The Dutch people and their government thus demonstrated that a woman's place was in the home.

Manners books that appeared before World War II did not give much advice to working women, and the few exceptions were mostly (adapted) translations. At the beginning of the century, one such book passed negative judgement on the question of whether granting (more) equal rights to women should have implications for courtesy. Women at work, it said, 'should not lay claim to exceptional politeness: the woman who practises an occupation is exterior to male courtesy; this courtesy only attends the woman who performs her female functions' (Foerster, 1911: 135). In the 1930s, another such book presented the following advice to women at work: 'If you have a boss, treat him as such; don't play the part of the mundane lady, but be a reliable, good worker and accentuate just that; that there will be no intimacies' (Haluschka, 1937: 148). And another adapted translation showed that comparing female office workers to machines was not restricted to the USA: 'A woman achieves valuable successes with her brain, not via coquetry and pose. A good secretary is a machine, not a female ... that may be hard for her, but her female side may be given its due after office hours when she can be as seductive as she pleases' (Latouche, 1946: 166). On the other hand, the boss was recommended to greet his subordinates courteously and 'to view them as people, not as machines'. Moreover, he was advised to keep clear of intimacies:

> Many girls are afraid of losing their job, if they do not grant the advances made to them by a certain type of man. There are employers who like to have their secretary and their beloved combined in one person. Eventually that goes wrong, for it is impossible to avoid disappointing either the secretary or the beloved. (Latouche, 1946: 123)

From the first to its thirteenth edition (1939–66), an originally Dutch and highly popular manners book advocated that 'there is nothing against a woman being 100 per cent woman, but if a business woman is to succeed, she will have to be more than specifically feminine' (Groskampten Have, 1939: 313; 1966: 328). In the early 1960s, another Dutch author addressed the old question of whether granting (more) equal rights to women should have implications for courtesy. He pointed out that women do want to be equal and on a par with men, but that they do not want to become identical to them. For it is not her ambition to become a man, he argues. 'Just as a woman sees the man in her husband, not the lawyer, the man married to an MD will not see her as a doctor, but as the women he loves.' Similarly, he continued, whatever a woman does in the social world, important or not, is irrelevant in contacts between men and women as human beings: 'the woman is a woman, a symbol of eroticism and motherhood' and courtesy should accordingly be defended as a tribute to this symbol (Knap, 1961: 12–13).

Between the mid-1960s and the early 1980s, a period in which virtually no manners book was published, the wave of informalization in the Netherlands was strong enough to catch up in many respects, one of them being a considerable increase in the number of women who escaped being confined to their home by going to work. Every manners book published in the 1980s made some mention of the new independence gained by women by going to work: 'Nowadays the daily contact among male and female colleagues has become much freer and less constrained' (Gorz, 1983: 133). And: 'In the military as well as the civilian world, the woman's right to a career of her own has become a part of everyday life, though she retains her right to some extra courtesy if she so pleases' (Grosfeld, 1984: 86). On amorous affairs at the office, a pragmatic and individualistic type of advice was given: 'soberly consider the growth of such an affair, accepting in principle that the people concerned should know for themselves what they are doing' (Hout, 1982: 72). Because 'the firm brings men and women together in an *equal* role as workers and colleagues', an author objected to 'the assumption that women should always do the *little things* that have traditionally been their task ... such as making coffee and putting papers on other people's desks' (Hout, 1982: 70–1).

In the 1990s, developments in the Netherlands continued to proceed in the direction of a diminishing difference between the two codes, the one for business and the other for non-work occasions. The following advice represented a synthesis, a unified code, for it was directed at both sexes and counted for business situations as well as for others: 'Whoever issues the invitation reserves a table and pays. Also if a woman is the host, she pays the bill. The whole bill. In these cases, some male acquaintances tend to assume power. Don't do that and do not allow it' (Eijk, 2000: 301).

6
Developments in Courting Regimes

6.1 Introduction

The previous two chapters have shown national differences in two part-processes of female emancipation: in the process of women gaining the right to pay for themselves and in developments from a unified code of good-society manners towards a code of manners differentiating between gender relationships at work and on other social occasions. International comparison showed a relatively late and incomplete acceptance of the right of American women to pay for themselves and the development in that country of a relatively strong double code which separated business relationships from others. My hypothesis is that these differences are related in an explanatory way to the earlier emancipation of American youth from the constraints of the parental regime through the establishment of a 'dating system' or 'dating regime'. In this long chapter I shall present a comparative analysis of developments in chaperonage and in manners dealing with encounters between the sexes, specifying the prevailing restrictions and opportunities for young people to meet, to get closer or keep their distance. These manners provide a view on the socially defined range of accepted behavioural and emotional alternatives in matters of sex and love. How did these courting regimes change? My attempt to understand and interpret these changes focuses particularly on the rise and fall of the American dating regime, for it is in these developments that my hypothesis can be tested.

In studying my sources, I have focused on a set of changes related to courting regimes. The main focus has been on connections between changes in these regimes and on changes in the self-regulation expected of the individuals who live under these regimes. In other words, I have focused on changes in the balance of external controls and self-controls in the matters of sex and love. At the same time, I have searched for changes in the balance between sex and love, that is, in social codes (ideals and practices) regarding the relationship between the longing for sexual gratification and the longing for enduring intimacy. This balance between emotive charges in both desires I have called the *lust-balance*. Another focus has been on changes in the relationship between group identity and personal identity, on changes in the We–I balance. And last but not least, I have looked for structural connections in the changes in all these (tension) balances.

Before presenting my findings, first the concept of the 'lust-balance' needs some further clarification. This concept is taken from Norbert Elias who used it in a wider sense to refer the whole 'lust economy' (Elias, 2000: 378, 441).[1] I use it more specifically to focus on the relationship between sex and love, a 'balance' that is perceived to be polymorphous and multidimensional (just as in Elias's concepts of a power balance and a tension balance): the attempt to find a satisfying balance between the longing for sex and the longing for love may be complicated by many other longings; for instance by the longing for children or by the longing to raise one's social power and rank.

The two types of longing, for sexual gratification and for an intimate relationship, are interconnected, but the connection changes in both the histories of peoples and the biographies of individuals. Nor is the interconnectedness unproblematic. Today, some people (mostly men) even view the two longings as contradictory (Hekma, 1994). In the spurt of informalization in the 1960s and 1970s, traditions providing examples of how to integrate these longings disappeared; the old 'marriage manuals' became suspect or hopelessly obsolete, mainly because they hardly acknowledged the sensual love and carnal desires of women, if they acknowledged them at all. Statements such as 'the more spiritual love of a woman will refine and temper the more sensual love of a man' (Calcar, 1886: 47) typify a Victorian ideal of love that was as passionate as it was exalted and desexualized (Stearns, 1994) with a rather depersonalized sexuality as a drawback and outlet for the man's 'wild' sensuality behind the scenes of social life. This ideal of love as feeling mirrored the Victorian attempt 'to control the place of sex in marriage ... by urging the desexualization of love and the desensualization of sex' (Seidman, 1991: 7). The current of this ongoing Victorian process resulted in a lust-dominated sexuality for men and a complementary (romantic) love or relationship-dominated sexuality for women. The romanticization and idealization of love also implied that sexual intercourse was increasingly defined as *his* 'right' and *her* 'marital duty'.

From the 1890s onwards, throughout the twentieth century with accelerations in the 1920s, 1960s and 1970s, the processes of the 'desexualization of love and the desensualization of sex' seemed to go into reverse gear: there occurred instead a 'sexualization of love' and an 'eroticization of sex'. In these processes – which took place together with continuing changes in the courting regime – people were confronted again and again with what might be called the lust-balance question: when and within what kinds of relationship(s) are (what kinds of) eroticism and sexuality allowed *and* desired?

This question is first raised in puberty or adolescence when bodily and erotic impulses and emotions that were banned from interaction from early childhood onwards (except in cases of incest) are again explored and experimented with:

> Sexual education predominantly consists of 'beware and watch out'. The original need for bodily contact or touching, which has a very spontaneous frankness in children, also becomes prey to this restriction in the course of growing up. Sexuality and corporality are thus separated from other forms of contact. Whenever two people enter an affair, the taboo on touching and bodily contact has to be gradually dismantled. For most people, this is a process of trial and error. (Zeegers, 1994: 139)

In the twentieth century, especially since the 1960s, a similar process of trial and error has been going on collectively.

The Victorian ideal of a highly elevated marital happiness was an ideal of the bourgeoisie. The rise of commercial groups and their world of business helps in particular to explain this idealization and also why 'ladies first' became a characteristic of all the commercializing nation-states: deference to superiors was no longer the main ruling principle in nineteenth-century manners because business demanded, not deference, but trust and respect. The social existence of the bourgeoisie depended heavily upon contracts, for which a reputation of being financially solvent and morally solid was crucial. This solidity included (creating the impression of) an orderly life and a supportive wife (see Chapter 2). This may explain why, in comparison with the aristocracy, the bourgeois control of the dangers of sexuality rested more strongly on the wife's obedience and assistance to her husband, and on (other kinds of) social control such as chaperonage.

Chaperonage is the embodiment of external social control on (the segregation of) the sexes, functioning to confine (her) sexuality within marriage or, in other words, to protect her 'honour'. A chaperone functioned to protect a young woman from strangers trying to intrude or worse, as well as to guard her from giving in to her own 'foolish and improper' inclinations. And last but not least, the chaperone guarded against status anxiety, that is against the status decline that results from destructive gossip. Simply to be seen alone with a man could raise suspicions of dissoluteness and stain her reputation. More generally, to be seen in what counted as an improper situation or with the wrong person or the wrong kind of people could damage or even ruin a reputation, whether or not something improper in fact had taken place. An unmarried woman, for instance, should never be in a situation where she was alone with a man, regardless of their activities and intentions. This explains why, at the end of the nineteenth century as these controls loosened and chaperonage became less strict, this aspect of diminishing social segregation was discussed so often in manners books. Until the 1920s, however, the social control of chaperonage (and its inherent inequality) still remained dominant; there was little or no faith in self-control over these matters.

From the 1890s onwards, this regime went through profound changes. Until the 1920s, courting manners generally showed the same overall development: young people started to go out together alone, without a chaperone. In the USA, this was called 'to date', and particularly in that country, dating spread rather quickly while dating codes became elaborate enough to speak of the development of a dating system or a dating regime. The practice of dating itself, however, was not an American invention because, in all the countries under study, full surveillance via the chaperone system was eroding. Yet the elaborate dating system as it developed in the USA did have specific characteristics. These become apparent from the 1920s onwards in advice on dating, on 'the line', petting and necking. The rise of the dating regime was the expression of a specific youth culture and a manifestation of the emancipation of a young generation and their sexuality. These emancipation processes also occurred in the European countries under study, but they proceeded differently and, until the rise of the second international youth culture in the 1960s, they occurred at a slower pace. In this chapter, I will sketch these trends and their differences by focusing first on the European countries under study and then on the USA. My presentation of a sociogenesis of the dating regime – and subsequent twentieth-century changes in dating, courting and sexuality – will be preceded by a sketch of changes in chaperonage in order to bring out differences in American developments compared to the European countries.

6.2   Chaperonage and the Courting Regime in England

In the early 1960s, an English author sighed: 'Boy meets girl and girl meets boy in so many different ways that it would be quite impossible to enumerate them' (Bolton, 1961: 15). This impossibility became taken for granted and was no longer expressed after the early 1960s. However, before that time, enumerating the various places and ways of meeting had been a quite normal procedure. For this reason this sentence indicates an important moment, a point of no return, before which, changes in ways and places of meeting often attracted special attention.

Throughout the nineteenth century, 'respectable' women and young girls were confined to the domain of their home, but a question like 'Can I with a lady friend visit a bachelor at his house?', sent in the mid-1890s to the editor of a 'Courtship Column', can be viewed as a harbinger of changes to come. However, the editor still came up with an unequivocally strict answer: 'It is thoroughly understood that married ladies should be accompanied by their husbands, and unmarried by their father and mother, or by a married couple with whom they are on terms of great intimacy. Under no circumstances can this rule be broken' (*Woman's Life*, 28 December 1895). By the end of the nineteenth century, however, alternative models of femininity had made other authors of manners books less restrictive. From the choir of history, here is Mrs Humphry's voice: 'But girls, nowadays, are not brought up with a single eye to matrimony, as they used to be. At this end of the century one is first a woman, then a possible wife. There is one's own life to be lived, apart from the partnership that may be entered into by and by' (1897: 58).

At the end of the nineteenth century, in England (and in the USA as well) the seaside is mentioned as a place where meeting someone of the opposite sex is informal and easy. In 1897, in her *Manners for Men*, Mrs Humphry wrote:

> Picking up promiscuous male acquaintances is a practice fraught with danger. It cannot be denied that girls of the lower middle classes are often prone to it; and there are thousands of young men who have no feminine acquaintances in the great towns and cities where they live, and who are found responsive to this indiscriminating mode of making acquaintances ... The seaside season is prolific in these chance acquaintances – 'flirtations', as they may perhaps be called. Bicycling is well known to favour them. (quoted in Porter, 1972: 33) [2]

Warnings like these show that there was now greater toleration of sexual licence. According to Davidoff, the phrase 'you can do anything that you please as long as you don't do it in the streets and frighten the horses' was a common expression (1973: 66). 'Flirtations' were frowned upon, but nowhere near as critically as in Germany or the Netherlands.

Women, especially young women, wanted to go out, and even chaperones were under the influence of this longing. In her *Manners for Girls*, Mrs Humphry noted in 1901 the arrival of the dancing, flirtatious chaperone, no longer keeping a 'sharp eye on the movements' of the girl she was watching over. She complained: 'The class of girl who likes the irresponsible, dancing, flirting chaperone is not as yet a very numerous one; but yet English Society is well aware of her' (quoted in Porter, 1972: 85).

Some middle- and upper-class ladies were beginning to go out in public without a chaperone, although rich and aristocratic families kept up chaperonage with greater strictness than did the middle classes. According to Curtin, 'there was some hint that the "new woman" with her bicycle and athleticism was a product of the middle classes'. The upper classes lagged behind, Curtin explains, because they were more strongly motivated 'to ensure she met only proper candidates' (1987: 243). These class differences were still mentioned in the first decade of the twentieth century. In 1909, for instance, Mrs Humphry wrote about a young man wanting to know whether he could take his fiancée to a concert without any one else, and her answer was that 'there are grades of society in which this would be absolutely correct. Even at the level of the upper middle classes it would be far from impossible.' She went on to point out, however, that this kind of laxity was not seen in 'the aristocratic and better bred classes of the community' (quoted in Porter, 1972: 67). In good society, she wrote:

> that is, among the professional and well-to-do classes, a girl could not attend a dance, theatre, etc., alone with a young man. Matters are much more free and easy now, than they were some ten years since, but were a girl seen alone with a young man in such circumstances, her friends would naturally draw the conclusion that they were engaged. This might or might not be agreeable to the parties concerned. (1909: 133, quoted in Porter, 1972: 67)

Soon, subtleties of chaperonage such as these became irrelevant. Around 1910, chaperonage was declared to be on its way out: 'Young ladies are now frequently asked to dinner-parties without a chaperon, a hostess constituting herself chaperon for the occasion' (*Manners and Rule*, 1910: 228).

After World War I, 'jazz had become universal ... the shimmy was "shaking Suburbia"' and one saw 'girls in the debutante stage not only dispensing with chaperones, but actually giving dances of their own without even a presiding mamma in the offing, and issuing invitations in their own names' (Graves and Hodge, 1941: 42–3). Indeed, the 1923 edition of *Etiquette for Ladies* said: 'Girls nowadays can give luncheon and tea parties in their parents' homes, receiving their guests and acting absolutely as hostesses. The mother will amiably absent herself on the occasion' (1923: 65). Engaged couples in particular saw their range of action widened. It was explicitly stated that engaged girls were now allowed to go with their fiancé almost anywhere, unchaperoned: 'theatres, dances, picture galleries and exhibitions, etc., or walking, riding, motoring and visiting friends' (Burleigh, 1925: 78; also Troubridge, 1931: 7). About girls not (yet) engaged, an etiquette writer concluded: 'An unmarried daughter is no longer socially her mother's pale shadow, kept closely under the elder lady's wing, never allowed to be alone, unless under her vigilant eyes, for she may now form her own social circle, entertain friends of both sexes, and be entertained at their homes.' Yet, traditional restrictions on young people's freedom to negotiate the dynamics and borderlines of their friendships were still quite strong as becomes clear from the way this writer continued:

> When any gentleman, newly introduced to a girl, has escorted her home from the scene of the introduction, it is not correct for her to ask him to call, or for him to seek permission from her. Any such invitation must come from the girl's mother, or any friends with whom she may be staying, so if she wishes to see more of her cavalier, she should introduce him to her mother or hostess. (Burleigh, 1925: 230)

This appeal to tradition did not keep this author from acknowledging that 'girls in various grades of life admit to their acquaintance, and accept as escorts to theatres, dances, etc., men with whom they have become acquainted in the course of their business or professional interests, without ever having had any actual formal introduction effected by anyone who knows them well' (1925: 233). This may no longer have been considered to be a serious breach of etiquette, but that did not mean, she warned, that this delicate matter could be dealt with light-heartedly; one had to be very careful. In the early 1930s, Lady Troubridge was among the last authors of English manners books to use the word chaperone. She did so in the context of bachelor parties: 'there should invariably be a married lady present or an elderly unmarried lady to act as chaperon' (1931: 292).

On the way from complete surveillance to greater freedom came new inventions like boarding schools for girls and ladies' clubs, both welcomed for enlarging the possibilities of making contacts outside the home: 'In the old days it was the custom to say that women were not clubbable, but the number of ladies' clubs which now exist demonstrate the fact that the club is a necessity of modern life' (Armstrong, 1908: 216). In the 1920s, '...to the business woman, the lonely woman, or the woman who is not comfortably or conveniently settled at home, the club has become one of the greatest of boons and a necessity to happiness' (*Etiquette for Ladies*, 1923: 136).

Greater freedom ran in tandem with greater intimacy and a chance of friendship between the sexes, both signifying a diminishing social and psychic distance:

> There was a time, not so long ago, when a marked reserve was required between men and women in public. But today, following upon the CAMA-

RADERIE between the two sexes bred by the War, and with the advent of women into almost every profession, art, and business, this social barrier is disappearing and a more friendly relationship is springing up between the two. The former stiff formality has been replaced by friendliness and under-standing. (Troubridge, 1926–31: 311)

'Chance acquaintances' or chance contacts were no longer depicted merely as 'flirtations' but taken more seriously: 'Very often a man will come into contact with a girl, through business affairs, at a dance or other function, or under even still less formal circumstances, and a friendship will spring up' (Devereux, 1927: 119). Surveying these developments from a larger dis-tance and with greater detachment, Davidoff concludes that by the inter-war period,

the reduced scale of living for most of the middle class, the decline of chaperon-age and new freedom for girls, meant that even the 'career' sequence of schoolgirl, deb (or provincial variant), daughter-at-home, matron and dowager wielding power in the social/political world, had ceased to have much cogency ... It was the time of the 'flapper', the 'roaring twenties'. (Davidoff, 1973: 99)[3]

This process may have been experienced as slow or fast, but its direction was undisputed; it was leading towards greater freedom to control the dynamics of one's own relationships, whether romantic or not, and to decide about the respectability of meeting places and conditions. There was grow-ing appreciation of the 'new woman' (who was often the 'fast girl' in the eyes of others):[4] 'The "new woman", by easing her demands for deference, allowed gentlemen to enjoy themselves in a relaxed fashion in her company – an advantage which lower-class women and prostitutes had always exploited' (Curtin, 1987: 280).

In the 1930s, the escape from being under the parental wing and a more rapid pace of making overtures were consolidated. This was brought out in the warning that 'he should have met her at least three times in the house of some mutual friend before he suggests a "spot of dinner" with a movie to follow. Nor should he get on Christian name terms before she gives him the hint that this is agreeable to her' (Troubridge, 1939: 176).

After World War II, the emancipation of the younger generation had again accelerated, as is apparent from the observation that:

many parents have dropped out of the scene and the young people have it all to themselves ... Today there is a tendency for the young man to meet his girl at a friend's party, to date her at the cinema or the club and drop her off at her home. And parents have got used to it. In fact, parents are growing to accept the idea that their offspring go out when they like, and few questions asked. (Edwards and Beyfus, 1956: 240)

This growing acceptance resulted out of a multitude of negotiations about the time at which young people were to return after an evening's outing. Advice on this 'very vexatious question' was usually against attempts 'to enforce a rigid rule'. This was rejected as 'probably very unwise'. Parents were advised to differentiate and to allow more latitude, for example, when the outing was to a dance or a party (Bolton, 1955 and 1961: 49).

Parties were also discussed for another reason. After World War II, under the heading 'Entertaining on Her Own' it was debated whether a 'single woman' was permitted to give a party in her bed-sitter, for such a party 'presents its own administrative and social problems. The heart of the matter is the bed.' This statement was explicated by the following retrospect:

> The mere presence of a bed in a corner of the room was once considered an irresistible invitation to wickedness and precluded any nice girl from giving a party in the same room. Even in the 1930's women undergraduates at Oxford were forbidden to entertain men in their bed-sitting rooms, even if there were several men and several women around too ... Today, a couple of cushions plonked on a divan bed is enough to give the room an aura of respectability. (Edwards and Beyfus, 1956: 136)

This retrospect, particularly the formulation 'irresistible invitation to wickedness', suggests that in mixed company the presence of a bed would automatically trigger sexual longings, moreover, that both men and women would have to give in to these longings. Thus, this retrospect also demonstrates a lack of confidence in the power of self-control. External social controls were believed necessary to avoid these 'irresistible' situations. In the mid-1950s, a couple of cushions apparently sufficed to keep the dangers under control. But not entirely, for the discussion was continued by a reference to the law and to the embodiment of external social control, *Mrs Grundy*, that watchdog over 'respectability' – her 'honour', her status and reputation:

> Girls ask their boy friends to the bed-sitter in the evenings but a Mrs Grundy of a landlady may complain. It is worth recording that as the law stands a judge can accept as evidence for divorce the fact that a man and woman were together in a bed-sitting room alone at night for some hours. But the judge might be wrong. They might have been drinking cocoa all the time. (Edwards and Beyfus, 1956: 136–7)

Obviously, respectability was still at stake, which shows that this was written in a period of transition. Young girls now had to learn how to be their own chaperone and how to react adequately when their visitor or an escort on an outing would loom closer whilst displaying 'the masculine skill of making a girl feel prim and a little ungrateful. How to say No without being made to feel absurdly proper?' (Edwards and Beyfus, 1956: 11).

This discussion about the bed-sitter was removed from the revised 1969 edition of this book. In between the first and the second editions, many external and situational pressures like *Mrs Grundy* and the law had been marginalized, and the women and men as individuals had come to the fore, signalling a significant shift in the balance of controls. The introduction to the 1969 edition of this manners book observed: 'The Modern Woman who, as we saw her, was an emergent character when first we wrote this book has now established herself as a force to be reckoned with.' This is substantiated by enumerating some of the new possibilities for women: 'to make the running with a man, taking him out and paying for him and gradually behaving in an independent way. She goes into pubs on her own, gives parties and goes to them on her own.' In short: 'The Single Woman has come into her own.' Some transitional ambivalence was still present in the remark that women have 'had to pay a price for it. She's had to give up many pleasing aspects of the protective masculine etiquette' (Edwards and Beyfus, 1969: xi).

By the 1970s, such traces of ambivalence had disappeared, and comments had become less celebrating or nostalgic, and more factual:

> The convention that demands that the man should issue the first invitation dies hard. The idea that the girl might do so is gradually becoming acceptable among the young in North America but it has not taken hold in Britain. It is no longer incorrect, but at this stage of social development it is certainly ill advised. (Debrett, 1981: 272)

The question whether courtesies such as offering a seat are still part of good manners 'in the age of equality' was now left open as being dependent upon the variables of any particular situation and relation. On the other hand, however, 'etiquette is certain only on one point: what is *not* good manners is refusing ungraciously' (Courey, 1985: 81).

From the Sexual Revolution onwards, a variety of topics connected with sexuality came to the surface, indicating significant changes in the lust-balance: 'Masturbation comes a poor second to sex combined with love, but it performs a useful and necessary service ... After all, God gave us fingers – in his great understanding, he probably knew quite well what the middle one was for!' (Kandaouroff, 1972: 81). The emancipation of sexuality coincided with advice to clearly express intentions and/or degrees of (relational) commitment:

> Because sex can be an expression of such varied emotions – affection, love, lust, even aggression – its introduction into a relationship does not necessarily signify a deeper commitment between two people, although it may be. It is considerate of each party to make sure that the other knows how much commitment is intended. (Debrett, 1981: 276)

During the 1980s, in the choir of voices on these matters, those defending a more traditional lust-balance and attacking 'excessive permissiveness' became somewhat louder again:

> The term sex equality is false for in the Western world, there is really little or none ... 'Love is of man's life a thing apart, 'Tis woman's whole existence.' ... It is part of woman's nature that she is less aggressive and the physical side of sex tends to remind her of her femininity. For the male penetrates whilst the female accepts is the way nature has arranged us ... Debate

about permissiveness being all right if the pair love each other has always been a white washing excuse for fornication ... Permissiveness has resulted in a loss of discipline not only in sex but in all areas, yet, without discipline civilised life would become impossible. (Lady Penelope, [1982] 1989: 148–9, 154–5)

On the whole, however, voices advocating a return to traditional discipline remained a minority, while a majority of others began to sound increasingly calm and factual:

> Flirtation is to sex what reading the menu is to a meal: one may not eat all one reads about, but the anticipation is delightful ... 'Courtship' seems to be divided into two categories – comparable to fast food and dinner at a restaurant. With women whom they just like or desire many men want the fast food approach. But when deeply drawn to someone they will accept, and even want, a slower pace. The same men who talk of a three-date 'score' admit to courting special women for months – if need be ... Many men admit to taking less trouble getting to know a woman after bedding her than they do before – when they are trying to charm her and understand what makes her tick. And some men value women largely for the difficulty of the chase. Indeed, for some the chase is the real excitement and the rest an anticlimax. And, though men still make most of the running, much the same can apply in reverse. So, for success, if someone isn't being guided by morality (old fashioned but rather successful) he or she should perhaps consider human nature and be guided by long-term goals rather than by immediate inclinations. (Bremner, 1989: 24? [6])

> And most important of all, your condom or mine? (Graham, 1989: 136)

> *One-night stands and thank-you's.* There once was a sort of rule that the man would contact the woman the following day, by phone or with flowers, to say thank-you or just to acknowledge that something had taken place... in today's climate [only] if the relationship is going to take a step further forward, then some such gesture would seem to be mandatory after a 'first time'. (Rees, 1992: 180)

These quotations, particularly the distinctions made in them, show how rapidly and widely the range of socially acceptable courting manners had expanded, while at the same time demanding an increasingly intense and lasting alertness, a heightened sensitivity for the slightest change in the relationship and/or the situation. This is how these interconnected changes were rendered in the introduction to a 1990s' manners book: 'Nowhere is the uncertainty more rife than in the field of what is considered acceptable behaviour between the sexes ... Approaches to sexual encounters in which both parties seek assurance from each other about protection from possible risks, call for a particularly sensitive awareness of mood and timing' (Beyfus, 1992: [7]).

A short retrospect by the same author clearly brought out the increase of accepted alternatives as well as the expansion of demands on a person's self-regulation:

At one stage it could reasonably be assumed that if an eligible male paid court to an eligible female, marriage was on the cards. Nowadays no such thought may dwell in either party's mind. Courtship may lead to live-in affairs in which marriage is not even considered, to passionate friendship without ties on either side, or to sexual fulfilment of a passing fancy ... misunderstandings may easily occur. No general advice holds except to try to avoid self-deception and idle promises. (Beyfus, 1992: 9)

This wide range of courting possibilities and relationships would hardly have been possible or imaginable without the emancipation of young people from the regimes of their parents. Already in the late 1960s, parental authority was sent up – 'Young people can have it all their own way today, marrying whom they like ("Anyone I know, darling?" asked one mother when her daughter announced that she was going to marry), marrying when they like and how they like' (Edwards and Beyfus, 1969: 261). Towards the end of the twentieth century, parents are still mentioned, but only in the context of children and teenage parties: 'Parents tend to make themselves scarce until the agreed hour of the end of the party. Parental presence at this stage is to be recommended as it backs-up the more responsible elements' (Beyfus, 1992: 224).

6.3   Chaperonage and the Courting Regime in Germany

In German, the word chaperone exists but only as a foreign word. The German word is Anstandsdame, but it seems significant that I have not found it in German manners books. These do not pay much attention to chaperonage and courting. Indeed, in many of them, these topics are entirely absent. This may be because the topic was considered to range among the 'matters of the heart' for which the main rule was to be very careful, because in these matters, 'delusion is brief, whereas remorse persists' (Ehrhardt, 1905: 141). Manners between husband and wife as well as manners between friends were usually discussed at some length. Both friendship and marriage have in common that the offer to marry as well as the offer to address one another in terms of the familiar 'Du' cannot be revoked without losing the love and the friendship, 'because one cannot possibly go back on a Du' (Dietrich, 1934: 80). In developing the personal and intimate relationships of love and friendship, however, rules and manners were considered inappropriate. In the Cambridge-Eichborn German-English dictionary, the word *Anstandsdame* is followed immediately by *Anstandsdame spielen* which is 'to play the chaperon (gooseberry)', and this impression of 'not being serious' is confirmed by the synonym *Anstandswauwau*, indicated as 'familiar', and *Anstandswauwau spielen*, which is 'to play gooseberry'. *Wauwau* is the sound a dog makes. It is a reminder and another symptom of that German tradition of branding large parts of the code of manners as outward superficialities (see Elias, 2000; and Wouters, forthcoming). The chaperone did exist in Germany, but I have not been able to find much about this institution. In discussing 'matters of the heart', authors often restricted themselves to the basic rule of thumb to be open and honest. They may have discussed manners in the relationship between spouses, but hardly anything, if anything at all, was written on manners in finding someone to marry. The 1900 edition of Von Franken's famous manners book does mention a few possible ways of meeting a girl: 'at an acquainted family, as a friend of your sister, in the countryside, at a social gathering, at a ball, playing an instrument together, doing a sport'. This list is found in the opening sentence of the chapter on marriage, in a paragraph on 'how to approach the girl I desire to become my fiancée?' In manners books of a later date even these clues are absent. The 1959 edition of the same book simply proceeded from 'Have you met a girl you would like to marry ...?'

Apparently, until late in the nineteenth century, escorts for young ladies and engaged couples were taken for granted; the writers of manners books simply assumed their presence and did not present many details. In 1878, Ebhardt wrote that only after they have passed the age of thirty were women allowed to make their own home and live as they pleased. Younger girls who were obliged to earn a living were mentioned as another exception to the rule that young women were to be accompanied when going out. The promenade and the skating rink were mentioned as places where it is taken for granted – 'of course' – that this rule would prevent a young lady from entering unaccompanied. A tight escort regime was also advised for engaged couples; they should never be left alone together, in public or at home, until very shortly before their wedding day (Ebhardt, 1878, quoted in Krumrey, 1984: 350). A book from 1893 was still presenting the same rules in a more pragmatic tone:

> If she has to travel a long way at night to get home, it is safest to instruct the maid to come and fetch her at a particular hour. If no other escort is available, we can see no harm in having a male friend of the family accompany her home. This should remain the exception, however, never become the rule. (Schramm, 1893: 166)

At the turn of the century, retrospective remarks clearly show escorts or chaperons to be on their way out:

> It used to be demanded that young ladies should visit the ice rink only when accompanied by older persons. Today, however, the world of women allows a far wider range of action than before and this restriction can no longer be maintained so rigidly. Today, young ladies may visit theatres and concerts without any protective escort, so why would they not be allowed to venerate the pleasures of the ice rink alone, as long as they live up to the demands required from all cultured human beings. (Marschner, 1901: 155)

The new freedom of movement spread, but in contrast to England (and the USA), without leaving a trace of social class differentiation; the upper and middle classes were not mentioned in this context. Changes were depicted in general terms. For instance, in 1908, an author wrote: 'Young girls and ladies are also allowed, of course, to visit coffee houses alone, all the more since these often have a special ladies section. Taverns are a different matter' (Eltz, 1908: 472).

Expanding latitude regarding the range of possible contacts between the sexes can also be inferred from a new topic in German manners books: flirting. At first, the word was used to refer to women's behaviour only. Apparently, this understanding indicated that girls and women were increasingly showing erotic attention to men, whereas before, such demonstrations had tended to come only from girls of easy virtue and from prostitutes. For men, paying erotic attention to a girl was, of course, part of traditional courting behaviour. They were expected to take the initiative in this sphere, but they had to be serious, and flirting was not. In his famous eighteenth-century manners book, Knigge had used the word 'villain' ([1788] 1977: 198) for the kind of man who courts by making false promises to innocent and inexperienced girls only to enjoy himself and then desert them.[5] Around the turn of the nineteenth to the twentieth century, the verb 'to flirt' spread in Germany to refer to a similar kind of behaviour by women: paying attention to a man without serious intentions, a show of affection for amusement only. In 1905, Dr Fritz Ehrhardt warned young girls in particular not to indulge, for most of them would want to get married and 'it is just these coquettish girls who like to play with fire who experience being left on the shelf and becoming a spinster as their most abysmal punishment'. These girls, he wrote, 'flirt indiscriminately, ... until they finally find themselves deserted; for all admirers, one after the other, even the most nearsighted ones, eventually discover they were merely being led up the garden path' (1905: 140). The following tirade against flirting also had a nationalistic ring; it is taken from a book which carries no date, but which must have appeared before World War I since the author mentioned the 'derailment' of young girls from good families who correspond with Negroes in 'our' colonies and send them pictures of themselves (Krampen, nd: 437):

> The mere fact that we have no translation for this foreign word ['flirt'] is suspect, demonstrating its contents as alien to our nature, just as the people of other countries cannot express our 'Gemütlichkeit' [cosiness]. To flirt is to lie and, therefore, flirting is disgraceful. Flirting is the sport of igniting hope, desire and passion in others, whilst being fully aware that they will never be returned. (Krampen, nd: 270)

The 'pragmatic American woman, who happily accepts that "making money" takes up the whole life of men', and the 'cool-natured English woman' were cited as the real masters of flirting or 'man hunting'. And although this author understood that 'a woman may experience herself to be a grace-bestowing goddess when she uses her weapons, sending inviting and alluring glances', nevertheless he warned against indulgence, for such 'allusions and teasing have instigated many couples into a love affair that could not pass the test of authenticity and have stirred many couples to part' (Krampen, nd: 271–2).

Although the male counterpart of flirting was not (yet) called flirting, it was repeated with renewed emphasis that a man should not incite false hopes by near-promises and promising suggestions. Dressed up as Madame Etiquette, this author wrote:

> My friend, don't you see you are compromising the young lady with your complaisance? That the exclusiveness of your devotion to her in the ballroom and on the ice rink chases off other admirers? One assumes you approach her with 'intentions', with 'serious intentions' ... You, however, succeeded in finding a suitable moment, as you laughingly assured us, at which it was still just possible to withdraw your head from the noose. That is unscrupulous, my dear! You 'dodge' at the very moment when you have excited her hope up to the sharp edge of fulfilment ... A gentleman does not behave like that.' (Krampen, nd: 274–5; the original German also used the English word gentleman)

This emphasis on 'serious intentions' in courting and courtship contrasts strongly to the non-serious attitude towards chaperonage as expressed in the words used for 'playing the watchdog'. It seems probable that both are connected: on the basis of the serious *inner* virtues and values that are connected to love and friendship, chaperonage is not taken so seriously. Even the very word *Anstandswauwau* suggests that playing the watchdog is viewed mainly as an *outward* superficiality.

In the 1920s, growing numbers of women began to take part in all kinds of (non-body contact) sports and many German manners books came to have sections or chapters on sports. In sports, one author explained, young girls learn to trust their own judgement and gain the kind of poise and composure that will silence those who still dare not allow a young girl to walk through the streets alone or who damn all sports for being unfeminine (Ebhardt, 1921: quoted in Krumrey, 1984: 358). This author also allowed young women not only to make regular bicycle tours with a gentleman friend, but also to skip his obligation to fetch her from her home, but instead to arrange to meet her half-way. In these matters, this author explicitly claimed to be on the side of the young women against the majority of their mothers, 'who still cling to the narrow prejudices of their own upbringing' (Ebhardt, 1921: quoted in Krumrey, 1984: 358).

In the next decade, it was proudly proclaimed that the days when young ladies were not allowed to enter an inn or even a lunchroom without an escort, were over. 'The growing independence of women has brought this about' (Meister, 1933: 362). Flirting also became more accepted, although the connotation of 'not being serious' remained dominant. One author was rather exceptional by defending (secret) short-lived affairs, thus offering a glance behind the scenes. 'Not every flirtation ends in engagement and marriage,' he started out his public acknowledgement of the indeependent force of sexual desire, and continued:

> It happens a thousand times: one feels attracted to someone, there's a heated

tension between two people, but it is immediately clear that nothing serious can come of it. From the beginning it is clear that differences in the education, social position, manners, religion, world-view, interests, and the whole make-up of the couple are immense and so important that both exactly know: this will never ever turn into marriage. ... It is painfully known: one should not lose oneself in the affair. This 'flirtation' should not turn into a great passion. However, perhaps fate may allow them a delightful time together. (Weißenfeld, 1941: 61–2)

Apparently a gnawing conscience made this author aware of a double morality shining through his argument, for he continued to defend such affairs by disclaiming any connection to the men against whom Freiherr von Knigge had fulminated so furiously, those who abuse an innocent and inexperienced girl without scruples, only for their own enjoyment. He claimed the flirtatious affair to be very different, admitting, however, that a girl who secretly entered such an affair runs far greater risks than the man does: 'Her whole future is always at stake; the man simply carries on when "it is over"' (Weißenfeld, 1941: 62–3).

After the war, the housing shortage and the large number of women living in one-room apartments were used as arguments for allowing women and men to entertain in their bed-sitter. It was advised, however, that at the end of parties when the last guests are leaving, her boyfriend should not stay behind. He, too, should leave (Meissner, 1951: 248?[9]). Twenty years later, in 1971, women were told that accepting an invitation to a bachelor's house 'does not in any way imply an obligation to share his table and bed. Similarly, a single woman may invite a friend or acquaintance to her house, for example for dinner, without arousing the suspicion of trying to "nail him down" or of compromising herself in any way' (Hanstein, 1971: 71). These words expressed many of the fears that had haunted women, and they expressed them more clearly and directly than at any time earlier in the century. Ten years later, in the 1980s, all this no longer needed to be said as these implications and suspicions had become outdated. However, shortly before the old social codes faded and the new, emerging ones hardened, the fears connected with them found the very direct expression that is characteristic of a transitional phase. Before that moment, the frank and informal manners that were later to be assimilated in the dominant code were still regarded as being too fearfully indecent to be more than hinted at in enshrouded ways.

During the 1950s, courting came to be discussed more often in German manners books. It was noted that 'a lot that used to give offence, is a matter of course today', and that both sexes have gained many opportunities for getting to know each other: at work, in sports, and during theatre and concert visits 'which today have become socially accepted without the protection of motherly or parental wings' (Oheim, 1955: 119). However, a clear concern was expressed about young people withdrawing too far from under these wings and complaints were made about the 'incomprehensible aversion many young couples have against introducing one another to their parents' (Weber, 1956: 371). Each young girl was advised to become sceptical if her friend did not want to introduce her to his parents (Weber, 1956: 376). This author noticed that young couples now spend time alone together in many ways and places: they go on cycle and canoeing tours, they visit pubs and cinemas; they go on weekend trips and camping holidays. She warned them not to go without parental permission and not to present themselves along the way as a married couple nor buy brass rings or indulge in any other degrading mischief. It was advised to make these trips preferably as a group, because in a larger company, 'final problems [an enshrouded formulation hinting at sexual intercourse] together with the confusion and embarrassment connected to them, can be postponed for a while without therefore being narrow-minded or old-fashioned' (Weber, 1956: 377).

Indeed, the concern that too many youngsters were 'going too far' seems to have been a major motive for the increased discussion of courting in the 1950s. An author advised her female readers to break off a relationship if it 'threatens to be getting into murky waters' – the language still hinting more than being direct: 'Always remember that no "experience" offsets the enchanting and irreplaceable things you would lose in this experience ... For these hard male words are valid still today: "She is very good in bed, but marry her? Never!"' (Oheim, 1955: 124). Another author wrote that, as in the past, love flourished in schools and dancing schools, and then she added new places such as at work, in student haunts and ice-cream parlours, etc., where 'the atmosphere is often somewhat frightening'. This was because the young 'existentialists' in student haunts and the so-called 'teddy boys' (*Halbstarken*) in the ice-cream parlours were rather unbridled and careless in their friendships, which would become dangerous when these relationships became intimately physical. 'Then, they often cause a big disaster, hardly repairable later in life, particularly for girls' (Weber, 1956: 371).

> These young girls have probably detected that basically they did not enjoy these activities ... In these matters, a woman is by nature not superficial. She can only become so after undergoing a series of experiences and having been disappointed again and again ... Women who have had these experiences too early often stay frigid during the rest of their life. (Weber, 1956: 373)

On the other hand, although 'going too far' certainly should not happen 'too early', a house regulation allowing the visits of a woman or a man, until 22.00 only, was called austere. The reader was comforted by an assurance that most landlords do not stick so rigorously to this time limit when they get to know you better. 'Once they have observed it is always the same girl friend visiting, they will not voice disapproval, even if it does sometimes get a bit later than ten o'clock' (Weber, 1956: 376). This author also raised the question whether an engaged couple 'is permitted to behave in the way that, from a moral point of view, should really [*eigentlich*] be reserved for spouses'. The use of the word 'really' here is telling. Indeed, the discussion ends by stating that 'both persons concerned have to settle the last decision in this precarious matter with their [own] conscience' (Weber, 1956: 381). However, the status of an engagement should not be ambiguous: 'If people only have the slightest ulterior motive, or the faintest suspicion that it may not really be a lasting bond, they should not get engaged' (Weber, 1956: 379).

In the 1950s, it was said that women could walk alone through the streets at night, provided they were cautious and behaved inconspicuously. By behaving thus, they would be unlikely to be accosted or troubled by unknown gentlemen. 'If this happens all the same, coolly ignoring it will offer the best defence' (Bodanius, 1957, quoted in Krumrey, 1984: 368). The same attitude was advised for women visiting restaurants alone. Krumrey adds the observation that increasing freedom simultaneously obliged women to be on guard against pawing by unknown men (1984: 401). And the fear of Mrs Grundy had not faded altogether, for a firm statement like 'going alone to a pub will give no offence in these times of completely equal rights', was still followed by a comma, and then the words, 'but a woman who values her good reputation will not go there anyway' (Andreae, 1963, quoted in Krumrey, 1984: 373).

Again and again, increasing possibilities for getting acquainted with persons of the opposite sex were mentioned. In the 1960s, adverts in newspaper columns were commented on favourably – 'They used to have a tinge of unseriousness, but that needs no longer be the case' – and the same was true of marriage agencies and computer matchmaking (Graudenz and Pappritz, 1967: 437–8; see also Hanstein, 1971: 44). The question was also raised whether a man was allowed to address a woman in the street with the intention of getting acquainted, and the answer was: 'No, actually he is not', followed by an example presented as an inventive and charming exception, ending in a happy marriage (Graudenz and Pappritz, 1967: 436). Another author answered that it should be possible to address 'an unknown female without being clumsy by coming up with something she can react to without feeling harassed', and adds: 'the words "meeting in the street" [Straßenbekanntschaft], inadmissible in the eyes of our grandparents, is no longer regarded pejoratively' (Hanstein, 1971: 43).

Camping was mentioned as a way in which young people and unmarried couples preferred to spend their holidays because they allowed a much less regulated kind of life, offering relaxation without constraints, and also because hotels don't like to offer their double beds to unmarried couples (Wachtel, 1973: 326). And Goethe's words 'permitted is what pleases' were used to refer to sexual positions as a way to combat routine as well as to swapping partners: 'if both partners have discussed what they expect from the relationship and what will not harm it, then here too what is permitted is what pleases both'. The addition – both – explains why adultery was excluded: 'increased sexual leniency cannot legitimate adultery' (Hennenhofer/Jaensch, 1974: 140–3).

By the 1980s, the wish of an unmarried woman to register at a hotel under her own name, not as the wife of her male companion, was called legitimate (Zitzewitz, 1986: 17). And it was observed that women obviously go to restaurants and pubs alone (Schliff, 1981: 237). Women were also allowed to ask a man to dance: 'They may go alone to a pub as well as on the dance floor; they no longer need a guard who protectively decides for her.' Girls have become so independent that they will weather these situations alone. The other side of this coin, though, is that, today, women can also be turned down. 'But we will get over that' (Zitzewitz, 1986: 70–1).

Unmarried living together was mentioned not just as an acceptable possibility, but even as nearly common-or-garden. 'Getting engaged has become almost old-fashioned nowadays' (Löwenbourg, 1987: 240). Another book offered a somewhat different observation: 'It is an established fact that living together without a marriage licence has been socially accepted for a long time. However, the tendency to get engaged and have a wedding is growing again' (*Umgangsformen Heute*, 1988 and 1990: 189).

By the end of the 1980s and the beginning of the 1990s, women were also allowed to address an unknown man on the streets (*Umgangsformen Heute*, 1988 and 1990: 102). The male gender perspective is now removed from the question: 'Is one permitted to accost "her" or "him", or not?' And the answer is: 'On the whole, it can be affirmed for the younger generation that each person may do as he or she pleases. One only needs to be friendly' (Wolter, 1990: 16).

6.4   Chaperonage and the Courting Regime in the Netherlands

Until the end of the nineteenth century, a courting regime prevailed in the Dutch upper and middle classes, too, that obliged young people to seek their parents' approval to become engaged, and only then was it accepted for them to hold and kiss and touch – a little. A high degree of parental control over the chances of their children to meet the opposite sex is apparent from the description of an engagement as a 'lovely and carefree period', in which

> the couple is supposed to get acquainted, but actually they don't, because in their happy mood both present themselves at their most advantageous; there are no worries nor collisions or internal complications. Those who already quarrel during their engagement, should break it off. In one month of marriage, for that matter, one gets to know each other better than in a whole year of engagement. (ECvdM, 1911: 112)

At balls and other dances, before he could ask a girl to dance, a young man should be introduced to the girl as well as to her parents, if they were present (ECvdM, 1911: 102). By this time, however, this custom had become somewhat controversial, for in a manners book of an earlier date, one reads: 'Apparently, it is considered less necessary among young people to have themselves introduced to the parents' (*Handboek*, 1905: 42). The young man is advised not to dance more than twice with the same girl, for if he did, one would suppose he had 'eyes for her' (*vues*), arousing expectations and, therefore, obligations. If a young man had danced more than twice with a girl, and he did want to get to know her somewhat better than was possible in the ballroom, her parents could not be missed out:

> you go to the girl's parents and ask them personally for permission to pay
> them a visit. If the parents are not present at the ball, you ask the girl and
> inquire about her mother's 'day at home'. Nevertheless, you should still ask
> her parents to be received, and pay the visit within two weeks after the ball.
> If your person is appreciated, they will ask you to come again and not wait
> too long before inviting you. And if Cupid puts his quiver at your disposal, I
> hope that your hand will be skilful and determined. (ECvdM, 1911: 106)

This description clearly brings out the large distance the sexes were
expected to keep between them, and also how every step towards diminishing that distance was at the centre of the public eye and well guarded by
the girl's parents and family.

The trend towards increasing latitude in chaperonage and courting
regimes was noted in *The Code of Madame Etiquette*, a Dutch manners book
that was highly popular in the first two decades of the twentieth century:
'The young girl of today enjoys almost as much freedom as a married
woman. She goes alone to a comedy or concert and travels alone at night in
trams' (ECvdM, 1912: 268). And: 'The young girl used to be prostrated by
the corset of convention. [Today, however,] she is no longer in her mother's
shadow ... When the daughter has completed school, where she often sat
next to boys in the same classroom, she is an independent being' (EcvDM,
1912: 266). The author of another Dutch manners book provided similar
statements: 'In our country,' she wrote, adding a little national sentiment,
'young girls, whether engaged or not, happily enjoy a large amount of freedom. They can move about without some Cerberus, whether a nanny or a
maid, always close on their heels.' This author also referred to co-education
as, in general, causing 'a pleasant and enjoyable sphere between young girls
and boys in our country, for the most part free from the slur of affectation
and mannerism' (Viroflay, 1916: 83–4).

Early in the twentieth century, a man and a woman were allowed to go
unescorted to the kind of bar or inn that is frequented by ladies. They were
warned, however, not to do that too often for people would soon gossip and
thus damage the girl's reputation (ECvdM, 1911: 48). It was noted that the
sight of a young man accompanying a young woman has become rather
common, that it draws less public attention and, therefore, has become less
titillating for the couple themselves:

> Only a few years ago, if a young man were to accompany a young woman
> home after a social gathering, and repeated this, for example, three or four
> times, the parents knew what to make of it, or they hurried to prevent what
> they saw coming. Today, one no longer draws any conclusion from such
> escorting, and girls who still do, will have to put up with many a disappoint-
> ment. (ECvdM, 1912: 180)

The author of another manners book from 1912 still noted that one of the
ways to announce an engagement is to go for a walk together, but immediately

added that 'nowadays this measure is outdated, for today young girls are no longer kept apart from young men as meticulously as before. One sees so many young people of the two sexes walking together that it would be foolish to suppose that all these couples are engaged' (Rappard, 1912: 73).

Private balls and dinners with dances were reported to have diminished in frequency, most probably because (recreational) sports came to provide many new possibilities for young men to meet young women. Whereas before, balls and similar gatherings used to be the only meeting places, now boys were also able to meet girls at sports like tennis, hockey, skating or bicycling (ECvdM, 1911: 98?[9]). Observations such as these suggest that ballroom manners were lagging behind and for about a decade remained more traditional than sports manners. Skating rinks were mentioned by a Dutch author as gatherings where the barriers between people break down particularly easily (ECvdM, 1912: 170). In the chapter 'on the ice', she wrote: 'If you are ice-skating with a gentleman and he offers you some form of refreshment, you can accept his offer with no misgivings at a private club; at a public rink, it is advisable to refuse, since the clientele there is always more mixed' (ECvdM, 1912: 173). On a previous page, this advisor had already explained that it was acceptable behaviour to refuse a gentleman's invitation to skate around the rink with him. 'One would not do that at an invitation ball', but it is acceptable at an ice rink

> because people become acquainted much easier there, and one might come into contact with the kind of people one would prefer to avoid. One might run into one of those 'would-be gentlemen' who make it their specialty to meet young ladies at an ice rink, knowing how easy this is in these surroundings. In this way, they try to work their way up. (ECvdM, 1912: 172)

In Dutch manners books, just as in German and English ones, sports were often mentioned favourably for enabling easier and freer contacts between the sexes, permitting young people to get to know each other more closely (ECvdM, 1912: 168). In this context, also clubs, club life and co-education were reported to have a liberating effect on contacts between the sexes. Both co-education and club life stimulated more personal and confidential ways of relating. Clubs allowed young people to go out in groups, for instance, to skating or on bicycling tours, picnics and competitions with other clubs, without being watched over by the traditional older couple whose task it was to ensure the maintenance of propriety. As it was expressed in 1912:

> Today, this old-fashioned silliness is ridiculed, and young people go out together. Only at dancing clubs has the old convention of older couples presiding been retained, as is customary at a ball.

> Gentlemen usually address the ladies by their Christian name and *vice versa*, and the timid deference that once characterized a young man's approach of a young lady has almost become a thing of the dark past. There is much good in this free intercourse between the sexes. They know and appreciate more

of each other; they don't stay blind to each other's defects; they are more natural towards each other than in the days when every single grown-up girl was
kept at a deferential distance from every male creature that crossed her path,
thus involuntarily turning each young man into a potential suitor. Thank God
those days are over. (ECvdM, 1912: 176–8)

Throughout the twentieth century two nostalgic themes were discussed
persistently as the other side of this 'golden coin': the decline in courtesy
towards women, and the 'decline of poetry' or romance in courting relationships. For example:

Brothers and sisters do not compliment each other. They are not courteous
to each other; they quarrel and are rather unconcealed in speaking their mind
... and quite often this is exactly how young people today treat each other.

Once, an elderly lady asked a young girl, a member of a large tennis club:

'Well, I bet an engagement occurs quite regularly among the youngsters in
your club?' The answer, however, was: 'O no, madam. We know each other
far too well.'

Wasn't this a telling answer? It demonstrates, I think, that there is an element
of truth in the assertion that a man likes to see his future wife enveloped in
a somewhat mysterious veil of idealism. The young girl is like the enigma that
the young man wishes to resolve. And as in today's club life girls present
themselves completely as they are, with all their good and bad characteristics
on show, it is quite natural that the young men regard them more as sisters
than as potential future wives.

Yet, to know each other thoroughly well has this large advantage, I would
almost say this large blessing, which countervails against all poetic old-fashioned courtesy: if among these young people a marriage is realized, their
chances for a happy marriage are all the better because both parties have had
ample opportunity to get to know each other informally. The enlarged confidence in the social intercourse of unmarried men and women has made these
contacts more confidential and also less dangerous. (ECvdM, 1912: 179–80)

These words cover a fair degree of both evaluative sides of the process. At
the time, and also much later in the century, it was not difficult to find far
more one-sided assessments, as for example:

Due to her more licentious way of associating with men (and also due to her
freer way of dressing), the woman has removed almost completely that
inscrutability, that air of mystery she was once enveloped in. Was this only in
their imagination, nothing but a stubborn myth, and thus disdained by some
people today? No, whoever talks like this does not realize the great importance of fantasy in our life. Even if he were right, he should regret that the
illusion has not persisted: a human being cannot make do always and everywhere without the golden sheen of appearances. (Alsen, 1936: 72)

Dutch manners books also contain many warnings against flirting. As in
Germany (see 6.3), connotations of the word were at first mainly negative.

Playful attention to someone of the opposite sex was soon branded as such. An early impeachment of tennis clubs for the intrigues and the coarseness of their self-proclaimed 'select company' also contained the smear that, among the members of these clubs, 'the fine, delicate and sacred feelings that one once used to hide anxiously and shyly, and were called love, nowadays are toyed with openly and without diffidence. Today, love is almost extinct; coarse "flirtation" has taken its place. What delicacy! Good heavens!' (A, 1894: 91).

Another author formulated a less conservative view, although she did perceive 'flirtations' and 'flirting' as the dark side of enlarged freedom. The bright side, she emphasized, however, is that 'girls are no longer expected to present themselves as naive or hypocritical by shyly and demurely looking down; today, they are easily permitted to talk to young men and to present themselves as amiable and cheerful.' To flirt, however, was to 'desecrate a heavenly emotion by turning it into merely a merry distraction'. If these girls marry, 'their heart is invalidated and no longer warm, because they have played the game of passion'. It is a dangerous game, for what begins as a pastime can turn into suffering. Therefore, a girl should not arouse feelings that she is not willing to rebuff. (Staffe, 1900s: 74–7). In one advice book, girls are warned a little more explicitly against 'losing the noblest and greatest gift of heaven to a girl'; it is described as the first but irrevocable step into an abyss of pure misery (Seidler, 1911–15: [10]).

A related topic, also revealing a fear of the 'slippery slope', was knowledge about 'the facts of life'; it emerged in the first decades of the twentieth century and was discussed until the 1960s. Conventionally, women should be and remain innocent until they *had* to be informed, which was shortly before marriage, but now it was reported that some of them were giving in to 'their pathological inclination to fathom the secrets of life', and reach for books that 'reveal the wounds of our society' and which bring them 'nothing but disenchantment'. They 'enjoy a poisonous liquid that will have a disastrous effect on their young brains, even more disastrous than the effect of that devil, Old Genever gin, on the brains of the masses' (Stratenus, 1909: 111–12).[6]

Another author also perceived 'flirting' to be a product of incresed freedom between the sexes, but she optimistically viewed it as transitional: 'Unfortunately, there are still a few foolish, nymphomaniac girls, who compulsively flirt and always imagine every man to be in love with them, but in our healthy, sports loving era, opportunities for unhealthy thoughts will continue to diminish' (ECvdM, 1912: 178). In a manners book for gentlemen, the same author advised young men to associate freely and merrily with young girls, but never to make them believe you have fallen in love with them when you haven't. 'A gentleman who is a "flirt" is even more contemptible than a coquette' (ECvdM, 1911: 25).

As the Netherlands did not take part in World War I, it seems likely that segregation between the sexes did not decrease as much there as in the countries that did participate in the Great War. And yet, the author of

Etiquette for Gentlemen (ECvdM, 1917) felt the need to add a whole new chapter to the second edition of her book (1920?), constituting one long plea for *Madame Etiquette* to preserve courtesy: 'as long as there are sexual feelings between men and women, courtesy should be preserved as the beautiful bridge that does away with the distance between them' (ECvdM, 1920: 36). She defended conventional courtesy by proclaiming among other things that the conventional feelings of women were their natural feelings: 'Any good psychologist, or good connoisseur of women, knows that every female soul is inhabited by a child's soul. He knows, that no real woman feels happy in her strength, but only in her weakness' (ECvdM, 1920: 38). These words are a strong expression of identification with the established, men, and of the fear of giving up any of the traditional female sources of identity and power based upon this identification such as submissiveness and surrender (see Stolk and Wouters, 1987a). As such, this strong defence mirrored the force of attack experienced in the accelerated emancipation of women and in the decline of segregation between the sexes. Another indication of this acceleration is that women and young girls from 'good families' were reported to be going to public dances, something they had never done before (see Chapter 3). At these dances, held at restaurants and hotels of 'good standing', women may have stuck to the old rule not to dance with strangers, that is, without being introduced, but introductions were made easily, and thus their circle of male acquaintances started to grow rapidly (Viroflay, 1919: 54–5).

In this period, it was predominantly unsupervised visiting that expressed most clearly the trend of diminishing segregation: 'probably the only position mothers today would still dare to defend is that a young girl should not visit a young man in his room. This is about the last bulwark of convention and it will possibly last a few more years' (Viroflay-Montrecourt, 192?: II, 68). That this was not sheer irony can be deduced from a discussion of this convention in another manners book. Here, the sentence – 'Nor does a gentleman visit an unmarried lady, who lives on her own' – is followed by:

> In the student world this rule is nowadays violated thoughtlessly and without compunction. Yet I'd seriously like to advise every single female student not to overdo it ... It does not become a young lady to go to borrow a book or find some other excuse for calling on a student. Behind her back she will often be ridiculed for it. ... If a student calls on a female colleague under some pretext, the young lady should receive him standing, thus signalling that she would not appreciate a protracted visit. ... Our modern young ladies seem to be keen on distancing themselves from all diffidence towards the male sex, but this pose is not becoming! (Margaretha, 1921: 29–30)

The same author complained about children in certain circles who showed no respect to their parents by confronting them with the established fact of being engaged (a complaint also made in Brummell & Co., 1927: 17). Such a bond, she continued:

is usually preceded by a period of flirting and fooling around together [*schar-relen*], and half the town or the whole village knows about it, except for the parents. Quite often such flirting and fooling around [*scharrelpartij*] do not even eventuate in a steady relationship [*vaste verkeering*]. And any girl who has experienced more than one such *scharrelpartij* is characteristically called in popular, not quite parliamentary, language: a 'licked roll' (or 'town bicycle'). (Margaretha, 1921: 143)

In the first three decades of the period covered in my research, the term *verkeering* (later spelled *verkering*) spread and became popular to indicate the phase preceding an engagement. Previously, the term had the more general meaning of having a relationship, being in contact with or in the company of one or more others. Examples and references in the *Woordenboek Nederlandse Taal* (comprehensive dictionary, Dutch equivalent of the Oxford English Dictionary) suggest that in this period the word was used increasingly to denote a courtship relationship, which gradually replaced becoming engaged as the main way of getting to know each other better. If such a *verkering* lasted and the bond between the couple got closer, the relationship would become known as *vaste verkering* (*vast* = steady and stable), indicating the preparatory phase before an official engagement. Although the practice will have spread with the word, in the manners books of this period *verkering* was rarely discussed. Engagement was. More authors jeered at the 'startling unconcern' shown in getting engaged, and extended their scorn to breaking engagements and falling in and out of wedlock with similar freedom from care. One of them declared it to be very incorrect for a young girl to tell her parents out of the blue that she was engaged to ... , and she adds: 'And yet, today, this happens all too often. There is a tendency today simply to eliminate the parents from these important life events and to take decisions into one's own hands. How shallow and wrong!' (Kloos-Reyneke van Stuwe, 1927: 26–7). Another author observed a fading of the ritual procedure for getting engaged and a proliferation of anarchy:

One person courts in a car, another on the beach, a third one seals the case with a kiss, a fourth person first kisses, proceeds courting the following day, and accomplishes an engagement within a week. The parents' consent has become a factor of third order. In certain prominent circles, consent isn't even asked for; parents are informed of the engagement only as sort of a 'notification'. The younger generation has progressed!
  According to both old-fashioned and modern views, however, it is beyond all doubt that a kiss is a kiss and not yet an engagement. A young innocent girl should not consent to being kissed before she is engaged. But ah!, countless are the girls who violate this prohibition. One kiss, stolen in a car, on a staircase, in the moonlight, on the beach, such a kiss is so easily and soon forgotten. It entails no further obligation for either party than to keep their mouths shut and under better control next time. But an engagement is a social deed, which has to be preceded by serious mutual checking of social positions, proportion of fortunes, etc. (Brummell & Co., 1927: 17)

Again and again the question was raised as to where the boundaries of decency were to be located. Obviously, several of these boundaries had moved up or had even been pushed aside, and one author presented the following examples of rules that had recently become obsolete:

> the rule that a well-bred girl is never allowed to be boisterous in public, that she has to lower her eyes demurely in front of every man, to move distantly and in a subdued manner, never to shout or to run, nor to laugh loudly, to romp about with other girls, that to enter the company of gentlemen with bare arms or loose hair is extremely indecent, as it is to walk in ways that might offer others a glimpse of leg above the ankle. (Zutphen van Dedem, 1928: 166)

These changes were summarized and symbolized, this author continued, in the changing boundaries of the skirt: from the long skirt to the ankle to the short skirt to the knees. The woman who lacks a sense of decency or a sense of embarrassment is immediately recognized by her desire to exceed the latest boundaries, even though these allow far greater freedom than preceding ones (Zutphen van Dedem, 1928: 168).

In the 1930s, manners books continued to warn against kissing too often and too easily: 'A kiss may set a fire where before not even a spark was suspected; it is capable of uprooting an existence and of building a future.' And yet, this author continued, so many people kiss thoughtlessly, thus debasing the practice (Alsen, 1936: 73). The fact that people could develop a courting relationship without being 'properly engaged', motivated this author to complain that, 'in recent years, a breakdown of moral consciousness has come about', for 'many young people would not be able at any moment to tell with certitude whether they are engaged or not; several also leave it to your discretion whether or not to call their relationship with someone of the opposite sex an engagement' (1936: 60). These words indicate that it had become accepted for a couple to present themselves as being engaged without having gone through the formality. The weight of a formal engagement also declined by the rising frequency of engagements being terminated. This author and others expressed serious concern about such 'rash engagements' that oblige friends and relatives to buy presents and pay a visit, but that are easily and silently invalidated: 'Pim? Oh ... didn't you know? That finished a long time ago!' (1936: 61; also Haeften, 1936: 47). In this decade, the recurrent question regarding the boundaries of decency was raised as 'How far can one go in flirting?' (Haluschka, 1939: 149). This was held to be a thorny question. There were many different kinds of flirting, but whoever takes love seriously could not approve of flirting, because 'a flirt gives too little and takes too much. The person who knows what love is, knows that flirting is accepting a loss, it's trading gold for copper' (1939: 150).

In another book by the same author, the decreased segregation and the arrival of friendships between the sexes were regretted, for in this way 'men have become habituated to such openly displayed female beauty that their hearts have been dulled and are no longer capable of high spiritual flights'. In this context this author came up with a graphic metaphor: 'One never dreams in front of an open gate, only before a closed one' (Haluschka, 1937:

30). For this reason she advised young women to 'stay away from beauty contests' and 'the same pride should keep you from allowing men to address you in the street, except if they ask you for a service' (Haluschka, 1937: 147). In the same tone of moral indignation, this author points to the 'girl-epidemic' and the 'vice-epidemic'. The first was specified by this invitation: 'Look into any illustrated magazine and you will see their legs, naked or half-naked, at a ball, a theatre, at home, in the streets, swinging above their heads, put on a table, dozens of them, hundreds; no wonder the concept "girl" loses every meaning other than "legs"' (Haluschka, 1937: 23). 'Apart from the girl-epidemic', she continues:

> there is also the vice-epidemic among our female youth. They really are ashamed of the word virtue, not to speak of the honourable word virgin, because these words are indissolubly associated with words like 'old' and 'shrivelled' ... A girl no longer wants to convince her neighbour of her good-ness, her chastity and purity, but of their opposites. Running risks is trump and ideal; we could almost say that to be dangerous has become a woman's life task. (Haluschka,1937: 69–70)

Reading this description of the vice-epidemic may further incite awareness of how strongly the long and virtually uninterrupted history of cultural crit-icism and romanticization is rooted in a continuous process of women's emancipation.

Talking about 'the facts of life' counted as both dangerous and shameful, and the same went for knowing or wanting to know about them. Ignorance was still presented as innocence and purity, and it was in the name of these virtues that the author poured shame on those young women who

> feel the need to be completely candid with the other sex; they must discuss the most daring topics. They know that behind such conversations dangers are looming, but it is just that that they find so exciting: balancing above the abyss. Another group, usually girls with brains, coquette with their naturalis-tic world view, pieced together out of highly peculiar books. Their quest to acquaint themselves with all the secrets of life never stops and they are obsessed by the urge to inform others ... In the name of reality, they have to demolish every ideal and tear up every benevolent veil. (Haluschka, 1937: 71–2)

Playing with danger (see Elias and Dunning, 1986: 91–125), whether by flirting, reading 'peculiar' books, or any other such shameful activity, was even depicted as 'our greatest enemy!' (Haluschka, 1937: 75). As before and invariably, increasing frankness and devotion to reality and truth were equated with greater acceptance of sexuality and with rejection of the ideals of love that shunned physical realities.

In the 1930s, parental control over the younger generation had softened to the point that wise parents would not even think of asking a young man for his 'intentions' when he paid a little extra attention to their daughter, not even if he were to take her out frequently. They might talk about this among themselves, but 'usually they leave these things completely to the young people themselves' (Veen-Wijers, 1936–40: 93; also in 1946–50: 108). But parents certainly were annoyed if a couple would not confide in them or only did so in a late phase (Post, 1938: 116). In view of such enlarged leeway, parents were advised to give freer rein to their adolescent children bit by bit, for if they were kept from availing themselves of the freedom now permitted too strictly and too persistently, 'they will escape from these restrictions anyway, and then run the risk of starting, in some dancing or other, totally condemnable affairs' (Paeuw, 1934: 205).

From 1939 up to the 1960s, each one of the 12 editions of Amy Groskampten Have's manners book contained the following observation: 'Due to co-education and freer contacts between the sexes, the young people of today have become more natural and particularly more honest towards each other than they used to be' (1939: 12). This bestseller contained advice on becoming engaged and on breaking off the engagement, but not on courting and going out in the sense of dating; only in the tenth edition, which came out in 1953, did she add this:

> The young man who knows his world will pay a visit to the father of the girl he feels attracted to, after meeting her a couple of times, and ask his permission to take his daughter out now and then so they can get to know each other better ... Most parents will appreciate this attitude: it prevents sneaky encounters and lies. (1953: 25)

The trend towards greater freedom also necessitated other revisions and additions. An interesting addition to the twelfth edition of this book said: 'An unmarried couple planning a summer hiking tour or some other trip together should agree in advance on how much money each one will contribute' (Groskampten Have, 1957: 52). Another addition was a paragraph on bachelors, revealing another sign of the time:

> Bachelors invite male and female friends, they go out with members of the opposite sex without raising any suspicion, they ask girls and young women out for car trips, for going to a dancing, the cinema, etc. ... There is nothing unusual if young people play tennis, swim, ski, or do whatever other sports together, but ...

> A small (actually a big) 'but' to all this regards the question as to where the well-bred girl facing all this freedom has to draw an invisible borderline. Nowadays, determining that borderline is infinitely more difficult than it was in former days, when free contact between the sexes was simply altogether unthinkable.

These words were followed by unclear, ambivalent advice such as not to go alone to a bachelor's house, or at least not too often. These words indicate that the rules of manners had become increasingly difficult to formulate in general terms. Courting manners as well as manners in general were becoming more varied and elastic, increasingly demanding reflexivity and flexibility instead of being merely the automatic expression of a fixed habit. It was probably for this reason that Groskampten Have called the borderline that was to be drawn vis-à-vis the new freedom 'invisible', an interpretation that is substantiated by her pointing to 'a positive attitude towards good manners' as being 'decisive' in these matters (1957: 336).

In the 1950s, authors scoffed at the 'stupid chuckling, scallywag whistling, not to speak of the rest' of what happens when a few boys meet one or more girls. Another target was a scene on the pavements of every city: boys talking to a girl whilst disrespectfully hanging on their bicycle, one leg over the crossbar. Young people hanging about in groups at street corners at night was called 'one of the most banal practices' (Keulaerds and Tienen, 1950s: 23; cf. Bruyn in Chapter 3). These words ranged among the many expressing great solicitude about the emerging 'youth culture', a concept indicative of a generation gap in the sense of parents losing their authoritative grip on the young.

Round about 1960, parents were advised to extend hospitality to all their children's proper friends, male and female, not expressly, but casually and lightly. In that way, the authors suggested, parents would be able to keep an eye and at least some control over the contacts of their children. And this policy was recommended also as the best way to prevent secret courtships at a far too early age (Palts-de Ridder and Eikhof, ca 1960: 4). By the 1960s, 'it is quite normal, also in circles where good manners are held in high esteem, that a girl is asked out by several young men without anyone disapprovingly saying that she "has so many boys". A girl is entitled to have male as well as female friends' (Palts-de Ridder and Eikhof, ca 1960: 3).

In the early 1980s, after a publication gap from the mid-1960s onwards, all the new manners books reported the relationship between women and men to have become far more equal. Indeed, a forceful wave of women's emancipation had made 'the weaker sex' strong enough to eliminate this expression from general usage. Manners books now included passages about how women themselves can ward off unwelcome advances. They were advised not to hesitate to speak up for themselves and to fight back: 'Repeat what he has said loud and clear: "Oh, so you want ..." (Grosfeld, 1983: 48). 'However', another author thought, 'level-headedly or critically raising one's eyebrows is frequently sufficient' (Hout, 1982: 73). Increased equality also implied less passivity on the part of women when it comes to welcome advances. Several books reported that women nowadays introduce themselves to a man even though some of the authors did express a preference for the old way of being introduced: 'A girl or woman who would like to become acquainted with a certain person would do well to take the official way, especially if that certain person is a nice man' (BakkerEngelsman, 1983: 13). Most advice was less formal: 'With increasing frequency, people introduce themselves. This holds true for women as well as men' (Groskampten Have, 1983: 269). Another author elaborated: 'If there is no opportunity for you to get into a conversation with someone in an inconspicuous way that does not seem forced, perhaps the best thing would be simply to walk up to him/her and say you would like to make his/her acquaintance.' After several examples of how one might do this, the fading general applicability of rules and the rising demand to be a reflexive and flexible self-possessed individual were heard in the lamentation: 'It is difficult to give advice, since it is largely you yourself who will have to decide which way of "getting acquainted" suits you best' (Eijk, 1983: 162).

In the 1990s, the genre of Dutch manners books was expanded by the publication of *Your Place or Mine? Erotic Etiquette*, a manners book dealing with courting, sex and sexuality only. In these matters, its author wrote in the introduction, 'conventions have all but disappeared, but boundaries and limits still exist. The problem is just: where?' (Eijk, 1994: 9). In a later manners book, the same author qualified this general statement by claiming that the difference between sexual harassment and making a compliment is often very subtle: 'a matter of boundaries and limits: who makes it, how, where, when, and to whom' (Eijk, 2000: 249). She also wrote about the 'misunderstanding that men are no longer allowed to be courteous to women'. No, she said, 'there are persons in authority who in their relationship to their secretary behave courteously in every respect'. Such behaviour is no longer the rule, but has become one among many possible options.

> *If you let women go first, they think you are paternalistic, and if you offer to do something for them, they growl that they are able to do it themselves*, some men complain. A misunderstanding, because why not make one another's life as pleasant as possible? It all depends on the way you do it [*C'est le ton qui fait la musique*] ... Nowadays it has become more a matter of courtesy; women and men relate to each other on a basis of equality. There are still women who appreciate a courteous gesture. There are still men who make such gestures without a patronizing hidden motive. (Eijk, 2000: 335–6)

These examples provide additional evidence of the general trend of increased behavioural and emotional alternatives running in tandem with rising demands on self-regulation: the task is to find out carefully and sensitively what in this situation and in that relationship is most pleasing as well as most effective.

6.5   Chaperonage in the USA

The dating regime in the United States developed from the 1890s onwards. It implied an erosion of chaperonage. However, as in England (see 6.2), this trend was initially accompanied by a countertrend: chaperonage was also spreading. These contradicting trends can be understood as stemming from different social class origins: chaperonage spread from the 'fashionable' circles in large cities whereas dating sprang from rich middle-class and good-society families all over America. In cities, the children and youngsters from families participating in good society were probably in greater danger of being seen alone, that is, of being approached by strangers trying to intrude and to be gossiped about.

According to the author of a manners book published in 1889, the effort to have young people from 'society' families supervised by a chaperone 'has been manifest for several years, and it has many earnest advocates' (Bradley, 1889: 100). This author gave in to them:

> Those who aspire to enter the 'fashionable' circles of our large cities (and it is claimed that even in so large a city as New York what is technically termed 'society' does not include over four or five hundred families, and some would even limit it to two hundred) must recognize the chaperon as a social institution that is slowly gaining ground. But outside of those circles etiquette does not yet require that all young ladies should be ceaselessly accompanied by chaperons, although it is entirely proper if they or their parents desire it. (Bradley, 1889: 322)

There is reluctance in these words, obviously stemming partly from a nostalgic outlook on the days when other forms of social control deemed chaperones unnecessary, that is, 'when the towns were small and every one knew every one else, where the children were neighbours and played together, and attended the same public schools and grew up surrounded by the same influences'. Then, young people were permitted a freedom of intercourse that was not suitable, as the 'earnest advocates' of chaperonage maintained, in large cities, 'where the young ladies go into society and come into contact with men of whom their parents know little or nothing' (Bradley, 1889: 318). The romanticization inherent in this nostalgic review also had a nationalistic ingredient: by frequently calling the system of chaperonage French and European, it was branded as foreign to the USA. At the same time, this stance against chaperonage was a stance in favour of co-education and against segregation of the sexes. The advantages of co-education were described once more as middle class and truly American, not foreign:

> A large part of the undoubted charm which our young ladies possess for foreigners, comes from this same easy self-possession, and no one acquainted with the world would venture to say that their morals were less pure than those of their more closely-guarded sisters ... The great mass of young ladies whose parents belong to the well-to-do but not extremely rich classes, who attend our public schools and associate from earliest childhood with those of their own age of the other sex, develop thereby a self-command, a self-possession and an ease of manner which is wholly unknown to the foreign or native young lady who is sent to a boarding school to mingle only with those of her own sex. (Bradley, 1889: 322)

Ironically, the same argument was used in explaining why 'fashionable' circles advocated chaperonage:

> foreigners coming to this country criticise and entirely misunderstand our freedom of manners. Knowing that no young lady with any claims to respectability would ever be allowed, in their own countries, to act with such freedom from restraint, they judge us by their standard and put their own construction on the matter – and that is the construction most unfavourable to the young ladies. (Bradley, 1889: 318)

In a chapter on unsettled points of etiquette, chaperonage of young ladies was mentioned explicitly as one such point. Here, another argument against adopting the custom generally was added: it would impose a 'heavy burden on the large class of well-bred persons of limited means who cannot spare the time to always accompany their daughters, nor afford such a costly attendant; while the parvenu will glory in the opportunity of seeing her [*sic*! CW] daughter thus accompanied' (Bradley, 1889: 364).

In accordance with this ambivalent, though mostly negative, attitude towards chaperonage, one reads a rather uninspired description of what the system of chaperonage actually consisted of. After having stated that 'the best and most natural chaperon for a young lady is her own mother', a rather strict number of rules were presented. For example, a young lady could not go anywhere with a gentleman unless a chaperone was present. This also means that all invitations were to include the chaperone, and that a gentleman who invited a young lady was to provide tickets for the chaperone as well. 'Even at home the chaperon's vigilance must not be relaxed, and whenever gentlemen call she must be present. It is said that "two is company, and three is a crowd" at such times; but strict etiquette requires that the young people should never escape from the "crowd"' (Bradley, 1889: 320–1).

A book published in 1905 still radiated the same ambivalence. On the one hand, mainly on the basis of national ideology, chaperonage was rejected:

> The necessity of a chaperon for young people on all occasions offends the taste of the American. It is even opposed to his code of good manners. That a young woman should never be able in her father's house to receive, without a guardian, the young men of her acquaintance, is alien to the average American's ideal of good breeding and of independence in friendship. (Harland and Water, 1905: 149)

On the other hand, after ideological lip service had been paid, these authors simply endorsed chaperonage: 'Driving parties, fishing parties, country club parties, sailing parties, picnics of every kind, – here the chaperon is indispensable' (Harland and Water, 1905: 151).

In *Manners and Social Usages*, published two years later, the same ambivalence is apparent. The book's Foreword said: 'In discussing the chaperon, the editor attaches less importance to European example than those fortunate conditions in America which limit the chaperon's activities to a few cities and circles.' And the chapter on 'Chaperons and their Duties' starts out with extensive praise of the American spirit for endowing young men and women 'with a freedom which is incomprehensible to the European, who belongs to an older, a more corrupt civilization'. On the same page, however, the author dryly added: 'it should be said that in our large Eastern cities the desirability of a modified chaperonage has long been recognized in certain circles, and it has always existed there. Whether the European idea or the American will ultimately prevail, is hard to tell' (Sherwood, 1907: 209). But it was made perfectly clear that if 'the

European idea' was to prevail, the Europeans were to blame for it, because of their dangerous misinterpretation of American freedom:

> A young Frenchman who visited America a few years ago formed the worst judgement of American women because he met one alone at an artist's studio. He misinterpreted the profoundly sacred and corrective influences of art. It had not occurred to the lady that if she went to see a picture she would be suspected of wishing to see the artist. Still, the fact that such a mistake could be made should render girls careful of even the appearance of evil. (Sherwood, 1907: 214)

In 1909, *Etiquette for Americans* reported that discussion about the chaperone was intense:

> Rampant articles are written on the absurdity of setting a watch over young women who cannot be trusted at all if they cannot be trusted in all. Anxious mothers uphold the necessity, girls decry it, and the chaperon herself, oddly enough – for the task cannot be amusing – insists upon the necessity. (1909: 189)

This book was rather positive about the chaperone, for a 'chaperon often averts great embarrassment' and 'innumerable cases might be mentioned in which girls have been thankful for the presence of chaperons'. It also added a reason for her existence: 'If men did not drink, there would be less need of chaperons' (1909: 191, 192–3).

In the 1920s, the presence of a chaperone was still very much taken for granted and also defended in the context of public dances. The argument against reported criticism was that these dances can be 'performed gracefully and without giving offence to the most squeamish chaperon' (Holt, 1920: 179; see Chapter 3). Yet, at informal dances, and there were many of these in the 1920s, the chaperone clearly had lost ground: there 'the hostess has always the right to regard herself as the accredited chaperon of any unmarried woman guest' (Holt, 1920: 144). Emily Post, however, disagreed. She took a more formal and conventional stance. In her famous manners book of 1922, she wrote: 'A well behaved young girl goes to public dances only when properly chaperoned and to a private dance with her mother or else accompanied by her maid, who waits for her the entire evening in the dressing room' (1922: 32). Although Post did admit that 'the very word has a repellent school-teacherish sound', she insisted that a young girl needs a chaperone as a 'protective defence' because, without one, 'she is in the position precisely of an unarmed traveller walking alone among wolves – his only defence is in not attracting their notice' (1922: 288). This metaphor may be related to the fact that Post was the only author who did not take for granted that the chaperone was an elderly woman: 'A lady may not be under the "protection" of a man *anywhere*!' (1922: 32).

The main reason, so it seems, why Post wanted her readers to adhere to the conventions of propriety by demanding that every young woman must be protected by a chaperone, was that 'otherwise she will be misjudged'.

Although from an ethical perspective, she continued, a young girl only needs her 'own sense of dignity and pride ... there are conventions to think of' (Post, 1922: 289). In a replica edition of 1922, published in 1969, Emily Post's daughter Elizabeth wrote 'A New Preface to an Old Edition'. After quoting that 'ethically the only chaperon is the young girl's own sense of dignity and pride' and that 'she who has the right attributes of character needs no chaperon – ever,' Elizabeth Post commented:

> At the same time, Mrs. Post's rules allowed the girl little chance to prove whether she had those attributes or not. Either Mrs. Grundy – the old lady living in the square brownstone house with a cupula ... equipped with a telescope – or a chaperon in the form of a relative or a lady's maid were constantly keeping an eye on the poor young thing in order to report at once if she strayed from the straight and narrow. (1969: 2)

Emily Post was not alone in attempting to guard conventions from attack. There were others such as Margaret Wade who tried to defend the convention of the chaperone against the counter-forces of women's emancipation: 'The idle girl of fashionable society cannot dispense with the chaperon,' she wrote, 'however emancipated she may consider herself' (1924: 271). The first season of a girl provided the main soil for the chaperone to stand on: 'Here is where the chaperon is an imperative necessity, if any girl is to come through her first winter with the respect of her elders as well as her contemporaries' (Wade, 1924: 278). This reason can be summarized as 'fear of Mrs. Grundy', that is, 'fear of falling' or status anxiety.

Conventions like the chaperone were also attacked straightforwardly or were simply declared to be a thing of the past:

> The chaperon is obsolete. The hostess at a private dance acts as chaperon for all her young guests and the patronesses of a subscription or club dance perform the same service. No longer is it necessary for a patient father or a bored maid to accompany a girl to a dance. Her escort calls for her with his own car or a taxicab. (Richardson, 1927: 41)

Eventually, the authors of all manners books moved to this position. In her 1931 edition, Emily Post had changed her chapter on the chaperone only slightly, but the changes clearly signified that the chaperone was on her way out. Now, she not only wrote about the chaperone, but also about the chaperoned position of a girl, explaining that such position 'may equally mean a solid family background'. Indeed, a young girl may be protected 'either by family background or other actual chaperon' (1931: 287). In a chapter, 'Letters and Answers', added to the 1931 edition, Mrs Post wrote: 'The sole reason for the chaperon was protection. If the modern girl is to go without protection, she must herself develop expertness in meeting unprotected situations. She must be able to gauge the reactions of various types of persons under varying circumstances' (1931: 688). In an answer to another letter, she suggested:

> Whether Cynthia may be allowed to go out alone with a man depends first

of all on the sort of girl Cynthia is, and what her training has been. If she has been brought up with the same lack of practice in the responsibility of look-ing after herself that her mother is apt to have had, the answer is, 'Decidedly No!' But if she is a clear-headed young modern, incapable of being non-plussed by any situation in which she may find herself, the answer so far as her personal danger is concerned, might quite probably be 'Yes.' But there is still the question of social position to be defined. (1931: 688)

This reference to social position suggests that the higher a girl's social posi-tion, the more she was expected to adhere to conventions.

From the 1930s onwards, manners books appearing in the USA con-tained statements like: 'Today a girl is her own chaperon to an extent never known in an earlier day, perhaps never before practicable.' At the same time, they continued to specify occasions that still demanded chaperones, such as long trips or when invited by a boy to a dance at his school or college. Then and there, 'either you take your own chaperon with you on the trip or else he provides one' (Landers, 1936: 95). The college dance is the occasion in which the need for a chaperone was most frequently and most elaborately dealt with. An example:

> When a girl, invited to attend a dance at a man's college, stays at a hotel, a chaperon is considered indispensable. The girl pays all travelling expenses and the hotel bill for herself and her chaperon. Sometimes several girls go together accompanied by a chaperon whose expenses they share. If you are invited to a house party at a man's fraternity house, neither you nor your mother have any responsibility about chaperons. Colleges will not allow a house party to be insufficiently chaperoned, and no doubt several women of standing in the community will act as sponsors. It is customary for the men to move out and turn their rooms over to the girls. At coeducational colleges a boy may arrange for his out-of-town girl to stay at the sorority house or at a women's dormitory, where the house mother or matron is official chaperon for everyone under her roof. (Pierce, 1937: 18)

Although Emily Post also took it for granted that chaperones would be pres-ent in the fraternity house where a party was given, she gave her new chap-ter on chaperonage in the 1937 edition the title 'The Vanished Chaperon and Other Lost Conventions'. As the 'most important change in the entire chaperon situation' Post marked out the change from protection by chaper-onage to self-protection by training:

> Since there are to be no chaperons – of any kind – the youngest age is none too soon to begin training a child in self-control and level-headedness, so as not to be overcome with dizziness in a netless world ... Since the modern girl is to go without protection, she must herself develop expertness in meeting unprotected situations. She must be able to gauge the reactions of various types of persons – particularly men, of course – under varying circumstances. (1937: 353–4)

Yet, although 'from an ethical standpoint, the only chaperon worth having in this present day is a young girl's own efficiency in chaperoning herself', as she had now formulated it, Post still remained cautious of the gossiping Mrs Grundy: 'there still remain appearances to be considered' (1937: 354). Moreover, in answering the question 'May a Young Woman Go Alone to a Man's Apartment?' – the title of a new paragraph – she even questioned any young girl's capacity to protect herself:

> And yet – any attempt to apply the rules of propriety to a young woman's going alone to the apartment of a man, would be the same as to attempt to give directions for applying a flame to a high explosive ... that is, granting a certain element of attraction between the woman and the man. (1937: 358)

Apparently, the chaperone remained for two reasons: first to accommodate Mrs Grundy, that personification of gossip and external social control, and second, for lack of trust in the strength of self-control. The period of transition, characterized by this ambivalence about the chaperon, lasted into the 1940s.

After World War II chaperonage was restricted, as a rule, to teenage and childhood – only few references to older youngsters were found. *Vogue's Book of Etiquette*, published in 1948, allowed girls of 13 and 14 to go to the movies in the afternoon in groups of three or four other girls without a chaperone. They were allowed to meet boys, in groups, in the afternoon, for a soda at the drugstore or in a tearoom, but girls of this age were not to be allowed to dine with boys in a restaurant or to go out in the evening unless chaperoned (Vogue, 1948: 49). Amy Vanderbilt explained: 'When we insist on chaperones for our children, it is to guard them from possible physical harm in the streets at night, from their own possible foolishness, and from destructive gossip' (1952: 537). By this time, whether one was to be chaperoned or not, increasingly marked the transition from child to teenager rather than that, as in the following example, from teenager to young adult:

> Is it proper for a single girl to have dinner in a bachelor's apartment without a chaperone? ... a girl not out of her teens would do better to avoid such a dinner engagement ... A career girl, from her twenties onward, can accept such an invitation but she should not stay beyond ten or ten-thirty. (Vanderbilt, 1956: 43)

The 1960 edition of Post's manners book still contained a chapter, 'The Chaperon and Her Modern Counterparts', but its main message boiled down to the insight that 'parental training had largely taken the place of the chaperon's *protection*' (Post, 1960: 168). The paragraph 'May a Young Woman Go Alone to A Man's Apartment?' had been deleted, and with it the doubt cast on the young girl's capacity to protect and restrain herself when alone with a man. This very conviction, however, was still expressed in the 1952 and 1963 editions of Amy Vanderbilt's famous etiquette book:

> If young people didn't want to make love most of the time during the period of their engagement it wouldn't seem normal ... For engaged people of all ages, society expects chaperonage of a kind. They may, of course, spend long days and evenings together alone, but they may not go off for a weekend or overnight unless adequately chaperoned. (1952: 126; 1963: 13)

These references to 'engaged people of all ages' were the last exceptions to the increasingly established rule that the words chaperone and chaperonage referred to children and teenagers, no longer marking the transition from teenager to adult, but that from child to teenager or adolescent. In the 1960s, this was often noticed, for example: 'The presence of a chaperon is still a standard requirement at certain teen-age gatherings, but otherwise the chaperon has all but vanished' (Miller, 1967: 83).

In her 1952 and 1963 editions, Vanderbilt raised the question of whether a group can chaperone itself, and thus, whether parents can feel safe in permitting their teenage children to go out at night. She thought not, 'for the group, once out of sight of parents, may break up into twosomes immediately, with the rules of behaviour determined by the boldest'. Vanderbilt, however, did not turn entirely against this 'independent course', as she called it, but it should be permitted only, she said:

> if the group is going to a specific, approved place and will return at an exact agreed-upon time. Its whereabouts should be known by the parents at all times, and no unaccountable junketing around the countryside in some boy's car should be allowed. Remember, adolescents want rules and need them. They do not respect the too 'easy' parent, or the one who is in bed and asleep when they arrive home. (1952: 538)

All this was removed from the 1972 edition, in which Vanderbilt had also deleted the reference to engaged couples wanting to make love most of the time and, therefore, being in need of a chaperone. She had changed the text into:

> While it is my conviction that decisions about pre-marital sexual relations are a private matter which each couple must debate for themselves, a couple do have obligations... any girl thinking of taking this important step, be she engaged or not, should consult a gynaecologist, or at least her family doctor, to receive preliminary instruction about contraception. (1972: 17–18)

The section on chaperones was now called 'Adult Supervision', and the word chaperone was used only in the opening sentence: 'The chaperone is not quite as dead as the dodo, but she is a very pale reflection of her former authoritative self. At the teen level she still exists, if only as reassuring background.' For no teen dance or party can do without 'some restraining presence' (Vanderbilt, 1972: 710).

In 1975 and again in 1984, Elisabeth Post first wrote 'Chaperons, like high-button shoes, are a thing of the past' and then continued by presenting her mother's insight that the chaperone has been internalized and needs to be internalized:

> From an ethical standpoint, the only chaperon worth having today is a young girl's own efficiency in chaperoning herself. The girl who has been taught to appraise every person and situation she meets needs no one to sit beside her and tell her what to do. She must be able to handle any situation herself, because today's girl is on her own. She must learn to gauge the reactions of

various types of people, particularly men, in varying circumstances. (Post, 1975: 909; 1984: 311)

Thus, after its first formulation in 1931, this insight was repeated for many decades, and with good reason. For the internalization of the chaperone represents a shift in the balance of controls: from external social controls to internal ones, that is, self-controls. In accordance with her description of a development from protection by others towards self-protection, both in the history of societies and in each individual's biography, Post made parents feel responsible for teaching their daughters this ability 'to handle any situation herself ' by advising them to steer in between two extremes: 'if she is too restricted now, she will have no experience to lean on when she is finally set free. This is as dangerous for a young girl as being allowed too much freedom before she is ready for it' (1975: 910).

> Many parents, unfortunately, become overprotective of their teenage children and restrict their activities and friendships unreasonably. Perhaps they are afraid that more lenient guidance would give the impression that they are indifferent to their daughter's well-being. They should realize that overzealous guarding will hamper their child's development of responsibility and judgment and that unnecessary restriction may separate her from her friends. (Post, 1975: 909)

The 1984 edition had only one addition to this text: *But in spite of the fears that alcohol and drugs inspire*, is placed before 'they should realize that overzealous guarding will hamper' (Post, 1984: 311).

At the end of the twentieth century, chaperonage was still discussed, but every trace of ambivalence had gone. No longer were chaperones depicted as conflicting with the ideology of freedom, and no longer as ill at ease in the USA. The chaperone was presented as just another supervisor, as

> an adult who supervises a social gathering of young people. To the young people, therefore, a chaperon is a killjoy; to the parents of the young people, however, a chaperon is a welcome proxy ... Teenagers owe it to their chaperon not to be late or rowdy; chaperons owe it to their teenage charges to extend them trust and not to bring up, in the presence of a date, how they used to wet the bed when they were little. (Segaloff, 1997: 34)

6.6 Chaperonage Compared: Some National Differences and General Trends

In the first half of the twentieth century, the topic of chaperonage not only attracted far more, but also far more ambivalent and more strongly nationalistic attention in the American sources than in those from elsewhere. Both the ambivalence and the nationalistic ring can be understood from the contradiction between chaperonage and the ideology of the land of the free in which chaperonage ought not to have been necessary. And the surplus of attention may be downplayed somewhat by pointing to the contradiction of the trend of eroding chaperonage coinciding with a countertrend of expanding chaperonage among the upper classes in big cities. However, the latter explanation is limited because a similar countertrend was present in England while English manners books did not pay anywhere near as much attention to chaperonage as American ones did.

In contrast to the USA, at the end of the twentieth century, the word chaperone was still known in England and in the Netherlands, but only as a thing of the past, like the word steamboat. In Germany, the word chaperone never became part of colloquial language. Instead, the Germans used words like escort or companion. The whole issue of chaperonage, however, was hardly ever mentioned in German manners books; it never seemed to be an issue. At the end of the twentieth century, in all European countries, whenever the word chaperone was used, it had predominantly negative connotations: external control by watchdogs signalling distrust and suspicion.

It seems likely that the strength of these connotations of chaperonage in Germany was also connected to a stronger distinction between private and public. It was related to a tradition of opposing serious *inner* virtues and values, such as those connected to love and friendship, to *outward* superficialities such as chaperonage. This opposition can be interpreted as a process-continuity deriving from the continued absence of a unified and central good society in Germany, where political power and the associated public sphere remained dominated by a military aristocracy for about a century longer than other Western countries. Representatives of the intelligentsia and of the bourgeois classes remained strictly excluded. Blocked from the political centres of power, the bourgeois intelligentsia in eighteenth-century Germany emphasized their 'depth of feeling', 'honesty' and 'true virtue' as against the 'superficiality', 'falsity' and 'mere outward politeness' of the nobility. As a social inheritance, Germans continued to behave rather formally in the public arena, whereas in private, relationships continued to be experienced as highly personal and immediate, intent on honesty and depth, not domesticated by general rules (Dahrendorf, 1969: 300; Elias, 2000: 15–26; Peabody, 1985: 113; Wouters, 1998: 287–8). Accordingly, chaperonage tended to be perceived as one of the superficialities that belonged to the public sphere, and was therefore liable not to be taken too seriously. In contrast, flirting was perceived as a breach of honesty and true virtue, as not acting seriously in a kind of relationship that required seriousness.

Early in twentieth-century America, exactly this interpretation of chaperones as watchdogs, signalling distrust and suspicion, had motivated strong ideological resistance against chaperonage. In the 1920s and 1930s, when discussing chaperonage at balls and parties at colleges and campuses, that resistance had already strongly decreased. That is because it was at these places, colleges and campuses, that the dating system emerged. Probably the evaporation of ideological resistance against the word and the practice of chaperonage was a side effect of the development of the dating system. It will have given parents something to hold on to in the face of their offspring freeing themselves in this and many other respects from parental control.

Whether there is more than irony in the fact that chaperonage remained an issue in American manners books, be it only in the context of children and teenagers, whereas the word vanished from colloquial usage in the European countries, is an open question. I think its continued presence is an indication of American parents relying more strongly on external controls than parents in the other countries – an indication of a balance of controls that was/is tilted a bit more to the side of external social controls than in the European countries (see Chapter 8, and my forthcoming book on differences in national habitus formation).

In spite of these national differences (and American ideology), the actual overall development in all four countries has been much the same. At the end of the nineteenth century, the patterns of chaperonage varied according to social class and degree of urbanization. In the countryside, differences between social classes were usually clearly understood, accepted, and preserved by means of powerful and virtually all-embracing social controls. Accordingly, chaperonage was light. The anonymous public life of big cities, however, required chaperonage not only to protect young girls and boys from physical danger but also from potential assaults on their respectability and reputations. Then, in the course of the twentieth century, the exercise of this form of external social control was largely stopped. It was only maintained to supervise children and (young) teenagers. Therefore, as a major general directional trend it can be concluded that where chaperonage vanished, its function was internalized. This 'internalization of the chaperone' represented a shift from protection by others towards self-protection as well as a shift in the balance of controls: from external social controls to internal ones, self-controls. Simultaneously, the principles for guiding and protecting young women and men were transformed from rather fixed rules into flexible guidelines, obliging the internalized chaperone to navigate far more reflexively, sensibly, and flexibly than the real chaperone ever had to. Parents, for their part, could only teach their children the necessary qualifications if they allowed for a controlled decontrolling of parental controls. They had to absorb themselves in a demanding process of sensitive probing, subtle timing, and proper dosage. In this way, they immersed their children in situations that were deemed necessary for acquiring and improving the skills of self-protection.

As the chaperonage system of direct external social control over potential lovers faded in the first decades of the twentieth century, the courting regimes in all four countries under study also changed. The courting regimes that emerged were all different, but the American dating regime was more different than the others.

6.7   The American Dating Regime

In the introduction to her study of the dating system, Beth Bailey distances herself from those who mourn the dissolution of this system in the 1960s as the death of romance by characterizing them as people from an older generation who ask: 'how can you fall in love with someone you see in the morning before he's even brushed his teeth?' Her generation answered: 'we see each other as people, not as dates ... romance can survive intimacy' (Bailey, 1988: 2). Victorian romance had an intensity of longing based on the virtual absence of intimacy, even proximity. It is this intensity of 'spiritual' love that Peter Stearns seems to mourn in his *American Cool* (1994). The *Cool* he describes evolving, however, is not characteristically American, for the development away from intensity and towards intimacy occurred in all four countries under study. For its part, the dating regime only developed in the USA. By the turn of the nineteenth century in all four countries, young people were beginning to go out together, with and without chaperones. In the USA, too, 'going somewhere' was beginning to rival 'calling'. Revealingly, in the nineteenth century the word date referred to a contact with a prostitute (Rothman, 1984: 22), but by the mid-1910s, the connotation of the word had changed. The association with vulgarity, however, lingered on, as this example from the period of transition shows:

> Any evening you've only to go along the river bank to see the men and girls (now please forgive the vulgarity!) 'spooning', holding hands, etc. Even the best girls here seem to think nothing of it. Here, a boy would think a girl very prudish, indeed, if she took any stand against such things. The boys expect these sort of thing of the girls! There, I'm sure I've shocked you. Or maybe I'm just a prude, am I? (Case, 1916: 38)

In these decades, the expectations of handholding and kissing were about to expand. Bailey assumes that in this period of transition, a man might have come on a 'call', expecting to be received in her family's parlour, while 'she had her hat on', expecting a 'date', that is, to be taken 'out' somewhere and entertained. In this process, having a 'good time' increasingly became identified with public places and commercial amusements. By the mid-1920s, dating had almost completely replaced the old system of calling (Bailey, 1988: 13–79). This implies the emergence of a 'youth culture' in the USA some three decades earlier than in the other countries under study. Moreover, as the practice of dating developed, differences between the USA and the other countries increased. Together with the word date, a whole 'family' of words and practices entered American (youth) culture.

One major difference between dating in the USA and courting in other countries is that the development of American youth culture and dating was most pronounced on colleges and campuses. These expanding centres of youth life and youth activities were uniquely American. A germ of their development can be found in the growth and structure of a national upper class in the nineteenth century. This growth was supported by various institutions, among which the New England boarding schools and the fashionable Eastern ('Ivy League') universities were very important. Then, 'at the turn of the century, and especially after the First World War, these national upper-class family-surrogates began to educate the children of the rich and well-born from all cities in ever-increasing numbers' (Baltzell, 1964: 390). In the words of a manners book from 1905:

> The idea of coeducation is a peculiarly American idea. Perhaps nowhere else in the world do such large bodies of young men and young women meet together for purposes of study and, at the same time, enjoy together such social freedom as is the case in the coeducational institutions of the United States. One may question the wisdom of the coeducational idea, but as to its popularity there can be no doubt. Coeducation is not only with us, but, if indications are correct, it has come to stay. (Harland and Water, 1905: 137)

Coeducational institutions in the USA usually had campuses: villages for the young.

> The campus mores were, of course, modelled after the adult world which the students in the Gilded Age were prepared to face. For the large corporations, banks and powerful law firms – in the big-city centres of national power – increasingly began to select their future leaders, not on the basis of ability alone, but largely on the basis of their fashionable university and club or fraternity affiliations. (Baltzell, 1964: 135)

As college attendance and life on campuses removed the students from courtship associations in their home communities, 'the control of the older generation over the sex behaviour of the young suffered a serious diminution' (Waller, 1938: 141). In 1905, etiquette authors already noted that: 'it is not hard to see that the somewhat informal conditions under which young people meet in these institutions, make a strict adherence to the code a matter of difficulty' (Harland and Water, 1905: 139). According to Paula Fass, there was a 300 per cent increase of attendance at colleges and universities between 1900 and 1930, while the increase in high-school enrolments was 650 per cent. In the 1920s two-thirds of all students were at coeducational residential colleges, where they engaged in a rich peer life (1977: 124, 130). At universities and colleges, in fraternities and on campuses, they were able to make their own code of courting behaviour in generational solidarity against the older generations (Waller, 1937: 729). 'The young were more and more orienting their behaviour to non-traditional institutions – peers rather than parents, movies rather than the local community' (Fass, 1977: 290). It is in the course of this process that 'punishments of middle-class children ultimately shifted away from the focus of disruptions of love to forced interruptions of contacts with peers and peer-based social life: "You're grounded" – that is, prevented from peer exchange – gained the place once reserved for "go to your room"' (Stearns, 1993: 14). Indeed, 'the rise of dating marked a shift in generational power' (Caldwell, 1999: 227) and 'Sex quickly became the key issue in the struggle that ensued' (Bailey, 1988: 78). It produced new appearances to be kept up: 'All colleges of good repute now insist on a list of patronesses who will give their presence as well as their names to the fraternity dances, as a guarantee that these amusements will be conducted with the decorum of the private ball'

(Wade, 1924: 272). College youth of the 1920s were able to redefine courting practices because their allegiance sapped the authority of adults. Of course, this redefinition left important continuities in the relationships between the generations untouched: campus courting mores remained 'closely bound to the values of the fraternity system, which are all too often still modelled on the country-club values of parents. On the fraternity-dominated campuses, moreover, the women students are likely to choose their dating partners on the basis of their status in the fraternity hierarchy' (Baltzell, 1964: 350). This author added that 'traditional fraternity values are being most vehemently challenged'. Baltzell's awareness of writing in a period of transition influenced the picture that he sketched. He was describing what was no longer taken for granted and was thus opening the window a little wider:

> Today, the debutante ritual is still in full force in most of the major cities in the nation. Yet, at the same time, it has far less meaning for the debutantes themselves, especially for those with the ability and ambition to go to one of the better Eastern Seaboard colleges for women. They now take their education seriously, and as a result, the campus community, on the whole but not entirely, has gradually since the war come to displace the local community with its country clubs and the debutante balls as the major upper-class courting environment. (Baltzell, 1964: 350)

These lines actually state that before the war, these dalliance relationships called dates, and the whole system of dating, were not seen as a real challenge to the traditional courting system in their local communities. They signify that the campus community was observed and experienced as a separate culture in which one could participate for a few years, that is, 'without significant long-term risk' (Bailey, 1988: 27). Moreover, they also signified, that campus communities in the 1960s did become a real challenge to the bonds with the community at home. In many cases, leaving home turned into breaking with the past – an old American tradition (Bellah et al., 1985: 198). In the 1920s, however, the bond between the colleges and good society was still strong: 'The twenties was, of course, the heyday of the businessman, of Wall Street glamour, and of the Chamber of Commerce hero. And college students saw themselves as part of the charmed circle' (Fass, 1977: 257).

Another major difference from the other countries is that in the USA, a date developed into sort of a dalliance relationship for the duration of the date and without any commitment to marriage. Another date might follow, but also follow-up dates did not imply marriage promises. Accordingly, the pair relationship of a date was not exclusive, on the contrary: simultaneous relations with numerous partners were encouraged. Young people were advised to get to know the opposite sex by dating many different girls or boys: Variety is the spice of life! It creates experience. So shop around, and 'have at least a dozen girl friends and boy friends that you like, that you are with often, that do things and have good times together' (Gillum, 1937: 31). This kind of advice was uniquely American.

A third major difference between dating in the USA and courting elsewhere was the genesis of necking and petting, and also the fact that these sexual practices were openly debated. Handholding and kissing and caresses above the neck became generally known as necking, whereas petting came to refer to caresses below the neck, to 'every caress known to married couples but does not include complete sexual intercourse' (Bailey, 1988: 79–80). In the 1930s, the question of 'how far to go' beyond kissing came up with almost any 'date' (Waller, 1938: 103), because courtship practices had permitted and stimulated a 'thrill-seeking behaviour' that had turned courtship into 'an amusement and a release of organic tensions', and kissing into an activity that 'may imply no commitment of the total personality whatsoever' (Waller, 1937: 728). Necking and petting as inherent possibilities made dating highly sexually orientated, but also sexually restrained as the sexual exploration was to remain without sexual consummation. In that sense, dating was orientated towards sex *and* marriage, 'with the corollary that intercourse between engaged or "serious" couples was both more likely to occur and more acceptable' (Fass, 1977: 75).

Women's bobbed hair can be taken as a symbol of the new lust-balance, away from the Puritan position in which good women took no pleasure in sex, and bad women took no pleasure in anything else, to a 'good-bad' middle ground between, on the one hand, their marital aspirations, demanding abstinence from all sexuality, even necking, and on the other hand, their own burgeoning sexual interests. In her fascinating study of dating in the 1920s, Paula Fass explains the significance of bobbed hair. At the time, women were wearing their long hair tied up. Not to do so would be improper because a woman would only wear her (long) hair loose in company if sexuality was (going to be) part of the relationship. Therefore, wearing loose bobbed hair was liberating in two ways: it allowed women to be more self-consciously erotic and also to feel equal to men. It did not destroy either old family standards or marital aspirations, and yet it certainly was a symbol of explicit female sexuality, signalling the possibility of petting, of restrained promiscuous sexual exploration (Fass, 1977: 280). Margaret Mead convincingly showed that, during the dating period, 'there is the imperative that one ought to be able to play with sex all the time, and win. The younger the boy and girl when they learn to play this game of partially incomplete, highly controlled indulgence of impulse, the more perfectly they can learn it' (1950: 292). This imperative stimulated increasing subtlety in the art of steering 'between the rocks of prudery and coquetry' (Hemphill, 1999: 110), for in order to 'remain the winner, she must make the nicest discriminations between yielding and rigidity' (Gorer, 1948: 116). This was the middle ground of the good–bad girl, the one that reminded Mead of a couplet from the early 1920s:

> Won't somebody give me some good advice
> On how to be naughty and still be nice? (1950: 291)

Manners books contain traces of the difficulties and controversies that accompanied the emancipation of the younger generation and their sexuality:

> The placid acceptance, a generation or two ago, that 'boys will be boys' in the face of college scandals by over-indulgent parents, has given place in badly-regulated families to an equally unfortunate idea that the modern girl must have her 'good time.' That the good time frequently leads to a Gretna Green marriage and an early divorce, the use of narcotics following the cigarette or a craving for alcohol so great as to wreck the life of its victim and disgrace her entire family – seems to be entirely overlooked by parents and guardians. (Wade, 1924: 279)

By the 1920s, 'sex had become an important feature of campus affairs, and peers restricted associations, directed introductions, and set elaborate criteria for behaviour, selection, and propriety' (Fass, 1977: 202). Petting soon became a controlled ritual, opening up possibilities of intimacy and response, but at the same time restricting spontaneity. Parents and authorities tried to control sex by restricting peer contacts and by limiting the privacy of youths: by allowing only verifiable destinations or supervised events, by controlling curfews and restricting access to the family car. On campuses, however, these forms of control were lacking, although 'many colleges and universities had regulations against students having cars' (Bailey, 1988: 86). The editors of college papers, we learn:

> were quick to deny any widespread evil in the behaviour or intentions of the young. They did not, however, deny the existence of petting or its importance in the social relations between the sexes. What they denied was the adult evaluation of such behaviour as promiscuous or immoral, as in fact it was by an earlier standard. Peer norms ... were now legitimate criteria for evaluating conduct. (Fass, 1977: 265)

Moreover, the strength of peer-group pressure turned petting into a convention and a necessary demonstration of conformity: 'One result of this peer compulsion was that experimental erotic exploration was often a group phenomenon. The petting party ... both forced erotic exploration and controlled the goal of eroticism' (Fass, 1977: 266).

The fact that the college behaviour of the 1920s had filtered down to the high school by the 1930s (Fass, 1977: 271) may explain why Mrs Post, in her new edition of 1931, finally paid some attention to the topic of petting; she even gave it a separate heading. She restricted herself, however, to just one line: 'Petting', she wrote, 'is quite outside the subject of etiquette – so far outside that it has no more place in distinguished society than any other actions that are cheap, promiscuous, or vulgar' (Post, 1931: 297). A few years later, Mrs Post was straightforwardly contradicted by another etiquette writer addressing girls who, as newcomers to the campus, 'are still an adventure to the men':

> So, of course, you want to make the most of your novelty. With skill, you can build lasting popularity for yourself for the rest of your four college years on

campus. If you date often, you will have many opportunities to 'neck,' in spite of Emily Post's claim that petting has no place in polite society. (College men, apparently, have never read her book.) ... All of them are frankly curious to discover if you are a 'hot number' or a 'cold proposition.' That you must determine for yourself. (Eldridge, 1936: 176)

Boys were expected to make sexual advances. Their attitude is captured in a 1920s fraternity phrase: 'If a girl doesn't pet, a man can figure he didn't rush her right' (Stearns and Knapp, 1992: 786). This may illustrate Bailey's conclusion that young people's sexual experience was governed by two codes, both

> the peer conventions that were insistently prescriptive, establishing petting, necking, and the 'right' sexual attitudes as essential criteria for belonging to youth culture; and the official conventions of adult culture and authority, which were dogmatically proscriptive. The two sets of conflicting conventions were both public, both seemingly 'universal,' and both extremely explicit. (Bailey, 1988: 96)

A fourth major difference between dating in the USA and courting in other countries was a more uneven balance of power in American dating in favour of men and their money. This difference was probably rooted in the relatively early decline of control by the older generation over the young. Parallel to this decline was the growing space and power of the younger generation to develop new relational ideals and rules among themselves and for themselves. That was how the American (peer-)code of dating emerged. In the constitutive process, the influence of young men must have been dominant, for in the new code it was pretty much taken for granted that 'boys will be boys', that they would 'naturally' want some sexual activity, and that they will 'go for it'. This implied that the responsibility for sexual restraint was put in the hands of women. They had to know 'how to meet the "jazz age" halfway, without destroying any of the old family standards' (Schlesinger, 1946: 54). Responsibility for sexual restraint was in the hands of girls, and therefore, to the extent that boys were allowed 'to be boys', young men could blame them for all sexual acts, whether unsanctioned or uncalled for: either she had not set limits (in time) or she was not truly virtuous.

In contrast to this dating code, here is an example of the old code of calling, quoted from an edition of the *Ladies' Home Journal* of 1905: 'No man, who is fit to be welcomed in your home, would refuse to release your hand if you asked him as if you meant it.' Bailey, who presents this example, comments: 'Here the man's liberties are not necessarily the woman's fault. If the woman is truly virtuous, and the man does not comply with her wishes, it is because he is not "fit to be welcomed [in her] home." That conditional term soon disappeared' (Bailey, 1988: 88–9). In the calling system, women were the hosts and they took the initiative. The dating system of 'going somewhere' made young women dependent on men's 'treats'. Boys came to be the host; they paid, and they took the initiative.

Of course, they assumed the control that came with that position. Bailey: 'Dating, like prostitution, made access to women directly dependent on money' (1988: 18–22). In short, her argument reads: 'Men paid for everything, but often with the implication that women "owed" sexual favors in return ... According to many, boys and men were entitled to sexual favors as payment for that debt; the more money the man spent, the more petting the woman owed him' (Bailey, 1988: 24, 81). The conclusion is that the transfer of power over young women from parents to the young men they were dating, the 'power-transfer' as discussed in Chapter 4, became an integral part of the dating system. In the words of an English researcher of American society, strongly influenced by Margaret Mead: 'A good-night kiss is almost the minimum repayment for an evening's entertainment' (Gorer, 1948: 116)

In exaggerated form, this type of relationship also materialized in the taxi-dance hall, a uniquely American institution, typical of that era, where all sorts of men (with the exception of 'American Negroes') could find access to young women and girls at 'a dime a dance'. 'Like the taxi-driver with his cab, she is for public hire and is paid in proportion to the time spent and the services rendered' (Cressey, 1932: 3). In the introduction to his *The Taxi-Dance Hall*, Paul Cressey wrote that since he had begun his study in 1925, 'taxi-dance halls have increased in number and in importance until they are now the dominant type of dance hall in the business centres of our largest cities'.

To some degree, money and dating were related in a similar way: '"nice girls" cost a lot' (Bailey, 1988: 23). Money purchased obligation; money purchased inequality; money purchased control. Young women were advised never to pay for themselves, even if they had money. The main reason given was: men don't like that (male pride). Here's an example, addressing women:

> Many men at college do not date because they cannot afford the expense. And ever so often, co-eds who are weary of staying at home on Saturday night decide it would be far better 'to go Dutch' than to sit. After the co-ed has paid her way for a while to be with him, he suddenly deserts her for some less generous youngster who wouldn't think of spending a penny on him ... Even when the co-eds wait to be asked before footing the bill, Dutch treats have not worked. Too much independence on a girl's part subtracts from a man's feeling of importance if he takes her out and can do nothing for her. So, if you want to date college men, resort to more feminine ways of succeeding. (Eldridge, 1936: 216)

A second example was written by a male author addressing men; now the main reason was: girls don't like that (feminine pride):

> Avoid the Dutch treat, no matter how broke you are. Any girl would rather sit in the park than dine Dutch treat at the Ritz. A young man who lets a girl pay for her entertainment deserves to lose her respect. Girls have decided ideas as to what your attitude toward money should be. They hate a man who's stingy. They like you to decide beforehand what you can afford to blow

– no matter how much or how little, and then to spend the money without registering pain. (Jonathan, 1938: 44)

Young men had monopolized the power resource of money, and young women had allowed them to keep it. But why? Until World War II, women in the USA were scarce, therefore in great demand (as the 'stag line' and 'cutting in' also demonstrate), which makes it even more incomprehensible why they consented to a larger amount of submissiveness than women in the other countries under study. Beth Bailey does refer to the 'scarcity' of men after the war as becoming 'a commonplace justification' for all sorts of female submissiveness (1988: 115), but this once more begs the question why the 'scarcity' of women before that war had not been used as a power resource, if only to prevent men from evaluating them 'as if they were show animals' (Bailey, 1988: 67) from whom they could buy sexual favours by paying their way on a date.[7] Why weren't there any voices to be heard in favour of women keeping their independence by paying for themselves? These questions are particularly intriguing because such voices of protest had been loud in the other countries under study.

The specific codes of manners and morals of American dating arose out of many part processes, of which three deserve special attention. Along with a critical degree of wealth and geographical mobility, co-education at universities and colleges allowed for an emancipation of young people from the regime of their parents. In the USA, these processes, amounting to the integration of the sexes and the segregation of the generations, had come to a critical point by the 1920s with the development of a national youth culture, which included dating. In the European countries under study, a similar critical point in these processes was reached only in the 1950s and 1960s, decades in which an international (western) youth culture emerged. The advantage of coming late, so to speak, was that in the European countries the wave of emancipation of young people from the regime of older generations was soon followed by a wave of emancipation of women from the regime of men: in the late 1970s, the women's movement in all western countries turned against sexual violence, that is, against male dominance. In the USA of the 1920s, however, liberation from the straitjacket of older generations and their morality was not followed by a liberation from male sexual dominance and male oppression. Dating codes, particularly the paying and petting codes, can be interpreted as proof of this absence. The younger generation had a common interest in breaking the taboo of the older generation, the no-sex-at-all taboo, thus creating for themselves a lust-balance with more sex. In the process of defining what sex, and on what conditions, young men and boys were clearly dominant. In that sense, the dating, paying and petting codes simply reflected and confirmed the uneven balance of power between the sexes prevalent at that time. This explanation would imply that most girls will have experienced the freedom they had gained in comparison to their mothers, but that it simply did not occur to them to raise cutting questions about their youth culture in terms of the balance of power between the sexes.

A third process, and a more down-to-earth reason why girls will have unquestioningly allowed the power resource of money to remain in the hands of boys, is to be found in the strong pressures of competitive conformity in dating as a youth culture. In their peer groups, a young woman was 'valued by the level of consumption she could demand (how much she was "worth"), and the man by the level of consumption he could provide' (Bailey, 1988: 58). These conditions favoured the boys who had money and the girls selected by these boys to spend money on. Dating became a 'competitive activity dominated by money and consumer one-upmanship' (Caldwell, 1999: 229).

The very competitiveness of dating is the fifth and last major difference between dating in the USA and courting in other countries. Dating as a way of courting soon became a contest for popularity, producing a peculiar mixture of competitive conformity. Each date and each person dated counted and was rated in a popularity contest: the 'rating and dating complex', a term introduced by Willard Waller (1937) and repeated by many, for instance Beth Bailey: 'You had to rate in order to date, to date in order to rate. By successfully maintaining this cycle, you became popular. To stay popular, you competed ... and being popular allowed you to compete' (1988: 30). Dating as part of a popularity contest on campus was less a competition of merit than a competition of position, fostering an acute awareness of the nuances of appearance, style, and personality (Fass, 1977: 254). Margaret Mead also confirmed that dating was primarily a competitive game in which publicly affirmed popularity was the prize. This could be illustrated, she wrote, by considering the behaviour of those who do not date, but withdraw to 'going steady'. For here we find two groups: young people 'in love' and young people who, 'without being in love, depend on each other for protection, the unpopular girl and the unpopular boy, concealing their failure in the popularity game by pretending to prefer each other' (Mead, 1950: 286). In part, dating became a competitive 'quest of thrill' (Waller, 1937: 729), pushing all participants towards further exploration of the path of lust.

In the 1920s and 1930s, American youth went down this path collectively, thus restricting petting to a ritual strongly controlled by peer-group pressure: 'youth were unlikely to bypass the restrictions and staged ritual associated with sexual behaviour. But neither was petting restricted to only a small minority of wildly experimental youths, for petting had become a convention and a necessary demonstration of conformity' (Fass, 1977: 265). Like petting, to some extent, drinking and smoking also became a necessary demonstration of conformity; Fass captured this in the sentence: 'Competition within conformity and conformity in the service of competition were the structuring facts of campus life in the twenties' (Fass, 1977: 323/226). Bailey added that, because youth and its institutions were a separate culture in which one could participate for only a few years, competition was without significant long-term risk (Bailey, 1988: 27).

The ritual of petting had opened up possibilities of intimacy and response, but at the same time it 'laid the basis for the emotionally inhibiting cat-and-mouse game of staged seductions and "scoring" that continued to govern sexual relations among the young throughout the first half of the twentieth century' (Fass, 1977: 271). This, as well as the importance of both popularity and the demands on the good–bad girl, functioned as a powerful motor in the process that led to dating becoming more sexed as time went on: 'Even in high school, at least by the early 1940s, middle-class boys talked in terms of pushing petting as far as their dates would allow, if not farther, describing the whole experience as "having fun" or "taking them for a ride"' (Stearns and Knapp, 1992: 786).

6.7a   The stag line, cutting in, getting stuck

Dating as a sport within a popularity contest may also explain a few other unique characteristics such as the (chat-up) 'line' as well as a number of words and practices at dances: the 'stag line', 'cutting in', 'getting stuck'. The stag line was the queue of boys waiting to cut in on a dance; particularly in the 1930s and 1940s this was an accepted practice among young people:

> When cutting in, the boy lightly touches the shoulder of the girl's partner. The partner either relinquishes her at once and steps aside, or he smiles and says 'Next time around.' He must make the change next time around; and he may not cut in again on that girl until someone else has claimed her as a partner. In other words, he does not cut in on the same boy who has cut in on him. The girl always says 'I'm sorry' when she leaves one partner for another. She should not show marked preferences but should be equally friendly and pleasant to all. (Eichler Watson, 1948: 476)

At a dance, both competition and success were highly visible: 'success was a dizzying popularity that kept girls whirling from escort to escort. An etiquette book for college girls (1936) told girls to strive to be "once-arounders," to never be left with the same partner for more than one turn around the dance floor' (Bailey, 1988: 31). Another 1936 etiquette book described 'getting stuck' as the opposite of being a 'once-arounder': 'If you get stranded with one partner, don't be overcome with embarrassment, don't get panicky or sick at heart; summon your self-possession and make a polite excuse to be taken to your friends or chaperon or even to leave for home' (Landers, 1936: 186). Getting stuck was seen as a highly visible catastrophe. It was taken quite seriously as a sign of social failure, worse than being a wallflower: 'Getting stuck meant, quite simply, not getting cut in on. Gradually the woman's smile would grow brittle and desperate; the man would begin casting beseeching looks at possible rescuers. Everyone would notice' (Bailey, 1988: 31). These quotations demonstrate the formidable force of peer pressure as a form of external social control: the pressure to conform and to compete for popularity.

6.7b   The line

Another typical bit of ritual in the American courting regime was the 'line', a well-rehearsed and oft-repeated set of phrases used in initial contacts between the sexes to flatter and charm; it was coquetry, a sort of exaggeration, and thus a clear symptom of the whole dating, paying and petting popularity contest. Paula Fass has presented the following interesting comparison: 'Like a woman without her cosmetics, a man without his line went out naked into the frightening wilderness of a newly sexual world' (1977: 288). The problem of this comparison, however, is the fact that girls used lines too. The same manners book for college girls that advised girls to strive to be 'once-arounders' also told them: 'If you are very popular at first, it is not surprising. Your line is new and so is the different way you smile and the smooth way in which you dance' (Eldridge, 1936: 176). Yet, Fass is not the only one who described the line as a male practice. She is in the company of, for instance, Geoffrey Gorer, who wrote 'The object of the "line" is to entertain, to amuse, and captivate the girl, but there is no deep emotional involvement; it is a game of skill' (1948: 116). The most probable reason why some authors have described the line as a male practice is, I think, because boys used it as a vehicle of offence in pushing petting as far as their dates would allow, whereas girls will 'only' have used it as a vehicle of defence and of charm. College girls were warned: 'Lines are dangerous weapons' (Eldridge, 1936: 178). In other words, if sex was the main topic, or central in the author's mind, 'the line' was viewed predominantly as an offensive tool, more or less skilfully used by boys, whereas if popularity was the central topic, both boys and girls were perceived as using 'lines'. The next quotation – from a manners book addressing boys – shows that both sexes were seen as sharing the ritual of lines in an ongoing process of open status competition:

> Let yourself go! Let compliments come irresistibly and spontaneously. Instead of a mere 'You look nice tonight,' you might say in a profoundly stirred baritone, 'That shade of blue does things to your eyes.' ... If a girl is 'handing you a line,' be pleasantly receptive. Take it with an interested smile, and hand one right back. Whatever you do, don't prattle, 'Oh, you're just giving me a "line".' Why be a lug and spoil her fun. You know how grand it makes you feel when you think some gorgeous number is swallowing your 'line'. Let the girl believe you're fascinated ... You'll be popular if you do. (Jonathan, 1938: 98–9)

Willard Waller presented an example of how 'true courtship' sometimes emerged from the dating process, in spite of all the forces, including 'the line', which were opposed to it. 'In the fairly typical case,' Waller wrote, 'the affair begins with the lightest sort of involvement', but later

> A becomes somewhat involved, but believes that B has not experienced a corresponding growth of feeling, and hides his involvement from B, who is, however, in exactly the same situation. The conventionalized 'line' facilitates

this sort of 'pluralistic ignorance,' because it renders meaningless the very words by means of which this state of mind could be disclosed. Tension grows ... [leading to a crisis and a] quarrel, in which the true feelings of the two are revealed. (1937: 733–4)

The line was there to stay; the ritual survived World War II, and was discussed by many, among them Geoffrey Gorer, who wrote: 'What distinguishes the "date" from other conversation is a mixture of persiflage, flattery, wit and love-making which was formerly called a "line" but which each generation dubs with a new name' (1948: 115). Not necessarily a new name, however, for the term remained well known and often used, as for instance in *A Girl's Guide to Dating and Going Steady*, published in 1968:

The first person tells the other how attractive and desirable she (or he) is. The receiver of the 'line' then faces the task of deciding how much is true and how much is false. As the game is often played, the boy who gives a girl a line that she falls for, to the extent that she does something he wants her to do, is the winner. On the other hand, the girl who lets the boy know that she sees through his line without 'turning him off' may be said to be handling it well. A certain amount of exaggeration is customary between boys and girls ... [W]hen a boy with a fast line meets a girl with a gullible disposition, she sometimes falls for him hook, line, and sinker. A line is basically flattery ... Few dating experiences could be more painful than falling for a line, believing a boy truly loved you, giving him your own love, and then discovering that he was only fooling. (McGinnis, 1968: 100–1)

A few years later, in the early 1970s, the line was reported to have spread as far as the black lower classes where it turned up as a male(!) courting ritual, as 'rap': '"Rapping" is an extremely important part of black lower-class sex life, and young boys work hard to develop an artful line. Girls assume that boys will try to have sexual relations with them and hold out for the one with the best rap' (Day, 1972: 165).

The 'line' can be understood as a specific expression of a more general American characteristic: the use of superlatives – overstatements, not only according to the English standard but according to those of the Netherlands and Germany, too – and relatively open displays of feelings of superiority. Wide use of exaggeration and superlatives is symptomatic of uncertainty of rank, of porous and changing social dividing lines. This characteristic is connected in explanatory ways to the process-continuity of the absence of a unified and centralized good society. In the USA, a relatively open competition between a variety of good societies and also a stronger reliance upon supervision and other forms of external social controls have formed a barrier to the development of lower-pitched or subtler forms of expression and negotiation; they continued to stimulate more pronounced and accentuated forms of impression management. In societies and circles where social positions are more stable and established, the use of superlatives tends to diminish. 'Bragging and boasting', 'exaggeration', 'national self-consciousness and conceit' appeared as generally recognized American characteristics in a 1941 review (Coleman, 1941). Cole Porter dealt ironically with this tradition in his lyric 'Anything you can do, I can do better. I can do anything better than you.' A later example is a 'line' used by businessmen: 'You're a real pro; you can charm a monkey's balls! But there's a difference between you and me: I can do it *all* the time.' And Judith Martin, who joined the tradition by calling her books *Miss Manners' Guide to Excruciatingly Correct Behaviour* and *Miss Manners Rescues Civilization*, told me in 1992 that the use of superlatives in negotiations leave many with the question, 'What's the bullshit degree?' (Wouters, 1998a).

6.7c Dating, necking and petting in the 1930s and early 1940s

In 1931, in the edition that declared petting to be 'quite outside the subject of etiquette', Mrs Post loudly wailed over parental power lost:

> The modern home is like nothing so much as the Tower of Babel. Parents say words that have no meaning whatever to their sons and daughters. Sons and daughters say words that utterly terrify their parents, who try to interpret the sounds according to archaic definitions, and find their meaning unintelligible. Exclaim, 'How shocking!' and the modern girl laughs. Tell her she is outrageous, and she is delighted. (1931: 690)

In the 1930s, most authors of manners books took sides, thus predominantly representing one of two prevailing dating codes, either the adult one or the peer-group code. At the time, both codes were still far apart. I will document this by contrasting examples of 1930s' authors, the first examples representing the adult code followed by examples representing the peer-group code. In the adult code of the 1930s, the practice of dating was largely accepted, necking might be accepted, but petting most certainly was not.

My first example of an author who represented adult authority is Emily Post, who in her new edition of 1937 had inserted a new paragraph, entitled 'When Young Women Are Not Particular':

> Continuous pursuit of thrill and consequent craving for greater and greater excitement gradually produces the same result as that which a drug produces in an addict; or, to change the metaphor, promiscuous crowding and shoving, petting and cuddling have the same cheapening effect as that produced on merchandise which has through constant handling become faded and rumpled, smudged or frayed and thrown out on the bargain counter in a marked-down lot. (1937: 355)

Another example is a manners book in which the voice of adult authority was raised against couples seeking isolation 'in a secluded spot or a parked car', but not rigidly against 'letting him kiss you good-night when he leaves': 'Much depends on whether he is expressing a sincere fondness for you, whether he is merely curious to see if you will permit it, or whether it is just a casual habit of his. ...[I]f in doubt – don't' (Landers,

1936: 187, 194). The third author representing the adult code apparently took for granted that dating is a popularity contest in which those who lag behind suffer:

> Without boy friends, a girl misses many good times and soon thinks of herself as a failure. The same is true for boys, but to a lesser degree, since they are able to take the initiative in the matter of dates. Even so, to be repeatedly snubbed at dances and to be refused dates with girls he particularly admires is likely to make a boy grow introspective and unhappy. Thus it is important for boys as well as for girls to find out what to do to be popular. (Pierce, 1937: 12)

In regard to petting, this author was rather negative, although not rigorously forbidding. There is some insecurity or ambivalence in her words:

> Some people regard petting as a moral question; others look on it as a matter of taste. Most people who have lived long enough to know something about life feel that promiscuous petting cheapens a girl. If you do not want to be petted, keep the conversation impersonal, change the subject, or laugh and make light of any sentimental remarks. Most boys will give up a sentimental vein if the girl does not fall in with it, or if she says laughingly, 'Not tonight, Jim.' You can even say, 'I like you ever so much better when you aren't so silly.' But usually such bluntness is unnecessary. (Pierce, 1937: 13)

This author implicitly admitted that some did not reject petting but rather saw it as a matter of taste. Her advice on how to stop a boy from 'taking liberties' was rather new to this genre of literature, but it was not directed at girls who pet. She feared falling on a steep and slippery slope, for a girl might get sentimental, she might kiss a boy goodnight, and then:

> it is practically impossible to refuse to do so again. It may in time become the most important part of your evening instead of just the finishing touch, and having started it with one boy, it will be difficult to think up a good reason on the spur of the moment why you should not kiss other boys ... [R]emember the old saying that everyone's sweetheart is nobody's wife. (Pierce, 1937: 13)

Of the manners books representing the peer-group code of the 1930s, I will present one example addressing women, and another one addressing men. The author of a book relating the peer-group code to young women declared: 'I travelled to forty-three universities. I dated college men and learned to know them by their lines' (Eldridge, 1936: 19). She verbalized evocatively why the peer-group code demanded a good–bad girl:

> No, honestly, I don't think the girl who lets herself get the reputation of being an 'icicle' can hope to compete with her more audacious (note I did not say promiscuous) sister who can handle men with dexterity. Most college men expect a certain amount of familiarity from the girls they date; most older men, seeking wives, want girls that other men can't touch. By the time they are ready to marry, they are just a little suspicious of the girls who are too 'easy.' And just how you are going to be the college boy's flame and the mature man's sweetheart is only one of the difficult problems that chaperones solved for your mother. (Eldridge, 1936: 177)

The same author observed some important changes between 1929 and 1936, after the flush of the 'Roaring Twenties' had faded:

> Fundamentally, of course, our nature is still the same (sugar and spice and other things nice), but we think differently. We smoke with more abandon and we kiss with more restraint ... We are on the upgrade of the new cycle where the girl is sought who cannot be readily 'made' (take that word advisedly, for it is good, collegiate slang that can have a lily-white meaning, and here reads 'necked'). Even in the jazz age, promiscuity never achieved secure popularity; today the wise co-ed knows that she doesn't have to kiss every man who takes her out merely because he insists. And she smiles at him naively while she parries his advances with subtlety. (Eldridge, 1936: 178)

This author also presented practical advice on how to resist insistent men, but her words had no trace of the fear of falling:

> 'I never thought you'd be a puritan.' That line produces results, so you will hear it often; for no girl with spirit likes to be told that she is a prude. Laugh and say, 'Miss Prude to you,' or 'Think so?' There are many ways to keep from kissing the man you don't want, once you identify his line. The first and most important is never to let yourself be left alone with him in a romantic atmosphere ... Never say, 'How dare you!' to a man, for that is a dare. (Eldridge, 1936: 181)

The author of another book that represented the peer-group code addressed boys and young men. His book contains both instructive and amusing descriptions of several types of boys and girls ('You don't win prom princesses. You buy them – like show horses', Jonathan, 1938: 9). Among his advice was the rule always to avoid girls who expect more than you can afford to spend – don't try to compete with 'Freddy Manybucks'. He supplied the following example:

> We know of a foolish young man who saved his allowance for weeks, planning to take a prom princess to an expensive supper club. He arrived with enough money to pay the minimum charge and a small tip. He spent a miserable evening wondering if he would get by. The girl was wholly unimpressed. She had been to the place often, and was rather tired of it. The next night she went to a skating rink with a smarter young man and had a grand time. (Jonathan, 1938: 161)

The example is somewhat ambivalent because the smarter young man presumably also had a grand time without having had to spend lots of money, but the explicit message is clear: 'travel with a crowd of your own financial standing'. This author also considered that trying a 'sentimental vein' and creating a 'romantic atmosphere' were instrumental in leading to necking and petting, but before making this point, he insisted upon staying detached. He advised taking kissing in a romantic atmosphere lightly, not seriously, at least not during the formative years when you are dating many different girls – gaining experience and learning about women kind in preparation for the great day when you'll discover *the* girl. So have a great time under the yellow moon... If a girl seems to want to be kissed – kiss her. But don't try to make something terribly serious and important out of a pleasant moment which is merely a part of being young and happy. Don't get all tangled up emotionally. Good sense and self-control are a prime necessity, and they're the best combination brake and safety valve in the world.

The first burning question is: To park, or not to park? If it's the first date, the smartest thing is to take the girl straight home and not even hold her hand ... If she lets you kiss on your second date, you will know where you stand on the third ... When you stop your car to survey the moon and the girl looks pleased and smiles dreamily ... But if she makes a beeline for the far side of the seat, ... start your motor and go home ... Some girls believe it fitting and proper to protest when you try to kiss them, no matter how much they may want you to. There are others who really don't want to be kissed. It's the facial expression and the tone of voice which usually tell the story.

Never ask a girl if you may kiss her ... If your 'date' seems to be having a hard time making up her mind whether she wants romance or a platonic friendship, you can take a chance. Live and learn! You'll either get your ears knocked back, or she'll nestle in your manly arms ... Don't paw like a horse. Taking advantage of her because you're stronger than she, certainly isn't romance. It's simply moronic behaviour ... For the most part, pitching and flinging the woo is up to the girl. (Jonathan, 1938: 107–10)

Another interesting part of this manners book was an early warning against 'going steady' for being a form of 'puppy love' – as it came later to be called. This warning was early in the sense that the topic was new to the genre, and it is interesting for being an extension of the warning not to take getting sentimental in a romantic atmosphere seriously, illustrating once again how and why an instrumental attitude towards girls was advocated:

Butterflies as big as bats. Daisies ten feet tall. And floating through this supernatural landscape like a cloud shadow on a summer day is a heavenly sweet young thing made of sugar and spice and everything nice. The most wonderful girl in the world!

All this, with entrancing variations, may happen to you, a normal young man, once or twice a year... There's nothing unusual about the experience ... 'But,' you protest angrily, 'this is *the* girl.' Maybe. Anyway, we don't care if she is. Unless you're in a good position to slip a ring on the third finger of her left hand and promise to love, honour, and perhaps cherish, you had better lend at least a tolerant ear to what we have to say ... No matter how infatuated you may be with an angel who walks and talks and eats, don't enter into that sad state of suspended animation known as 'going steady'. If you're anxious to become a man of the world, if you want to make many friends, and if you're anxious to acquire that elusive quality known as social polish, don't 'go steady.' Doing so cramps your style. Variety is the spice of life. It creates experience. High school and college years are formative ones. Make as many friends as you can, of both sexes. Competition will be good for you. It sharpens your wits, teaches you how to get along well in spite of difficulties. Date many different girls, gaining experience and doing your best to interest them all. You'll need that practical experience all through life. It will make you a good judge of women when at last you're ready to choose a partner for the most important years of your life. Of course, you'll like certain girls better than others. That's natural and inevitable. But it's money in the bank to have lots of girls on the knowing list and the date calendar. It means more people to meet, more places to go, more things to do. It means more popularity for you. Asking a girl to 'go steady' is a purely selfish action on your part. It flatters your ego to be a headman. It shows that you are afraid of competition. Really you are asking the girl to accept the restrictions of an engagement without giving her a ring and the promise of marriage, which an engagement is supposed to mean. All you're doing is taking an option, and an unfair one. ... Going steady isn't fair to the girl, and it isn't fair to you. It means you fall into a rut during years when life should be exciting and ever-changing. The really popular Young-Man-about-Town is the fellow who avoids entangling alliances. (Jonathan, 1938: 112–15)

Apparently, the status competition and popularity contest of dating and rating, petting and paying, also functioned to support the young in maintaining their distance from the danger of becoming too seriously involved; the contest supported them in avoiding a 'surrogate' engagement. Obviously, a 'real' engagement and marriage remained serious aims, but they could be achieved only with 'real' money in the bank, enough to afford a wedding ring and everything else it symbolized. In this way, 'real' money was the basis of both marriage and dating; in dating the boy paid in preparation for his later position as 'head of the house', playing to be the 'head man' for the duration of the date. To stop playing by getting too serious too soon was contemptible and ill motivated:

If you as much as smile at the girl, he will be around to ask you what your intentions are. He'll tell you of their great and beautiful understanding. If you like the girl and she seems to like you, tell her frankly that you want to date her. If she's pledged to somebody else, you've had the information from the right person. If she isn't, she'll appreciate you're speaking frankly, and she can set the other man right about his place in her life. (Jonathan, 1938: 201)

Obviously, to 'go steady' was perceived as breaking the rules of the dating regime, a kind of treason, inviting other boys – as sort of a punishment – to break in and continue to play where the game was stopped by taking it too seriously. The instrumental approach to dating, necking and petting, was backed up by a carrot and stick mechanism, the carrot being the celebration of necking and petting as simply belonging to 'being young and happy', the stick being the destruction of popularity by falling for romance: only a coward or a jealous sissy would lose that instrumental approach. This example shows how the entire game of promiscuous popularity, the demonstration of competitive success through the number and variety of dates commanded, functioned as a weapon against getting more serious by 'going steady'.

A manners book of 1941, presenting the adult code to girls, still breathes the atmosphere of the 1930s. The basic outlines of the dating regime were accepted and adopted – college girls should meet lots of boys, they should go with as many different ones and types as possible, and study them just like any other subject, all for the sake of popularity and, eventually, of being able to make a wise selection of a husband. However, petting was rejected as cheap: *'The intelligent girl does not have to "pet" to be popular. ... If a girl is a nice girl ...* she will remain a nice girl, despite her new freedom ... *If she is a cheap girl,* she will have her future hours of deep regret' (Wallace, 1941: 179; 193–4). After having repeated a couple of times that a well-bred girl did not pet, it was admitted – this time without showing a fear of falling down a slippery slope – that girls sometimes fall for the 'sentimental vein' and the 'romantic atmosphere':

> Oh, there will come a time when almost any girl will be carried away. If she is truly well bred, she probably will be heartily ashamed of such a moment and determine that it shall never happen again. Such a girl can be as fine as any girl in the world. She was inadvertently cheap for a moment but has risen from it. But, that girl who 'pets' because she likes to 'pet' with any man with whom she happens to be is dulling the pleasure that would be one of the most divine in the world when true love finally arrived. The girl who so 'pets' is more likely than not to be the heroine of the famous legend, 'Always a bridesmaid but never a bride.' (Wallace, 1941: 204)

6.7d Dating codes after World War II

After World War II, many authors advised parents about what freedom to allow their teenage daughters: at what age should what freedoms be allowed, or not (yet). Some were amazingly detailed in connecting ages with conditions of meeting such as the hours of meeting and the sort of places: drug stores, tea rooms, movies, dances, night clubs, and restaurants. All these details show both the intensity and insecurity of the ongoing negotiating struggle between the young and their peer groups and adults.

Conservative authors such as Emily Post remained abhorrent of the peer-group code. In her revised 1950 edition, Post had moderated her pre-war stance that young women should never live on their own (1950: 168) and she had also softened a little by telling parents now at what age and to which places they could permit their daughters 'to go out alone with a man' (1950: 171–2), but she still refused to use the words 'date' and 'dating', and she was still adamantly against petting, of course. Other authors, too, advised negatively: 'If a girl is smart and socially mature, and a credit to her well-bred parents, she's clever enough to have lots of dates and good times *without petting*' (Eichler Watson, 1948: 479).

Another author, addressing girls, started an argument against petting by writing 'Dating should be fun', but many girls 'are made uncomfortable by boys who want to spend dating time in love-making'. She continued to describe 'the pressure of petting', which consists of the 'fear that they will be considered poor sports, or that they will lose opportunities for dates, if they are reluctant to include "necking" on their dating programs', which boils down to the fear of becoming 'a social failure for not having a heavy schedule of dates'. The readers were reassured: 'there is no law that says you must kiss your escort at parting!' and 'to gain the approval of boys and the assurance of further dates by "buying" them with the coin of integrity and self-respect' is not necessary: 'A sense of humour, wide and diversified interests, and a healthy liking for members of the opposite sex will bring attention and dates. You don't need to "buy" them,' so 'don't feel compelled to "pay" for every date ... Petting or necking will solve nothing – not even genuine questions about sex.' The advice this author gave was simply to have 'plenty of plans for activities on dates, and have 'them often with other couples', have 'group dates' (Sweeney, 1948: 26–7).

Hardly anything in this argument differs from what was written before the war by representatives of the adult code, except the direct reference to 'genuine questions about sex'. Indeed, sex was now discussed more openly. The need for such discussions had risen because there was more sexual activity: 'So many young people use the freedom of the parked automobile for unrestrained, irresponsible sexual activity that anyone who parks is suspect' (Duvall, 1958: 191). Perhaps these discussions served parents, who were concerned 'that their sons and daughters don't get caught in some sexual jam that will spoil their future', as well as their sons and daughters, who reported being 'unable to talk about love, sex, and courtship problems with their parents' (Duvall, 1958: 193). Yet, as the rules loosened up, there was a need for alternative strategies. Having group dates or double dates and planning plenty of activities were hardly ever missing among a wide range of practical advice on how to avoid (too much) necking and petting. This latter type of advice became more frequent and detailed:

> She wards off unwelcome behaviour with a firm refusal to co-operate, accompanied by a knowing smile and a suggestion of some alternative activity. She may say, 'Not now, Ambrose – let's go get a hamburger; I'm hungry.' Or she may take a tip from Marianne. When her date seems about to do something objectionable, she takes both his hands in both of hers, squeezes them affectionately, grins into his eyes, and says, 'You're quite a guy.' By doing this, Marianne lets her date know that she won't go along with his intimacy, at the same time that she shows she likes him as a person. A girl's best protection is in *anticipating* a situation and deflecting it. (Duvall, 1958: 189)

In the 1950s, warnings against being 'picked up' were new to the genre: do 'not get into a pickup situation', for even if 'a man picks up a girl and finds out that, in spite of the pickup deal, she is a nice girl and he falls in love with her, there will always be that cloud, that reservation' (Ludden, 1956: 20). Negative advice on 'pickups' continued into the 1960s: 'The fact that the girls are willing to date in this offhand way often gives the boy the idea that anything goes' (McGinnis, 1968: 113).

Another novelty of the 1950s was the 'blind date'. It was defended by Mrs Post, who had finally adopted the term 'date'. She defined it as 'a peculiarly American variation of the formal introduction, which in this case is made indirectly and for the express purpose of arranging a date' (Post, 1960: 174). Later, an addition made explicit what was at first taken for granted: 'The dangerous blind date is the one arranged through a chain of people, or people you do not know' (Post, 1975: 914).

The main change in courting after the war, however, was that 'youth turned to "going steady"' (Bailey, 1988: 26). Sometimes, this new practice was communicated differently: 'Instead of using the words, "going steady," some girls simply say they are out of circulation just now, and the man understands – and for the time being files her name away for future reference' (App, 1947: 29).

6.7e   In and out of circulation

After the war, girls went in and out of circulation, shifting in between experiments of going steady – also in 'going further' – and experiments of being in circulation. Thus, courting was differentiated into dating and going steady, while dating started at an earlier age and had spread to wider social strata. 'Definitions of social success as promiscuous popularity based on strenuous competition had given way to new definitions, which located success in the security of a dependable escort' (Bailey, 1988: 32). Much greater emphasis was now placed on the necessity of restraining sex for the sake of love. The lust-balance question of what should be the ideal relationship between love and sex was now addressed more straightforwardly and more often than before. The appeal to morals had often become subtler without losing any of its force:

> When conscience and unacceptable impulses are equally strong, a girl may become a hypocrite who does one thing and preaches another, acts one way and pretends to be acting another. She cannot consciously reject her parents' values, but neither can she accept them as her own. Her attitude is simply: *as long as no one knows* about it, I can do anything I please. Notice that *she* knows (with a part of herself), but she's never learned to see herself as somebody who really *counts*. (Unger, 1960: 55)

These lust-balance discussions are another indication of sexuality having become more important and less rigidly restrained. The author who reported so factually about girls going in and out of circulation, also presented an example of a highly sexually orientated discussion. His argument starts by labelling the early dates of any boy as 'dangerous' and 'critical':

> For, psychologically, the girl is still just 'a moment's ornament' to him. He will of course want to kiss her as much as if he had known her for two years. But if she lets him, she will almost automatically switch herself into the lane of girls that men forget. She will remain–just a moment's ornament. His reverential love will be nipped in the bud. *Sex will begin before love has got a good start.* She will become pleasure for him instead of contentment. She will 'startle, and waylay' him. And really any 'dancing shape' can do that – and very probably soon will. (App, 1947: 50–1)

The suggestion clearly is that she has no time to waste. Relations between the sexes were becoming more equal and informal, but the divisions were still stark. Only if she were to stay by his side and play it right, which included 'no parking where parking is suggestive', then 'he will grow to think of her not merely as a "lovely apparition" but as a lovely presence'. Courtship should not become largely sexual pleasure, it should be romantic, 'always far short of sexual fulfilment,' for 'love grows on desire restrained'. Therefore, she should have to teach him 'a fixed habit of respectful desire for her' in order to be able to trust him. The development of reverential love *and* trust 'requires the constant sublimation of sex to romance, of a physical urge to a postponed hope, of a passionate desire to a sweet promise. That sweet promise is a happy marriage' (App, 1947: 50–1).

This argument leans heavily on this 'sweet promise': in its name young girls were expected to 'catch' young boys early in their dating, and help them to transform their sexual longing into a romantic longing (and, if possible, to keep them away from 'dancing shapes'). If not, his ability to love would be nipped in the bud. In this argument, there was no reference whatsoever to campus years as a youth moratorium with its 'good–bad' middle ground and its 'good–bad' audacious girls, able to act with the dexterity needed to equal the cool and instrumental scheming of boys who insist on sexual favours. Moreover, the argument completely ignored *her* sexual appetite; she might have turned from being an apparition to being a presence, but in her the spark that could light a sexual fire was supposedly absent. Having no sexual desires of her own, this argument was, in fact, a sort of Victorian idealization of love, written in cynical Freudian terms. And it also boiled down to a plea for going steady, implicitly even for puppy love, for if he had to be 'caught' by the lovely apparition early in his dating, then both were puppies. Accordingly, or so it seems, the topic of puppy love emerged in Amy Vanderbilt's million-selling manners book. She took its occurrence for granted, reassuring her readers that:

> [these] passing attachments always do seem more of a menace than they usually are and should be accepted with a certain amount of humour untinged with ridicule. Puppy love is serious to the lovers, if a little ludicrous to parents, brothers, and sisters, but it should be respected, for it has its painful aspects. Very few daughters really wish to settle their affections for life on a teen-age boy when it comes right down to it, though the fantasy of undying devotion is very evident for a time. (Vanderbilt, 1952: 538)

These kinds of words addressed the feelings involved in puppy love, but they neglected the novelty it was. Before the war, it was not mentioned. That is, I have not come across it in my sources nor anywhere else. The dating regime had provided both sexes with easier access to each other, and it had also opened the doors to both the longing for sex and the longing for love as well as to experiments at balancing the two. At first, these processes had mainly involved young people at colleges, but soon their example had reached and influenced younger age groups. For several years, however, there had been no space for puppy love; if it occurred, it was likely to remain hidden, for puppy love was not taken seriously. Quite the contrary: expressions of it were seriously ridiculed. After the war, many of these

conditions had changed. Dating manners still formed an impressive example for young people, but as an extension and continuation of growing up in
more equal, more intimate and permissive relationships, they could now
give more leeway to their longing for the intimacies of both sex and love.
Romantic and erotic longings occupied the minds of increasingly younger
people, and adults half-heartedly allowed them expression. This outline of a
socio- and psychogenesis of puppy love also helps understand why boys and
girls, young women and men, developed the custom of going in and out of
circulation, in and out of 'going steady'.

Most authors of manners books were against 'going steady'. Some were
'only' critical, for instance by calling it a 'controversial question' and a practice that has 'confused' many people (Duvall, 1958: 214). One author,
addressing young women under 21, summoned his readers to stop 'this
"going steady" fad which had risen after World War II':

> It's possible for you and your friends to turn over to a new page. Let the sec-
> ond decade, post World War II teenagers grow up and stop playing games. Act
> your age and have some fun. At no other time in your life is it possible to
> know so many people so well, mix so often with people of your age, and have
> so many contacts with members of the opposite sex. Shop around. You're
> *supposed* to at your age. Later, it's wrong. Now, it's RIGHT. You're sure to do
> it *sometime*; so do it when nature planned that you should . . . Under 21!
> (Ludden, 1956: 12–13)

In her 1960s' edition, Mrs Post joined the choir of negative adult voices
against 'going steady' and 'pinning', defined by her as 'the presentation of a
fraternity badge by a college man to his girl ... another type of "going steady"
... or "engaged to be engaged"':

> To the chagrin of many parents and teachers 'going steady' has become a fact
> of American teenage life. Gone is the traditional stag line at the high school
> dance; today a girl usually dances only with her escort ... these young people
> are putting limits on the development of their own social personalities when
> they limit their dating friendships. Only by meeting many other young peo-
> ple of varied backgrounds and interests can a boy or girl broaden his or her
> own experience and gain enough insight to be capable of making a good
> choice of a partner when the time comes. (1960: 180)

In the 1975 edition, daughter Elizabeth Post added: 'The constant "togetherness" of going steady also poses a sexual problem. Boys and girls are put in
a position where it is difficult, if not impossible, to resist their urges, even
though they may want to' (1975: 915). In discussing this 'sexual problem',
this book was rather late – again. In 1960, for instance, it was dealt with as
'the problem of two people becoming so secure in each other's company
that there follows a natural desire to express affection more and more fully'.
This was admitted to be natural, certainly, yet 'within us, two different kinds
of feelings are at war with each other. What we've learned to feel about the
way a girl should act shouts at us, "Stop!" But other feelings say, "Go ahead.
This is what you want to do, isn't it?"' (Unger, 1960: 37). Understandingly,

this author wrote: 'we may feel torn apart by the struggle – a helpless victim', and yes, 'we all make mistakes', indeed, for 'impulses are often stronger than ideals.' He continued, however, by warning: 'Ideals have to be lived out consistently to be effective when we need them', and therefore, if you're not ready to cope with these serious implications, 'you're not ready to go steady ... The most direct way to solve the necking problems which arise in going steady is simply not to go steady' (Unger, 1960: 37–9).

Most authors briefly discussed the origins of this 'frightening' custom (Vanderbilt, 1963: 559), this 'emotional crutch' (Vanderbilt, 1978: 46). Conformity was often mentioned, and so was (emotional) insecurity; here are some examples: '"Everybody goes steady in my town. If you don't you're just a square ..."; just conforming with the local dating customs' (Unger, 1960: 36, 40); 'too many parents are being lulled by young sons and daughters who report that this steady dating is what everybody else does', a practice that 'apes the intimacy and closeness of formal engagements in its exclusiveness of other social contacts' (Vanderbilt, 1963: 559); 'Make sure you're not going steady just because everyone else is, or because it's unnerving to meet new people, or because you're afraid to be alone for an evening' (Ostrander, 1967: 56).

One author added (and scorned) an advantage boys have in going steady: money; it's cheaper. He brought this up after having raised the question: 'Who started this "going steady" movement? Talk to the boys and they'll say the girls force them into it. Talk to the girls and they're usually less positive about it.' He then proceeded by presenting a sketch of the 'undeniable advantages' from the boys' point of view:

> He is sure of an exclusive franchise on the girl of his choice. Competition has been eliminated for the nonce, ... the financial strain will be less ... It's no imposition at all to have a date in her living room, eating her popcorn, watching her television set. It's all part of the deal. And if the steady arrangement has lasted for some time, ... she can even be expected to pitch in with a little cash on occasions. (Ludden, 1956: 5)

Indeed, these advantages were 'undeniable', but what were the advantages for girls? The question wasn't even raised. In a way, it is raised by Beth Bailey in her study of dating, but her answer is rather incomplete. Like so many social arbiters, Bailey believes insecurity to be an important part of the explanation. In contrast to any social arbiter, however, she sees this insecurity as being rooted in a demographic change: the pre-war dating system, with its characteristics of 'shopping around', 'stag lines' and 'cutting in' 'succumbed to fears about what people saw as a new reality. After World War II, for the first time, women outnumbered men in the United States ... The dating system that had valued popularity above all was unsettled by women's concern about the "new" scarcity of men' (Bailey, 1988: 34). In other words, their fear of becoming a spinster was pointed to as the main motive for girls to give up dating, to go steady and marry young. This fear may have increased somewhat, indeed, but I very much doubt that it was strong enough to explain the whole new trend. I think girls experienced other and more important advantages in going steady, advantages with greater explanatory power.

To some extent, these advantages consisted of avoiding the disadvantages of dating. As before, dating presupposed some degree of familiarity and sexual activity, but the new generation of girls thought these degrees to be low, too low. Girls who were not going steady had to put up with 'the usually not-so complicated forwardness of boys. For example, "being out for what they can get" or "taking advantage of a girl"' (Unger, 1960: 64). Advice books might have offered useful examples of how a girl could restrain or stop a boy's sexual advances, but the problem she had to tackle was rather how to enjoy sexual activity. Among the conditions that would make this possible, trust was pretty basic. Traditional dating, however, did not allow much trust to develop:

> In a very real way, the game of dating is a contest ... you may consider the boys who are out there waiting to ask you for a date as your adversaries. Your part of the game is to cause them to want to ask you and to cause a particular one to ask first. It's quite a game! ... Whenever a woman fails to think of herself as an individual worthy of a man's courtly attention, she's giving a point to the other side. And you do it all the time. You do it every time you let a man see how eager you are ... Remember the object is to make HIM eager. (Ludden, 1956: 38, 39)

In this kind of contest between 'adversaries', each date was seen as a victory, but the game would go on. The contest might proceed by his trying to find out whether the girl was 'for kicks' or 'for real', and the girl 'who freely indulges in "heavy necking sessions"' was not 'for real'. Boys were willing to 'play around' with any girl who would allow it, but ... if a girl was "for kicks", not "for real", she frequently does lose his respect.' And once he decided she was not 'for real', insult was added to injury, for if 'you're now getting rough or indifferent treatment, didn't you perhaps ask for just that?' (Unger, 1960: 64). This is an example of women being responsible and, therefore, open to being blamed for all sexual acts, whether unsanctioned or uncalled for: either she had not set limits (in time) or she was not truly virtuous. On dates with a boy who was 'out for what he can get' the contest proceeded differently. These boys did not want to find out whether a girl was 'for real'; they were merely sexually aggressive, as was advocated by Dr Albert Ellis in his best-selling book, *Sex and the Single Man* (1963):

> get as much of her body bare as quickly as you can. Deftness and speed often pay off in this regard ... do it firmly, vigorously, in spite of some resistance on her part. Show her that you are determined to have her as nude as possible, even though you are not going literally to rip the clothes off her back and begin to rape her. (quoted in Bailey, 1988: 92–3)[8]

But even if she liked the boy and trusted him, she would still run the risk that at some point 'the boy begins to be insistent and urgent in his caresses

... his fondling gets rougher and more intimate' (Duvall, 1958: 210), and turns out to be unable 'to stop necking and petting at a "safe" point' (Unger, 1960: 60). Girls had to prevent their own but certainly his sexual excitement from 'reaching "the point of no return"' (Unger, 1960: 58). 'If a pregnancy ensues, it is the girl who is "in trouble"', while 'the fellow's future [is] at stake'. And you 'know how prevalent is the male "double standard"' (Duvall, 1958: 204–5). With these dating conditions prevailing, how could girls enjoy much sexual activity?

From this perspective, 'going steady' may be interpreted as part of a 'civilizing offensive' of girls against the double standard of boys that was embodied in the dating code. In that sense, the emancipation of women and the emancipation of women's sexual affects were running in tandem. Young women could not escape the double standard; they had to accept it or to fight it, for even when 'going steady', the threat of the 'dancing shapes' remained. In reaction to a young woman who had discovered her boyfriend had been sneaking dates with 'fast girls', an author wrote:

> Since many boys are restless for excitement and impatient to try their prowess in the sexual area, they often date 'trashy' girls. In this way they think they're getting this strong sex drive out of their system. And that means getting closer to readiness for 'no fooling' steadiness and marriage. What you've run up against here is the well-known 'double standard.' As time-honored as it is, in many countries through many centuries, it's definitely not so sacred in America today that you can't challenge your boyfriend on it. (Unger, 1960: 63)

The interpretation of the trend towards going steady as having been motivated by young women seeking more power and respect, more trust and sexual pleasure in their relationships with young men, finds further support in passages on female sexuality. No matter how overwhelmingly negative authors wrote about going steady, at the same time they advocated the practice by writing lines like

> Generally a girl who is fond of the boy she's dating enjoys his light caresses, especially if she feels that they're reserved for her alone ... the boy who likes a girl for herself will respect her wishes and not force himself upon her. So a girl has to run the risk of losing the attention of a few 'wolves' in her search for the kind of date who is willing to be a genuine friend. (Duvall, 1958: 186)

And:

> If a boy deliberately stimulates you sexually, ask him not to; if he continues, don't go out with him anymore ... But by far the best advice we can offer is to know your date and to know him well – his reputation, his background, and what his feelings are for you – *before* you let yourself in for this kind of situation. (Unger, 1960: 54, 56)

In the dating advice books of this era, advice in which young women merely appeared as sexual objects abounded. Obviously authors were worried about the fact that 'going steady also implied greater sexual intimacy – either more necking or "going further"' (Bailey, 1988: 51). They thought it neither necessary nor appropriate, however, to write positively about young women as sexual subjects. The only exception did not go beyond first date kissing:

> So forget your rule, and forget any generalizations you may have been frightened by. It is certainly not *necessary* to kiss a boy on the first, second, third or any date. If you don't want to kiss him, don't. A kiss should be a sign of affection, and there's nothing more tasteless than a DUTY kiss. On the other hand, if you do want to show your affection in that way, and you approve of the situation and the boy, kiss him. First date or not! (Ludden, 1956: 84)

This is the only way in which the power of a girl's sexual longing – 'like the boy? kiss him, first night or not' –, was acknowledged positively. And, 'boys being boys', which included the belief in the 'point of no return' from which moment on boys were still generally believed not to be mentally strong enough to resist their raging hormones, how could anyone expect more? In the early 2000s, this connotation of 'boys being boys' is still strong in the USA, while it is totally rejected in the Netherlands, England, and Germany. At every point, also in the middle of sexual intercourse, 'stop' or 'no' is expected to prevail.

And yet, the most important advantage for girls in 'going steady' probably arose out of their growing longing and capacity to become sexual subjects: going steady was a kind of play-marriage relationship with a higher level of mutual trust which provided young women with the basic condition needed for enjoying a fair share of sexual pleasure. At the same time, the basic importance of this condition brings out the theoretical significance of mutually expected self-restraints – MES. It had to be on a level where he could be trusted, that is, expected to restrain himself.[9]

6.7f   The Sexual Revolution in the USA

One of the changes of the Sexual Revolution was summed up by a change in the title of a paragraph in a popular dating guide: what in the 1958 edition had been 'Must you neck to be popular?' in the 1968 edition read 'Is "Making Out" Expected?' (Duvall, 1968: 186). The contents of the paragraph had been changed accordingly. For instance, the sentence 'A girl doesn't have to neck or pet to be popular' now reads 'A girl doesn't have to "make out" to be popular.' And a paragraph on 'Dates in Dorms' contains this advice: 'Keep the lights on. Don't close or lock the doors. Keep the feet on the floor' (Duvall, 1968: 196). The obvious hint in these sentences was also made more explicitly:

> Our society allows a great deal of freedom to young people. It says, in effect, to dating pairs, 'Go on out and have yourselves a good time. Enjoy each other in a variety of situations. You have privacy, an automobile, and no chaperonage. Get acquainted with each other. Become fond of one another, and make

plans for the future, if you wish. But one thing is to be left for marriage – going all the way.' (Duvall, 1968: 200)

Another author characterized all the advice of the recent past as a far too formal schedule, without any attempt

> to consider how well the girl liked the boy and how well they got along together. We have come a long way since that advice was given. Today, it seems more reasonable to say that how you respond to a boy should be tied much more closely to how you feel about him and how he feels about you ... The answer to the question of when to kiss, therefore, is not a matter of how many dates you have had, but rather a matter of how you feel about each other. (McGinnis, 1968: 116–17)

Advice like this signals the decline of general and formal social rules in deciding about behavioural alternatives and the rise of more flexible guidelines which were to be used in accordance with one's feelings and with an appreciation of the relationship and the situation: from an emphasis on fixed social formalities or external codes and regulations to an emphasis on the individual and relational fine-tuning according to internal and relational data, among which shared emotions are crucial. This author had developed a schedule, though not a time schedule, in which the 'nature of the relationship' and the 'physical ways of showing affection' all followed from 'the intensity of your feeling for each other' (McGinnis, 1968: 119). These feelings were understood to be romantic; it was still taken for granted that it is from their increasing intensity that sexual desires would rise. Sexual feelings and desires as relatively independent forces, influencing (romantic) feelings of affection, were not (yet) recognized. This stance reflected the moral position that 'physical ways of showing affection' should follow from the intensity of the feelings of affection.

A few years later, sexual feelings and desires, whether or not related to romance or affection, were recognized more fully by Jill Schary in *The Cosmo Girl's Guide to the New Etiquette*:

> Sometimes I don't wear a girdle, and sometimes not even a bra. The movement of the breasts and buttocks under the kind of soft, graceful clothes I wear speaks a language that almost all men understand. ... I am *soft* – in my manner, my voice, my touch and smile, in the way I walk, I am not a pal or one of the boys. I am many things he is not – I am *feminine*! I am a woman, and I know it – every single minute. And that is how I turn men on! (in Brown, 1971: 228)

Here, sexual feelings, sexual charisma and sex appeal were displayed indiscriminately. The promise of sexuality was out in the open: 'all are called', so to speak, and this had become possible because the selection process in which 'few are chosen' had become based upon the principle of mutual consent as much as on that of mutual attraction. This was implied in a section under the heading 'How sexually generous a girl should be', written by Gael Greene, in which she argued that 'the concept of sexual generosity is losing ground in this Age of Sexual Emancipation,' and concluded that 'sex, at least *good* sex', 'implies a *mutual* giving' (which is reminiscent of 'going Dutch' on a sexual pleasure; see Chapter 4). This conclusion was followed by a sharp argument against 'one unhappy side effect of our new sexual freedom':

> a strange distortion of sexual generosity. For some girls, sex has become ... calculated trading – bed for insurance of a date next weekend or a dinner at Trader Vic's or a weekend at Stowe. Bed, because she owes it to him ('He spent sixty-five dollars on me tonight') ... bed, because: 'If I make a fuss, we'll wake my roommate' ... bed because: 'Everybody does it' ... 'I know he'll never call again if I don't ... 'We've gone this far. How can I say no, now?' This is not sexual generosity, but sheer profligacy. It's not carefree liberation, it's a dreary slavery of habit. It's not giving, but a colossal waste of a girl's resources. Well, it *isn't* love and it *isn't* lust.

> Don't get me wrong. I'm not about to suggest that sex outside of marriage is doomed to despair, or that sex without love should be avoided. Of course, the grand passions are the greatest, but a magnificent love affair need not necessarily lead to marriage, and a lot of less-than-love affairs have a legitimate place in the sexual scheme of things. Sex is a form of expression ... sex *can* bring instant intimacy ... sex *does* stave off loneliness. A girl can have an absolutely fantastic evening in bed with a fascinating man whose name she might not necessarily know and whose face she may never see again. But it is pitiful to be deluded. (in Brown, 1971: 229–30)

Delusion and confusion, inherent in all processes of emancipation and accommodation (as will be argued later in Sections 7.3 and 8.3), have complicated the delicate process of proceeding according to the principles of mutual attraction and mutual consent. It was only on the basis of mutual consent that contacts between people could become increasingly frank probings of each other's erotic strength and sexual attraction. In the absence of a strong norm of mutual consent, for instance, women were not only expected to lower their eyes demurely but they also dared not look at men freely, as this would too often be interpreted as an invitation to proceed as he pleased, as giving a *carte blanche*. Moreover, without a fair degree of equality between the sexes, to give in to mutual attraction would remain dangerous: soon mutual consent would be lacking or absent. However, mutual consent was only a *necessary* condition for the choosing process towards having 'good sex', it was not sufficient. Greene's examples show, in her own words, that '[g]oing to bed out of passivity, habit, obsession, or nagging insecurity seems to build up a reservoir of sexual and emotional numbness and, in many girls I talked to, feeds both guilt and sexual hostility.' In this context she adequately borrowed the phrase: 'Bad sex drives out good' (in Brown, 1971: 231).

Here, conformity and (emotional) insecurity were raised as arguments against 'bad sex', whereas, as arguments against 'going steady', they had served the purpose of avoiding 'a sexual problem' and 'bad love', as it might be called in analogy. It was only now, in this phase of sexual emancipation, that the *whole* lust-balance appeared on the public agenda, that it was publicly admitted that both love and sex can be experienced as good, bad or even absent: 'it *isn't* love and it *isn't* lust.'

On the private agenda of individuals, finding an abidingly gratifying lust-balance had presented itself much earlier, of course, both as a task and as a problem. Mutual consent as a rule in courting and in sex had been the outcome of ongoing power struggles and collective negotiating processes, and they implied ongoing trials of power and negotiating processes between individual partners, demanding more sensitivity and flexibility from both, and also more play and foreplay. Thus, the development of mutual consent had as a rule reduced the dangers for women of being humiliated, and it had increased their chances for enjoyment in making love (and eventually also his) by prolonging foreplay. This is the significance of a statement like '*good* sex implies *mutual* giving'. Not only in bed but in every phase and moment of a love relationship, the process of pulling and pushing, attracting and repelling, became more subtle, playful, and demanding. An erotically promising eye contact might be followed by a disheartening verbal contact that breaks the spell. In order not to break the spell and to stay 'on that same wave length' where a relationship is experienced as 'it *is* love and it *is* lust', at least to some extent and for a longer period, new skills were demanded, for instance the skills of managing emotions, managing relations and relational conflicts. In these years of transition, conformity (keeping up with the Joneses in sexual experimenting) and insecurity ran rampant. Symptomatic is the statement that 'the most serious dating dilemmas involve drinking, drugs, and sex' (Whitcomb and Lang, 1971: 389).

Insecurity was writ large in and between the lines of a paragraph on 'Sex in College' in Amy Vanderbilt's manners book of the early 1970s:

> I doubt very much if every young man and every young woman entering college feels completely adequate in the matter of what he believes will be expected of him sexually in this new exciting and increasingly permissive world. On the contrary, I am sure many young daughters go with feelings of great personal inadequacies, as do young sons. Not to mention the fears and doubts of the parents who in their day probably faced a very different kind of college or university atmosphere where sex, although it of course existed, was not the open thing that it is now ... Parents of college men and women in this time of sexual revolution cannot be overprotective. Such an attitude is not only useless but creates seemingly insurmountable gaps between the generations. Parents should be receptive, available, and concerned rather than curious. (1972: 727–8)

Parents were addressed in terms of 'should', but their young daughters and sons (not once was 'their children' used) were addressed in the reassuring way that betrayed deep fears: 'Students who have had a good relationship with their parents ... will not use sex as a reward or as a punishment to prove their masculinity or their femininity.' And instead of the constraining word 'should', young people were reminded of their 'responsibilities to society not to produce children out of wedlock, not to use their bodies promiscuously' (Vanderbilt, 1972: 727–8).

In her 1975 edition, Mrs Post discussed some of the new issues, but she usually came up with old answers. For example, after the observation that 'Women's Lib, feminists, and the changed relationship between men and women in general are challenging the established order of "boy asks girl" for a date', she raised the question whether this order could be turned upside down: could a girl ask a boy out on a date? 'There is a certain amount of justice in this attitude,' Mrs Post started out her answer, but in a tone that seems more cramped than generous. She continued:

> but I believe it is self-defeating. Men *like* to think of themselves as the aggressors. They may be flattered by a woman who pursues them, but they may also feel that their masculinity is being threatened ... A girl who knows how to use her femininity and her charm to get the man she wants, instead of displaying her independence and 'strength' to bowl him over, has a far better chance of success. (1975: 911–12)

6.7g The 1980s and the 1990s

On one side of the spectrum of the manners books that appeared in the 1980s and 1990s, one finds a few unequivocally restorative and, in terms of the lust-balance, highly love-orientated expressions. The revised 1984 edition of Mrs Post's manners book, for instance, had left her insistence on women using their femininity unchanged, and so was the rest of her chapter on dating, except for one update. This was the reference to 'the fears that alcohol and drugs inspire' (1984: 311; see Section 6.5). A few years later, Mrs Post's stance on this issue was contradicted in a manners book for service men: 'In this modern age of equality, women of all ages often take the initiative in asking for dates' (Swartz, 1988: 136). Another example of a love (rather than lust) restorative orientation after the Sexual Revolution is:

> *Should you insist that your parents tell the rest of the family that you are living with someone?*

> Personally, I think living together in what in the old-fashioned way was called 'sin' is something to be ashamed about, not to boast about. If my daughter was living with a man without marriage I would want as few people as possible to know about it. I am sure that applies to the majority of parents, wherever in the world they may live. There are a few 'modern' young women who wish to boast not only of having an illicit love affair, but also of having a fatherless child. I think it is wrong, and the more people who are brave enough to say it is wrong, the better. (Cartland, 1984: 86–7)

In the 1980s, manners books expressing ideals of a lust-balance with more sex lost favour, except for another best-seller by Helen Gurley Brown, *Having It All* (1982). Most of her advice for 'getting it all' concerned getting all the things men used to have: love, success, sex, and money: 'Having work you love is as important as having *somebody* to love – not *more* important but just *as*. Men *know* this; women are learning' (1983: 373). The book also comprised an early acceptance of married women having affairs on the side, and an explicit praise of masturbation as 'one of life's free, harmless, deserved pleasures' (1983: 166). A much weaker attempt at integrating sex into 'it all' was made by Baldridge:

> My own feeling is that sex is much better when there is romance lurking around somewhere. Otherwise, it can become as matter-of-fact as a computer printout. If you think your date tonight is going to 'sleep over' and you welcome that thought, prepare for it. Have some treats waiting in your fridge ... A sparkling clean bedroom is enticing. (1990: 175)

Baldridge not only fought matter-of-fact sex with romance lurking in the fridge and sparkling in the bedroom, but also with politeness:

> When two people have been intimate, and the sexual encounter was a pleasant one for both, it should be considered a common courtesy the next day for one to get in touch with the other, if for no other reason than to say 'thank you.' Neither person should take a thank-you call as a profession of love or as an indication or desire on the caller's part to deepen the relationship ... You are not making a commitment or proposing matrimony with a short note or telephone call. (1990: 175–6)

This reads like a formal approach to an informal relationship; it seems characteristic of the period of transition from a formal period to an informal one: informality was accepted and appeased by an attempt at formalization. Another such example is the advice Baldridge gave when the possibility of having sex was frustrated because he had not brought a condom. In that case she was advised to tell him: '"Since you're not prepared, we'll just have to wait until you are. Let's skip sex tonight"' (Baldridge, 1990: 180). The possibility of him replying that she was not prepared either was not mentioned. Apparently, she was neither expected nor advised to bring some condoms herself, which (again) tended to portray her more as a sexual object than as a sexual subject.

In 1992, Mrs Post once again updated her book. Now she wrote: 'Women know it is socially accepted to ask a man for a date. How comfortable they feel doing it, however, may be another matter' (1992: 161). This edition no longer contains a chapter on dating; the subject was dealt with in two sections, one for 'older children' and one for 'singles', each no longer than one and a half pages (out of a total of 750). The section on dating for 'older children' starts out with three lines addressing parents, the last one being: 'Setting limits is your prerogative – no parties without an adult chaperon, and reasonable curfews – are two' (Post, 1992: 144), and it continued by providing some 'good general rules' for boys and girls, such as: 'Unless a couple has been going steady and they have agreed to share at times, the boy pays all expenses on a date except when the girl asked the boy for the date' (Post, 1992: 145). In the context of singles, only two questions were dealt with and they were dealt with briefly, 'who calls for whom?', and 'expenses': 'Many people have not yet overcome the awkwardness of having a woman pick up the check'. The next small paragraph, called 'The Etiquette of Intimacy', only deals with protection against sexually transmitted diseases: wear a condom! (Post, 1992: 163–4). This matter-of-fact way of writing was certainly politically correct.

Another example of the restorative trend as it continued in the 1990s was a book advocating 'The Rules' that were once called 'playing hard to get':

> Follow The Rules, and he will not just marry you, but feel crazy about you, forever! What we're promising you is 'happily ever after.' ... Why? Because he spent so much time trying to get you. You have become so precious to him that he doesn't take you for granted. On the contrary, he thinks of you constantly. (Fein and Schneider, 1995: 1–6)

Playing hard to get, also implied deferred sexual gratification:

> Now you might argue that you don't mind having sex with him on the first or second date and taking your chances, that it's okay with you if he doesn't call again ... We know from experience, of course, that most girls who say this are lying to themselves. Deep down inside it's not okay with a woman if she sleeps with a man and he doesn't call ... When you sleep with him on the second date, you don't really know if he's going to be a gentleman or a creep. *Rules* girls don't take risks. We wait until we're sure before having sex.(Fein and Schneider, 1995: 81–2)

Spoiled by other girls, the slow pace in getting physically intimate may make him angry, these authors admitted, but they reassured their readers by telling them that anger indicates interest: 'he will probably call you again!' When the time for having sex arrives, these authors advised, when in bed, 'stay emotionally cool no matter how hot the sex gets. The fact is, most women turn men off not only because they sleep with them too soon, but because they ... try to exploit the physical closeness of sex to gain emotional closeness, security, and assurances about the future' (Fein and Schneider, 1995: 81–2).

The cynicism of these authors does not appear to be of the tongue-in-cheek type. This appears, for example, from the way in which these authors defended why men should pick up their dates and pick up the checks. They referred to the double standard of a code for business situations and a code for dating: 'It's just chivalrous,' they wrote, for

> Equality and Dutch treat are fine in the workplace, but not in the romantic playing field. Love is easy when the man pursues the woman and pays for the woman most of the time. He feels that the money he spends on the food, the movie, and the cabs is the price of being with you and it's worth every penny. You should feel honoured, happy, not guilty. (Fein and Schneider, 1995: 38)

Confronted with the fact that 'The Rules exist without the slightest acknowledgement of anything the feminist movement has achieved in the past 30 years,' one of the authors, Schneider, said: 'Our way may be retrograde, but it works. If a chicken-soup recipe worked in 1940, why change it?' (Chrissy Iley in *The Sunday Times*, 23 June 1996).

Probably the most determining figure in the field of manners in the 1980s and 1990s, and certainly the best known, was Judith Martin's creation of Miss Manners. Her humorous irony, a tongue-in-cheek seriousness is brought out in this fragment on flirtation:

> Proper flirtation – and it is a proper pastime, or rather an improper one that proper people can properly practice – is an end, not a means. It is not the beginning of courtship, but a different, milder form of romantic activity ... The tone should be 'Ah, had I but met you earlier – had I but known that someone like you existed,' as opposed to 'How about giving it a whirl and seeing if it works?' It is the essence of bittersweet, a pleasure for the sophisticated palate.
>
> But how can one do this among literal-minded clods? Alas, Miss Manners regrets that flirtation is no longer possible when flirts open themselves to the insult of being held accountable for their actions. People who spoil such sport ought to be punished by being condemned to spend their evenings discussing inflation. (1983: 275)

To the question whether there is a proper way to make a pickup, she answered: 'Certainly. There is a proper way to do everything, and usually several improper ways. Pickups, to seem respectable, must be contrived to seem accidental' (Martin, 1983: 290). She declared she was against 'pushy tactics' because they 'are self-defeating. The real skill, in courtship, is to be able to play just slightly more slowly than one's partner' (Martin, 1983: 278).

On the question of whether or not to expect a call or a postcard 'when the hospitality extends overnight', Miss Manners answered a 'gentle reader' that:

> [the] night stand, whether it is the one- two- or three- variety, does not, by its very nature, require social continuity. You are confusing it with an entirely different social tradition, called courtship. Miss Manners cannot find your young men remiss, provided that they met the basic requirements of the night-stand act. (1983: 295)

In this way, Judith Martin had her Miss Manners deal with the 'problems arising from Modern Sex ... with a weary little smile', showing that she 'has nothing at all against modern trivial variations on behaviour, provided the traditions are observed'. And Martin really meant 'trivial' for she explicitly states that everything that is presented as modern either is the result of 'the custom of self-gossip' (the novelty of making one's own activities public) or of 'historical ignorance. Take, for example, the "modern" matter of ladies asking gentlemen for dates. Have you never heard of "I find I have an extra theatre ticket for Thursday night"?' (Martin, 1983: 277). The problem I find in treating Modern Sex this way, however, is historical: it belittles the significance of twentieth-century's changes in the lust-balance.

In *Miss Manners' Guide for the Turn-of-the-Millennium* (1990), Martin specified the difference between a one-night stand and courtship by raising the question 'why the openly and instantly committed person, male or female, is likely to be alighted by the object of his or her immediately declared attentions?'

> Miss Manners could dismiss this as a prolongation of the adolescent concept of romance as sport, in which winning a heart only inspires one to look for a more challenging one. Indeed, that is her usual diagnosis when she hears people complain that the lack of uncertainty in marriage eliminates the pleasure.
> Skipping the stages of courtship is another matter. It leads, Miss Manners believes, to scepticism about the value of the love being offered. It actually curtails the development of reciprocal love and the courtesies it should inspire.
> The Victorian heroine kept a check on expressing her feelings not only to torture her suitor but to give him, as well as herself, time to let that first excitement of romantic attraction develop into serious longing. (1990: 551).

The chapter on 'the stages of courtship' contains a plea for 'dating around', called 'social promiscuity', based upon a direct rejection of the 'submarital category' of couples going steady and living together. People in their teens or twenties should spend much time and energy on discovering the opposite gender,

> unfettered by the responsibilities of exclusivity. To dash from one person to another, revelling in the wicked pleasure of infinite possibility, is best accomplished, it seems to her, during youth. Miss Manners is tired of listening to the pathetic tales of those abandoned in middle life by overgrown boys or girls who have only just made that discovery. (1990: 554)

This seems to me a new argument for an old American tradition, the dating game: it tells boys and girls to get those raging hormones out of their system and be young and wild: Yee-ha!

6.8 Courting Regimes Compared: Some National Differences and General Trends

Changes in courting regimes and in the related relationships between children and parents, women and men, have triggered many similar questions and discussions to appear in the manners books of all four countries under study. This already indicates that the changes were going in the same direction. The question concerning in what places young women and men could acceptably meet (private dances, clubs, skating rinks) and where not (a bachelor's apartment) more or less faded when acceptability came to include the street. Discussions about the necessity to be (properly) introduced ended with the acceptance of people simply introducing themselves. Questions regarding appropriate ways of meeting changed from focusing on how to ward off unwelcome advances to a broader focus including questions such as how to invite and respond to welcome advances. Increasingly open access to the opposite sex and easier, more comradely contacts between the sexes coincided with discussions and laments about the decline of courtesy towards women and the decline of poetry or romance in courting relationships, about the trend to disclose the 'secrets' or 'facts of life', a trend in which women were thought to lose their innocence and purity, about the practice of kissing thoughtlessly and promiscuously, girls as daredevils for whom running risks is a trump and ideal. Manners books from all the countries under study contained queries about the boundaries of decency, about where this increasingly invisible borderline actually was. And authors came increasingly to address detailed lust-balance questions, enlarging the spectrum of the lust-balance under discussion. The accepted code regarding the pace of getting closer and expressing further interest accelerated from a three times meeting before suggesting a 'spot of dinner', via a three times meeting before kissing and a three-date 'score', to the instant intimacy of a one-night stand. And in all four countries under study the process of female emancipation was expressed in increasing acknowledgement of the principles of mutual attraction and mutual consent in courting.

All these changes in courting regimes were directly related to changes in the balances of power between parents and children and between men and women in favour of the latter. A general trend in the twentieth century in all the countries under study was that young women and men increasingly brought their courtship outside the direct control of parents and their representatives such as chaperones and Mrs Grundy. The main difference emerged in the early 1920s when American parents were dropping out of the scene earlier and further than in the three European countries, giving way to the development of a youth culture and a dating regime. This implied an earlier and more open integration of sexuality into courting practices and ideals in the USA (and also a somewhat different process and pattern of integration – to be discussed later). After World War II, when it became socially accepted that young people in the European countries would also practise some form of 'dating' and 'going steady', trends in all four countries more or less converged. Experimentation with multiple partners in 'staged seduction', however, was never endorsed, and certainly did not spread in the three European countries under study. There, until the Sexual Revolution, the emancipation of the younger generations and their sexuality was relatively limited. It consisted of the development of a type of courtship relationship that was to some extent similar to 'going steady', a kind of 'trial' relationship that could transform into an 'engagement to be engaged'. In both, some sexual experimenting came to be increasingly accepted. However, it is difficult to compare the extent of the integration of sexuality into these courting relationships because the European manners books provide far less information on these relationships than American ones, while the information they did provide was less open regarding sexuality. Lust-balance questions such as what an ideal relationship between love and sex might be, were merely hinted at between the lines or addressed vaguely in terms of 'final problems'. Some additional information, however, can be derived from changes in the functions and meanings of an engagement, in 'getting engaged'.

The following short excursion on this topic relies on a study of advice on engagement and marriage in Dutch manners books between 1850 and 1990. The author, Patricia Eggermont, concluded that the meaning of an engagement was changing in the 1920s: the period of getting to know each other was moving from the engagement itself to an earlier period, while breaking off an engagement was becoming less of a social calamity (1993). During the first decades of the period of research, getting engaged in the European countries under study remained the main socially accepted possibility for young people to hold, touch and kiss. Manners books contained warnings against light-hearted 'beaux' and 'coquettes' with a history of broken engagements (A, 1894: 27), and also against too short engagements, because they could give reason 'to suspect the young man's motives' (Engelberts, 1890: 78). The motives hinted at were sexual: to hold and kiss and touch. And the same motive was still included in the 1950s warning not to get engaged 'if people only have the slightest ulterior motive' (quoted from a German manners book). Over these decades, engagements tended towards further experimentation and integration of sexuality. When engaged, the couple were expected to limit their sexual explorations and experiments. Manners books were ambivalent in the sense that advice made it clear that one should not go too far, but also that exactly this did happen: 'The complete expression of love, however, should be kept for the future husband. If the exchange of kisses during an engagement becomes too frequent, kissing in marriage will have lost its value ... Taking all this into consideration, it makes sense, if possible, not to leave the couple alone' (Staffe, 1900s: 98). Another early twentieth-century manners book said that, as fiancée, a girl should not allow any liberties that she would have been ashamed off before, and continued:

> She should, however, show him that his presence is the most precious thing in the world for her and that there is nothing she would prefer above being united with him forever, but she should not go to lonely and secret places for this reason. If she did, the young man might rejoice this at first, but soon he will develop an aversion to it and his esteem for her will drop. (Seidler, 1911–15: 75)

Another indication of sexuality more or less accepted and expected of engaged couples, is the inclusion of engaged couples in quite a few titles of nineteenth- and twentieth-century introductions to sexuality: *Huisboekje voor verloofden en pasgehuwden* [*Housebook for Engaged and Newly-Married Couples*] 1823; S. Sr. Coronel, *De wittebroodsweken: Hygiënische wenken voor verloofden en jonggehuwden*, [*Honeymoon Weeks: Hygienic Advice for Engaged and Newly-Married Couples*] 1889; H.L Batenburg, *Boek voor verloofden en jonggehuwden* [*Book for Engaged and Newly-Married Couples*], published between the 1900s and the 1950s in many editions.

Because it was more or less accepted and expected that at least some sexual intimacies would occur during an engagement, good manners *and* her reputation demanded that it would be the young woman who breaks off the engagement. A man who did this was described as a boor. A manners book written for gentlemen added: 'It is a form, nothing else, a mere eyewash' (ECvdM, 1917: 114). Yet, the only thing he could do was to provoke her into breaking off the engagement (ECvdM, 1911: 114).

Early in the century, getting engaged was already losing some of its certitude as a solemn or holy pledge to get married in due time. In 1911, *Madame Etiquette* advised her readers not to make too much fuss over an engagement, for if it breaks off, which happens quite often, she said, then all those flowers and festivities will make the memory all the more sad (ECvdM, 1911: 188). In the early 1920s, increased caution is evident from the reason given for announcing an engagement by sending two separate cards: if the engagement is broken off, 'it is not pleasant that an engagement card is kept here and there or is left wandering about. Considering the number of engagements that are broken off, it is advisable not to send too many cards around' (Margaretha, 1921: 118–19).

In the 1920s and 1930s, the trend towards a more easy-going and trouble-free attitude towards (ending) engagements continued (Eggermont, 1993: 111). Many authors jeered at the 'startling unconcern' shown in getting engaged and expressed serious concern about the high frequency of these 'rash engagements'. Yet, breaking an engagement remained a very serious event: all presents and love letters were to be returned.

After the war, in the 1950s, it was observed that, due to the 'very free' contacts between young people, official engagements had dropped in frequency. Increasingly, the phase was skipped because even without being officially engaged, couples 'have all the freedom needed to come to a decision regarding the desirability of a marriage; they can have their intercourse as frequently and as intimately as they please' (Schrijver, 1954: 43).[10] Yet, through the 1950s until the late 1960s, engagements were still popular. In 1959, the sexual freedom that came with an engagement in the Netherlands was compared to the sexual freedom offered by the dating system in the USA. The comparison was made in an interview (*Het Vaderland*, 15 August 1959) with George Simpson, Professor of Sociology at Brooklyn College, New York, on the occasion of his return to the USA after a year teaching at Leiden University. Simpson defended the dating system against the then common attack that in it, boys and girls used to mutually exploit each other. Dating is not such a hard system, he is reported to have said, but a positive means to initiate American youth into healthy sexuality and to promote a mature choice of partner. At this point, in accordance with prevalent Dutch public opinion which was still strongly against pre-marital sex, the Dutch reporter criticized Simpson, for he wrote: 'Prof. Simpson defends his value judgement of the significance of "dating" by referring to the Freudian theory that repression of normal desires until the authorised moment of marriage will always be harmful to that marriage. Initiation and preparation are to be appreciated as functional, that is, as positive.' It is in the context of this defence that Simpson was reported to have pointed to the large difference in the Netherlands between engaged and non-engaged couples, and he is quoted as having said: 'Engaged couples suddenly permit themselves a much larger freedom. Is then an engagement here indeed conceived of as a warranted bond for life?' He had a point, but it offended conservatives who wanted to uphold the status façade. Over the decades, engagements and dating had both become increasingly sexualized, but the sexuality in engagements was kept hidden behind the ideal of everlasting love.

This interview was part of an extensive public discussion about youth and morality. At that time, the majority of the Dutch population was still rather conservative on this point, and conservatives, particularly those in positions of authority, worried about the morality of the younger generation, particularly 'among the lower classes'. A new branch of this discussion expressed moral concern for what was then (in the Netherlands, from the 1920s to the 1950s) called the '*amatrice*' (female amateur): 'The appearance on the scene of the *amatrice* as a *dramatis personae* ... is connected to the appearance of a premarital female sexuality that could no longer as a matter of course be localised only within the lower classes nor be lumped automatically under the heading of prostitution' (Mooij, 1993: 136).

An example is provided by a report about 'a search among salesgirls' (*sic*) and this report

> showed a large majority of them to possess contraceptives. The type of the *amatrice*, the girl who gives herself to a friend in a loose-fixed relationship for which she is rewarded by being taken out often – to be distinguished from the professional prostitute – is found most frequently among the salesgirls of our cities. (Saal, 1950, quoted in Mooij, 1993: 151)

This figure of the *amatrice* evaporated completely in the Sexual Revolution, and so did 'getting engaged' as a way to greater sexual licence. With the moral stigma removed, the *amatrice* became a girl with a steady relationship, a 'normal' girl who had *verkering* or *vaste verkering*. She was, in fact, 'going steady'. Thus, lust-balance trends in the USA, and in the Netherlands (and in the other European countries) converged. In the next chapter I will focus on trends since the Sexual Revolution.

7

The Lust Balance of Sex and Love since the Sexual Revolution: Fuck Romance!

7.1   Introduction

In the 1960s, as the international western youth culture and its Sexual Revolution surfaced and was soon followed by a strong wave of female emancipation, sex-for-the-sake-of-sex came to be discussed in all the countries under study. As a result, the *whole* lust-balance appeared on the public agenda. Moreover, both sexes came to participate in public discussions of lust-balance questions. Until then, the dominant social code regarding the sexuality of women and men had continued to involve a lust-dominated sexuality for men and a complementary (romantic) love or relationship-dominated sexuality for women. Now, much stronger than in the first (USA) youth culture, changes in lust-balance definitions and practices resulted from changes in the balance of power between both the generations *and* the sexes. And both, in turn, were directly connected to changes in the We–I balance and in the balance of controls as expressed in lust-balance relationships (relationships involving sex and/or love). In order to understand and interpret these interconnected changes more fully than would be possible on the basis of my study of manners books alone, I have looked for studies into the connections and the tensions between love and sex, but these are rare, and historical studies into this area that cover my period of research are even harder to find (see Blom, 1993; Hatfield and Rapson, 1994; Kooy, 1968, 1983; Zessen and Sandfort, 1991; Zwaan, 1993). Studies of sexuality do not usually pay much attention, if any at all, to the kind of relationship in which it occurs; and vice versa, studies of loving relationships usually do not take a systematic interest in sex. Both kinds of research are even reported as attracting different kinds of respondents (Schreurs, 1993b: 332). Therefore, in my attempt to sketch a coherent picture of these social and psychic changes within and between the sexes, I have made use of data obtained from sociological and sexological research, as well as my own experience of these decades. In addition, I have used evidence from sexual advice books and from a study of (changes in) the popular Dutch feminist monthly magazine *Opzij*[1] (Aside/Out of the Way!), established in 1973. The selection of *Opzij* as a source of empirical evidence implies (and allows for) a focus on women, the women's movement, the emancipation of women and, by implication, the emancipation of female sexuality. The reaction of men, their accommodation and the restraining of their sexuality will receive less attention, partly because for men there is no source of evidence comparable with *Opzij* that could be studied as diachronically and systematically: accommodation processes are rather 'quiet' on the whole. When they occur, those involved in these processes feel that the moral basis for raising their voices is lacking, as has happened, for example, from the late 1970s onwards, when women and their women's movement have been loudly attacking men for their domestic violence. Adding the study of *Opzij* to my sources implies a somewhat stronger focus on the Netherlands, but what follows has remained the discussion of changes in courting regimes that I started at the end of the previous chapter (section 6.8). It is a continuation based on expanded sources. What follows focuses on general trends since the Sexual Revolution. A few significant differences, particularly those between the USA and the European countries under study, will be elaborated upon in the next chapter.

Manners books in the first half of the twentieth century said little or nothing about sex, but introductions to sexuality did, of course. From reading them, it clearly appeared that in the 'traditional lust-balance', female sexuality remained highly subordinated to male sexuality: 'A woman does not *take*, but *tempts* in order to be taken ... Copulation is performed *by* a man and *to* a woman' (Wattjes, *ca* 1930: 34). And:

> The newly married woman *is as a rule*, more or less completely 'cold' or indifferent to and during sexual intercourse. She must be *taught to love*, in the complete sense in which we here use the term. The husband may perhaps not succeed in imparting this erotic education; generally that is because he takes no trouble about it. She then *remains* permanently *frigid*. (Velde, 1933: 271; It is no surprise, therefore, that the title page of the original Dutch edition of this international best-seller said: 'written for the physician and the husband', that is, not for women.)

Outside the genre of introductions to sexuality, discussions of female sexuality usually centred on the 'prostitution issue' and the issue of the *amatrice*. Up to the Sexual Revolution, a woman's sexuality and her reputation had remained interconnected with wider social codes in such a sexually repressive way that, in retrospect, it gives the impression that 'as far as her reputation was concerned, a girl who admitted to having sexual needs might as well take a seat behind a window in the red light district' (Dantzig, 1994: 1276). In the course of the century, more and more women will have deviated from this code behind the scenes, but whenever caught in the glare of public attention, they gave rise to scandal and were treated like 'fallen women'. Many scholars claim that, to some extent, the Sexual Revolution consisted of the decline of the enormous distance that had been growing between the public front kept up and actual behaviour (for instance, Bailey, 1994). The new generation, involved in a new youth culture, demanded more honesty.

The 'traditional lust-balance' was attacked in the 1950s when the topic of female sexual pleasure and gratification gained considerable importance in sexual advice literature – *The Adequate Male*, translated into Dutch as *My Husband, My Lover*, is predominantly a good lover (Caprio, 1960). Especially from the 1960s onwards, the sexual longings of all women, including the 'respectable' and the unmarried, could be openly acknowledged and discussed. Then, for the first time, women themselves actively took part in public discussions about their carnal desires and a more satisfactory relationship between the longing for sexual gratification and the longing for enduring intimacy (love, friendship) – a more satisfying lust-balance. Thus, the emancipation of women ran in tandem with changes in public morality as well as in the codes of manners and ideals individuals regarding love and sex. These changes coincided with rising tensions between the two types of longing. From the 1960s onwards, topics and practices such as premarital sex, sexual variations, unmarried cohabitation, fornication, extramarital affairs, jealousy, homosexuality, pornography, teenage sex, abortion, exchange of partners, paedophilia, incest, and so on, all part of a wider process of informalization, implied repeated up-rooting confrontations with the traditional lust-balance. People were confronted with the lust-balance question more frequently and intensely than ever before: when and within what kind of relationship(s) are (what kinds of) eroticism and sexuality allowed *and* desired? These repeated confrontations accompanied and reinforced the trend towards a collective emancipation of sexuality, that is, a collective diminution in the fear of sexuality and its expression within increasingly less rigidly curtailed relationships. Sexual impulses and emotions were allowed (once again) into the centre of the personality – consciousness – and thus taken into account, whether acted upon or not. As the social and psychic distance between the sexes and the classes decreased, both women and men became involved in a collective learning process – experimenting both in mainstream settings and in undercurrents – in which they tried to find new ideals and ways of gratifying their longing for both sex and love. The questions and answers with which they were confronted shifted and varied along with changes in the spectrum of prevailing interpretations of what would constitute a satisfying lust-balance. In this chapter, I aim at a description and interpretation of this collective learning process. It is subdivided according to four phases that can be distinguished. The first phase was the Sexual Revolution itself. The second, a phase of transition from the end of the 1970s to the mid-1980s, was characterized by the shift from 'sexual liberation' to 'sexual oppression'. In the third phase, there was a lust revival, and in the fourth, from the early 1990s onwards, a lust *and* love revival.

7.2   The Sexual Revolution

The Sexual Revolution was a breakthrough in the emancipation of female sexuality even though many women throughout these years continued to think of sex in terms of duty (Frenken, 1976), sometimes worsened by the new 'duty' to achieve an orgasm. Due to the contraceptive pill and an increase in mutually expected self-restraint (mutual consent) in interactions, the dangers and fears connected with sex decreased to such a degree that there was an acceleration in the emancipation of sexual emotions and impulses – allowing them into consciousness and public debate. Women's sexual desires were taken more seriously: Dutch men became 'more strongly directed at clitoral stimulation' and their aversion to oral sex decreased considerably – from more than 50 per cent reported in the early 1970s to about 20 per cent ten years later (Vennix and Bullinga, 1991: 57). This means that increasing numbers of them learned to enjoy the woman's enjoyment and that many women have opened up to sexual fantasies and titillations. The dominant image of single females, if not already 'old spinsters', changed accordingly from 'failed-as-a-woman' and 'sexually deficient' into the opposite: sexy and independent (for the USA: Ehrenreich and English, 1978: 258–9; Israel, 2003). In a relatively short period of time, the relatively autonomous strength of carnal desire became acknowledged and respected. Erica Jong had her multi-million audience dream about a pure form of instant sex, the 'zipless fuck':

> the incident has all the swift compression of a dream and is seemingly free of all remorse and guilt; because there is no talk of her late husband or of his fiancée; because there is no rationalizing; because there is no talk at *all*. The zipless fuck is absolutely pure. It is free of ulterior motives. There is no power game ... No one is trying to prove anything or get anything out of anyone. The zipless fuck is the purest thing there is. And it is rarer than the unicorn. And I have never had one. (Jong, 1973: 14)

For both genders, sex for the sake of sex changed from a degrading spectre into a tolerable and thus acceptable alternative, allowing more women and men to experiment with sex cheerfully and outside the boundaries of love and the law. Until around 1970, the slogan of the advice literature that accompanied this process was that 'men should restrain themselves somewhat more and women should be a bit more daring' (Röling, 1990: 90), a slogan that was obviously attuned to men who came too quickly and women who did not come at all. From then on, interest and attention shifted from joint pleasures towards discovering one's own sexual desires and delights. In close connection with this, the ideal of love shifted further away from the Victorian ideal of a highly elevated marital happiness towards individual happiness or satisfaction and greater scope for each partner to develop themselves – a development that was observed in all countries under study (Blom, 1993; Mahlmann, 1991; Swidler, 1980). For example, the American *Ladies' Home Journal* warned in the 1970s 'that it was a myth to believe that marriage "is free of conflicts, that it is an all-encompassing blend of two personalities fused into one. A marriage like this leaves no breathing space for two individuals to retain their own personalities"' (Cancian and Gordon, 1988: 309). In the early 1970s, the growing emphasis on individual development also came to be expressed collectively in the deliberately created 'apartheid' of discussion groups, refuge homes, pubs, bookshops, etc. 'for women only', expressing an outlook of 'emancipation-via-segregation' (Stolk, 1991), also pejoratively called 'self-segregation' (Lasch-Quinn, 2001).

Sex for the sake of sex was first and to a greater extent accepted among homosexual men, who almost seemed to realize the dream of the 'zipless fuck'. The far-reaching liberation of sexuality among them was a topic that was also frequently discussed outside their circles, both with an envious and a frightened tone. The comparison with homosexuals also had another function, put into words by Joke Kool-Smit (commonly credited with having triggered the second feminist wave in the Netherlands): 'feminists and homosexuals are each other's natural allies', she explained, not only because both groups are discriminated against, but from a 'much deeper similarity between the liberation of women and of homosexuals. Both demand the right not to behave like a woman or a man ought to, they do not accommodate to their sex role of strong man and soft woman' (*Opzij*, 1973 [11]: 26; see also Stolk and Wouters, 1987b).

However, as Kool-Smit continued, 'some male homosexuals ... are even more strongly adapted to male mysticism than the average hetero-man. And this group and feminists stand directly opposed to each other.' The struggle for liberation from the straitjacket of sex roles obviously had priority, but as far as sexual liberation was concerned, Kool-Smit referred to lesbian women as a model: 'lesbian feminists could be an example for other women with regard to their relationships and in finding a distinct identity. For in these relationships where men are absent, emotional warmth need not come from one side only, and erotics can at last be separated from dominance' (*Opzij*, 1973 [11]: 26). In 1974, Anja Meulenbelt, probably the foremost Dutch feminist, also contributed to this trend by announcing her love affair with a woman under the title 'Homosex en feminisme' (*Opzij*, 1974 [3]: 7–9).

In their quest for a more satisfying lust-balance, the two sexes tended to go in opposite directions. Led by their gender-specific definitions of lust, men (more openly than before) tended to go towards a lust-dominated sexuality, towards sex for the sake of sex as (imagined) in the world of homosexual men, and women towards a love and relationship-dominated sexuality in which physical love and psychical love are integrated and set apart from domination as (imagined) in the world of homosexual women. An undercurrent of women emphasizing lust by sharing the dream of the 'zipless fuck', also shared the mainstream women's longing for a sex that is pure, that is uncontaminated by power and dominance.

In these years, increasing numbers of women and men discovered with greater intensity that the relationship between carnal desires and the longing for enduring intimacy was an uneasy one, and that the continuation and maintenance of a (love) relationship had on the whole become more demanding. The feelings of insecurity, shame, guilt, fear and jealousy, as well as the conflicts, divorces and other problems related to their drifting lust-balances, were all perceived and discussed, for instance in the encounter and sensitivity movement, but hardly, if at all, by the women's movement. At the time, the spirit of liberation from the straitjacket of older generations and their morality prevailed, and the fervour of the movement did not allow much attention to be given to the *demands* of liberation.

7.3   From 'Sexual Liberation' to 'Sexual Oppression'

In several respects, the Sexual Revolution ended towards the end of the 1970s, as the voices against sexual violence became louder and louder. At that time, as the study of *Opzij* shows, in addition to sexual assault and rape, sex with children – incest in particular – and pornography also came to be included in the category of sexual violence. In the early 1980s, sexual harassment was added. As the women's movement turned against sexual violence, attention shifted from differences between the generations to differences between the sexes. Opposition to the sexual practices and morality of older generations decreased, while opposition to those of the dominant sex gained momentum (Daalen and Stolk, 1991). 'Greater sexual openness and more acceptance of sexuality had brought sexual abuse into sight' (Schnabel, 1990: 16), and this was another reason for the shift of emphasis from sexual liberation to sexual oppression. In the media, the misery surrounding sex came under the searchlight. In the women's movement, heterosexuality was sometimes branded as 'having sex with your oppressor', a sentiment also expressed in the lesbian slogan 'more sun, fewer men'. In 1976, one of two lesbian women was reported to have said: 'We are interviewed because of being lesbians, because we make love to women ..., whereas this is the perfectly normal result of seeing yourself as important and of refusing to live in oppressive conditions any longer' (*Opzij*, 1976 [10]: 4-6). Hardly anything but 'soft sex' – sex that is not aimed at penetration – still attracted positive attention, and the phrase 'lesbian consciousness' (potteus bewustzijn) became popular as a kind of yardstick for feminism. In 1980, in a report entitled *Women and Sexuality: Ten Years after the Sexual Revolution*, the author, a sexologist, excused herself for being 'obliged' to discuss male sexuality: 'Because most women still prefer to make love with men, we cannot talk about "her" sexual gratification without referring to "his" modelling of sexuality.' This author also advocated 'soft sex': 'Women can contribute a lot to the recognition of this "soft" pole. And this would not only liberate our own sexuality, but also that of men' (Bruijn, 1980: 4,23). Retrospectives on the 'years of sexual liberation' were also increasingly set in a negative tone:

> It is appalling to notice how many people's thinking became stuck in the ideas of the sixties, at least with respect to sexuality. 'Anything goes' and 'the sky is the limit' are still their slogans and these stimulate a tolerance regarding any daughter-sister assault, which is a slap in the face of the victims. (*Opzij*, 1983 [2]: 14)

The change of perspective and feeling from liberation to oppression which occurred from the end of the 1970s into the first half of the 1980s, was far less marked outside the vanguard of the women's movement, of course, but in most female–male relationships, female emancipation continued in less extreme ways. The women's movement, *Opzij* included, was running wild, so to speak, but at the same time, this very one-sidedness and its policy of emancipation-via-segregation added to the political force of the movement: they were successful in many respects, and in all walks of life women's emancipation was a high ranking moral and political issue. And in these discussions, whether on television or between neighbours, they all moved in the same direction: old male privileges that had been accepted as facts or bad luck, turned into oppressive practices.

Therefore, for most women the shift in focus towards fighting male oppression did not imply any increased attention to the demands of liberation, that is, increased demands on self-regulation, such as the capacity to negotiate a more ideal lust-balance. Whereas before, the fervour of the struggle against the old morality had prevented this, now moral indignation about oppression functioned as such a barrier. This indignation also produced a blinkered view of the (gender-specific) difficulties connected with the emancipation of sexual impulses and emotions. Directing public attention to the difficulties of women in particular was met with moral indignation by feminists; it was branded as 'individualizing', that is, as reducing structured male oppression to individual problems of women. While the perspective did shift collectively from the other (older) generation to the other sex (men), it remained almost exclusively directed *outwards*: the origin as well as the solution of all difficulties was in the opposite sex.

Banning the psychical demands of emancipation from public discussions and from sight did not, of course, facilitate the quest for a new lust-balance, as may be concluded from the two extreme ways in which it was sought. One extreme consisted of a romanticization of old we- and I-feelings – of traditional female solidarity and identity – and an attack on pornography as a form of sexual violence. Here, the implicit lust-balance strongly emphasized love and soft sex, coupled to tenderness and affection. This view was the dominant one, and also advocated by the intellectual avant-garde of the women's movement. Only one author deviated from the general trend by expressing regret that, in comparison with magazines for homosexuals, a monthly like *Playgirl* contained so few pictures evoking a visual pleasure that presupposed 'a pleasure in sex without the ballast of love' (Ang, 1983: 433; Wouters, 1984). Other contrasting voices did not go nearly as far and, taken together, in the early 1980s their force seemed to have shrunk to a marginal whisper. In that margin, the other extreme was to be found. It consisted of a tipping of the lust-balance to its opposite side. According to tradition, a woman should have sexual desires and fantasies only *within* a romantic relationship which was meant to last a lifetime. In a lust-balance that is tipped the other way, a woman's sexuality could be aroused only *outside* such a relationship, in almost anonymous, instant sex. All public discussion focused on the first of these two extremes, while the second remained virtually in the shadows. Ironically, in emphasizing male oppression so strongly, the difficulties connected with the emancipation of sexuality were indeed reduced to the psychic and/or relational problems of individuals, thus leading precisely to the 'individualizing' that was so fiercely opposed at the time. In the next two sections, a closer inspection of both extremes is offered.

7.3a   The anti-pornography movement

During the first half of the 1980s, protests against pornography were numerous and sizeable, sometimes even violent. Massive anti-pornography demonstrations were held. Slogans such as 'pornography is hatred of women' and 'pornography is sexual violence' became well known. In 1984, a Dutch ministerial report on sexual violence turned strongly against pornography and against 'the process of pornographization in the media, in the advertising industry and in mass-produced literature' (Nota, 1984: 47). To the extent that this stance was explained, reference was made to a romantic relational ideal of love, thus preventing any public recognition of the appreciation of sex, and certainly not of sex for the sake of sex.

Although pornography certainly contains many examples of images that are degrading to women, the rejection of the whole genre was nevertheless remarkable. For one thing, the numerous protests against pornography usually suggested that only men were susceptible to this kind of titillation of the senses, and that therefore only men were responsible for the process of 'eroticization', referred to as 'pornographization' in the ministerial report. At that time, there was already plenty of evidence – data derived from experimental research – to suggest that this is quite unlikely: images and fantasies of fortuitous sexual conquests by sexually active and dominant women could certainly titillate the female senses. This kind of research suggested that it is plausible to assume that both women and men are more strongly sexually aroused by fantasies and images of chance sexual meetings than by those of marital or paid for sexual intercourse (Fisher and Byrne, 1978), that fantasies about 'casual' and 'committed' sex make no difference in women's sexual arousal (Mosher and White, 1980) and that women, just like men, are more strongly sexually excited by fantasies and images of sex that is initiated and dominated by someone of their own gender (Heiman, 1977; Garcia, et al., 1984; at a later date also: Dekker, 1987: 37; Laan, 1994). Furthermore, research data also suggested that the difference between the sexes in experiencing pornography was relatively small, provoking more arousal and fewer conflicts and guilt feelings if women had been able to explore their sexuality more freely, just like men, and had developed a more liberal, 'modern' sexual morality (Sigusch and Schmidt, 1970; Straver, 1980: 55).

An interesting (later) finding in this context is from a study comparing women's responses to the 'regular' man-made pornographic film and to a number of women-made, female-centred pornographic films:

> Contrary to expectation, genital arousal did not differ between films, although genital response to both films was substantial. Subjective experience of sexual arousal was significantly higher during the woman-made film. The man-made film evoked more feelings of shame, guilt, and aversion. (Laan, 1994: 49)

This kind of study shows that, on the whole, genital arousal – vascocongestion – occurs 'even when the erotic stimulus is evaluated negatively or gives rise to negative emotions and when little or no sexual arousal is reported' and that 'the gap between genital and subjective sexual arousal is smaller for women who masturbate frequently (10 to 20 times per month) than for women who masturbate less often or not at all' (Laan, 1994: 78, 164, 169). This finding suggests the interpretation that women who masturbate frequently are better informed about their carnal desires and/or able to indulge more (easily) in them. In addition to frequency of masturbation, frequency of coitus also yielded higher correlations between genital and subjective sexual arousal (Dekker, 1987). And a few years later, research data showed that consumers of pornography appreciate and keep up gender equality to a significantly higher degree than non-consumers (Reiss, [1990] 1997: 145 ff).

Women's public opinion on pornography was also remarkable in comparison with that towards prostitution and 'pornoviolence' – a concept introduced by Tom Wolfe for the use of violence in the imaginary world of novels and movies:

> Violence is the simple, ultimate solution for problems of status competition, just as gambling is the simple, ultimate solution for economic competition. The old pornography was the fantasy of easy sexual delights in a world where sex was kept unavailable. The new pornography is the fantasy of easy triumph in a world where status competition has become so complicated and frustrating. (1976: 162)

There have been hardly any protests by women against the spread of 'pornoviolence' in the media. Prostitution, however, next to pornography, did become a significant issue in the second half of the 1970s. At first the women's movement was ambivalent about prostitution, but in the 1980s, the voices defending prostitutes increasingly drowned out the sounds of protest against them. Prostitutes even succeeded in winning the support of the mainstream women's movement. Yet, in fact, on even more adequate grounds than those which apply to pornography, prostitution can be seen as a perverted expression of a sexual morality directed only towards male pleasure and to keeping women in the position of subordinates and servants. As far as 'consumption' is concerned, they relate to each other as imagination (pornography) to overt action (prostitution), while the conditions and relationships of 'production' seem also to be in favour of pornography: the physical dangers for women are most probably larger in prostitution than on 'the set' or in a studio, and they are absent in the representation of sexual fantasies in books or paintings. In sum, the difference in terms of moral indignation aroused between pornography and prostitution is not likely to be explained by a difference in the dangers of production or consumption.[2]

A difference in image-formation may help to understand why women's solidarity was more easily and strongly directed at prostitutes than at female porn stars. In prostitution, women are 'real', whereas in pornography they are visually only a recording and tangibly absent. The concept of prostitution draws attention more strongly to prostitutes than to their customers, pimps or managers, whereas the concept of pornography predominantly evokes the image of wallowing male consumers. However, this difference in image-formation seems to be the result rather than a cause of the anti-pornography movement.

Except as a symptom of women's solidarity, the comparatively small extent of moral indignation at prostitution may be largely understood from women's sensitivity to the argument that there is little difference between the selling of sex in prostitution and in marriage – 'for the sake of peace, or as an expression of gratitude for a night out or a new dress' (*Opzij*, 1979 [7–8]: 41). In this 'sex-is-work' view, prostitutes (like swinging singles) may seem to have the upper hand by staying more independent and obtaining higher financial rewards. Applying this view to housewives, lust has no place and sex brings more displeasure than pleasure: women appear predominantly as sexual objects, not as sexual subjects. As such, it mirrors another view that was still widely held in the 1970s, the belief that men are entitled to have sex with their wives when they want it. In 1975, a detective of the Amsterdam vice squad was still shameless enough to say: 'I'm almost sixty years old now and I've raped my wife quite often. Yes, if she didn't want to [do it with me]' (*Opziji*, 1975 [3–4]: 38). In addition to this sex-is-work view, the image of the 'prankster' emerged: 'naughty' women who (more often than not) enjoy the sex they are paid for – an example of women turning traditional double morality upside down.

The protests against pornography also evoke surprise because they go against the flow of the twentieth-century process of informalization (increasing behavioural and emotional alternatives) and its inherent 'eroticization of everyday life': the emancipation of sexual impulses and emotions as part of a more encompassing 'emancipation of emotions' (Wouters, 1992; 1998a; 1998b). Together, all these arguments seem to permit the conclusion that the anti-pornography movement to a large extent was an 'emancipation cramp'. It was predominantly an expression of the problems connected with the emancipation of sexuality: the attack on male pornography was a sort of 'best defence', concealing as well as expressing a 'fear of freedom' (in Erich Fromm's famous phrase), a fear of experiencing and presenting oneself as a sexual subject.

7.3b   What is the price of sex?

In the margin of the public debate, some of the difficulties attached to the emancipation of sexual feelings sometimes surfaced more or less casually, one of them being the risk of tipping over to the other extreme of the lust-balance. At this other extreme, sex was isolated by excluding sexual intimacy from other forms of intimacy, since these had come to be experienced as obstacles to sexual pleasure. Sexual desires tended towards the 'zipless fuck', to a 'sex without the ballast of love', while the forces which formerly forbade this – the social code and individual conscience – still had to be avoided with such energy and determination that their absence, so to speak, loomed large. In his famous *The Culture of Narcissism*, Christopher Lasch presented these examples:

> more and more people long for emotional detachment or 'enjoy sex,' as Hendin writes, 'only in situations where they can define and limit the intensity of the relationship.' A lesbian confesses: 'The only men I've ever been able to enjoy sex with were men I didn't give a shit about. Then I could let go, because I didn't feel vulnerable.' (1979: 338)

It was expressed also by a Dutch woman who said:

> For years and years I did not want any emotional commitment with men ...
> What I did do regularly at the time, though, was pick up a one-night stand. In
> fact, that suited me well ... Because I was not emotionally committed to those
> men, I was able to take care of my sexual needs very well ... It also gave me a
> feeling of power. I did just as I pleased, took the initiative myself and was very
> active. (Groenendijk, 1983: 368)

Statements like these show more than a shift of accent in the traditional mixture of love ('emotional commitment') and carnal desire. Here, the price of
sex, to put it dramatically, was nothing less than love. In these quotations, the
formulation – particularly the word 'because' – indicates that the lusts of the
flesh could be given a free rein only if the longing for love was curbed radically, as radically as lust had been curbed before. For this reason, this was
called 'the new withdrawal method': 'Don't go for happiness, just go for
orgasm' (Rubinstein, 1983: 79).

The co-existence of an abhorrence of subordination to men with a longing for a loving relationship made many women suspicious of their relational
desires. They feared that if they gave in to this craving for love, they would
lose 'the feeling of power' since they would (as usual) almost automatically
fall into the devouring dependence of a self-sacrificing love (see Dowling,
1981). Therefore, what at first sight might appear to have been a fear of intimacy was in fact another expression of the 'fear of freedom'.

As an undercurrent, this lust-balance formed the negative of that
propagated by mainstream feminism, that is, the anti-porno movement. It
is an open question as to how many women who in public turned against
pornography and, by implication, against male sexual fantasies, to some
extent combined this attitude in private with an escape from emotional
commitment into volatile sexual affairs. What may be concluded, however, if only from the coexistence of these two extremes, is that in this
period there must have been a tug-of-war going on between and within
women; *between* women who ventured into giving free rein to sex for the
sake of sex, and women who rejected this; and *within* women to the extent
that women encountered both sides in themselves and met them with
ambivalence. The question of how many and how intensely women
experienced this tug-of-war or ambivalence cannot be answered. From a
longer-term perspective, it is obvious, however, that throughout the
twentieth century and especially since the Sexual Revolution, many
women have been involved in the quest for a more satisfying lust-balance, somewhere in between the extremes of 'love without the ballast or
duty of sex' and 'sex without the ballast of love'. No woman will have
been able completely to withdraw from this development and its inherent tug-of-war and ambivalence, if only because, before the Sexual
Revolution the social code allowed women to express only one side of
the lust-balance.

7.4   Revival of Lust

In the latter part of the 1980s, the outlook of leaders in the women's movement was less exclusively outward, that is, focused on oppression by men.
They developed a more relational view of oppression, a view that saw
oppression as incorporated in the social code as well as within personality
structures – the latter via the mechanism of an 'identification with the established' (see Elias and Scotson, 1994). Thus the difficulties and pressures connected with the emancipation of women and of emotions came to attract
more attention. This was aptly expressed in the title of the inaugural lecture
by a Professor of Women's Studies: 'The Burden of Liberation' (Brinkgreve,
1988). Its point of departure was the insight that 'greater freedom of choice
once again turned out to be a pressure to perform', as the historian Röling
summarized it (1994: 230). Consequently, emancipation (and assertive use
of the greater freedom of choice) were also seen as a learning process in
which problems were expected to occur as a matter of course: 'It is the complicated task of a "controlled letting go", making heavy demands on affect
control, and it is not to be expected that without a learning process this will
proceed spontaneously and "smoothly"' (Brinkgreve, 1988: 14).

In the latter part of the 1980s, this more reflexive outlook coincided with
further emancipation of sexual impulses and emotions. In magazines like
Opzij, more attention was given to themes like 'men as sexual objects', paid
sex for women, women's adultery, SM, positively evaluated passes and eroticism in the workplace, and also for 'safe sex' (owing to AIDS). These topics
were discussed soberly. When an early attempt at commercializing this interest was made through the establishment of a Dutch version of *Playgirl*, the
magazine had the cautious and typical policy of not publishing 'frontal
nudes'. It was defended by the argument that 'women have only in the last
five years begun to discuss their fantasies. Male nudity does not eroticise ... It
is power which makes men erotically appealing. Hence the popularity of
romance novels in which the male star is a doctor, a successful businessman or an elderly father figure' (*NRC Handelsblad*, 21 October 1987).
Yet the wave of moral indignation at pornography faded away and, in retrospect, the anti-pornography movement was characterized as a 'kind of
puritanism' by Anja Meulenbelt (see Section 7.2), still a leading feminist
(*Opzij*, 1988 [9]: 43).

From the mid-1980s onwards, a number of women-made, female-centred
pornographic films showing women actively initiating and enjoying sexual
activity appeared on the market (Laan, 1994: 163). In this period, a sexologist relativized the importance of 'intimacy'. She wrote: 'in many ways, the
need for intimacy can be a trap for women', and after having presented some
examples of women who like making love to strangers, finding sexual pleasure, she concluded: 'Indeed, at times there is this double feeling: you *do* want
that pleasurable experience of togetherness, you *do* want to have sex, but you
don't bargain for a rather too intimate steady relationship' (*Opzij*, 1986
[7–8]: 69). In 1988, in a special issue of *Opzij* on 'Women and Lust', this

argument was supplemented by a strong attack on the traditional lust-balance: 'Tradition teaches a woman to experience her sexuality as predominantly relational and intimate. But it is an amputation through traditional female socialization to represent a sexuality so weakly directed at pleasure and lust.' The article, directed especially at 'career women who live alone', continues first with a plea to have 'sex for the sake of sex, to be erotic and horny but not emotionally committed' and then warns: 'If a woman nevertheless (secretly) needs intimacy in order to enjoy sex, she will always be left with a hangover. After too many hangovers, she will stop having this kind of affair. Then, she may help herself, that is, masturbate. That can be gratifying too' (*Opzij*, 1988 [1]: 86–7). In later years, this appreciation of masturbation was supported, although sometimes only half-heartedly, as in a review of the first issue of *BEV*, a 'lust magazine' for women:

> I think we are on the brink of an individualization of sexuality, a development that very well befits the growing self-sufficiency of women and also fits in nicely to this age of video, telephone sex and special sex-shops for women. However, this image does not please me. What I sketch here, in fact, is an exact copy of what men are used to doing: they hurry to see a peep show during their lunch hour, or use the company toilet to take the matter into their own hands. (*Opzij*, 1989 [2]: 17)

A few months later, this author attacked a sexologist (Vennix), who had found that half of his female respondents repeatedly made love without the lust to do so, for creating the impression that women actually *are* like that. After having pointed out that these sombre data on 'the female orgasm' were derived from questioning 'only married people', she concluded: 'I think data like these should be connected above all to circumstances. Personally, I would resent it in any case if, from Vennix's research, even *one* man might jump to the conclusion that the importance of *my* orgasm could possibly ever be overestimated' (*Opzij*, 1989 [6]: 25).

A 'large study of sex and relationships' published in *Opzij* in 1989, comparing female readers of this magazine to a general sample of Dutch women, showed that the emancipation of women and of sexuality were running in tandem. It concluded that *Opzij* readers in certain respects had become more like men – a 'masculinization'. They were, for instance, more playfully thinking about keeping up more than one relationship, and they rated having sex (masturbation as well as coitus) higher on a scale. On the other hand, a 'feminization' was concluded from their pursuit of 'a sex between equals, allowing, even stimulating dedication': 'Traditional "femininity", including tenderness, foreplay and passion, is not weakened in this process of renewal. On the contrary, men are expected to behave like this, too. The renewal can be characterized as eroticizing feminization' (*Opzij*, 1988 [1]: 70).

In this period, the Chippendales and similar groups of male strippers (who keep their G-strings on) appeared on the scene, and their success shows that the public titillation of female lust had become a socially accepted fact.

Although the Chippendales did indeed make caressing movements in the direction of their crotches, their coquetry in military uniforms, however, was a continuing variation upon the tradition of the Mills & Boon romance novels in which women need to look up to a man before they are willing to nestle in his arms (Stolk and Wouters, 1987a: 136–72). This pleasure in looking up shows how deeply rooted in the personality the longing for (male) protection was/is, while all the same it is based on the woman's subordination. It also shows the significance of 'identification with the established' as a defence mechanism (and as an aphrodisiac).

Since all the changes described above were moving in the same direction, it seems plausible that, from the mid-1980s onward, the difference between men and women regarding their lust-balance – ideal and practice – decreased. There was a certain lust revival, an acceleration in the emancipation of sexuality. The revival was limited, however, as can be demonstrated from the lack of commercial success of magazines aiming at female sexual fantasies, magazines like *Playgirl* and *BEV*: both disappeared after a few issues. They were not (yet) commercially viable.

7.5 A Lust and Love Revival

A research finding regarding the difference in appreciation of qualities of one's own partner and those of a fantasy partner possibly expresses a characteristic tension of the female lust-balance that prevailed in the 1990s: women reported that they particularly appreciated their own partner for qualities that are traditionally female – not macho, but sweet, tender, sensitive, emotional, honest, faithful, caring, devoted, companionable, totalling 62 per cent – whereas dreams about a (sex) partner mainly referred to corporeal characteristics like robust, big, handsome, dark type, sexy; totalling 65 per cent (Brinkgreve, 1995). This tension in the lust-balance of sex and love, a tension between fantasy and reality, was not only experienced by many more women than before, but apparently also endured better. This means that women's conscience and ego-ideals in these matters had become less rigid, that is, more subtle and flexible.

In the 1990s, the further revival of female lust was expressed in the successful sales figures of mailing businesses and chain stores marketing erotic articles for women, in particular from the sale of vibrators: both in 1993 and 1994 there was an increase of 25 per cent (*NRC Handelsblad*, 6 April 1995). In Germany, the network of female sex shops had become so strong in the 1990s that *Die Tageszeitung* proclaimed the decade as that of the 'lusty lady' (6 March 1997). Owners of video shops reported women's growing interest in porn videos, a booming market and a multi-billion dollar business. A 'sexuality weakly directed at pleasure and lust' had become more of a humiliating spectre, while at the same time the sex that prospers in anonymity, sex-for-the-sake-of-sex, evoked fewer elated reactions, and not only in the context of AIDS. A Dutch trend-watcher claimed: 'Sex for the sake of sex is out. ... Sex is once again being perceived as part

of a relationship (as it seems to have been before the Sexual Revolution)'
(Kuitenbrouwer, 1990: 48-9). And an assertive heading in a book on 'erotic
manners' read: 'Sex for the sake of sex is old-fashioned' (Eijk, 1994). These
statements are backed up by research data on young people. They confirmed: 'Free sex certainly has not become a new sin, but it is losing popularity.' As an ideal, 'most young people think of love and sexual pleasure as
two sides of the same coin, and this goes for both boys and girls' (Vliet,
1990: 65; see also Vogels and Vliet, 1990). In 1995, 'having strong feelings
for each other' sufficed for three-quarters of the Dutch school population
(aged 12 years and older) as a precondition for having sex (Brugman et al.,
1995). This attitude was reinforced by their parents: 'Many report the presence of a "relationship" to be decisive for their consent to a teenage child
wanting to have sex. Some indicate that depth and stability of a relationship, more than age or anything else, makes having sex acceptable' (Schalet,
1994: 117). Teenagers themselves in no way exclude the possibility of having sex for its own sake, but in the longer run the ideal of lovers being
matched to each other, including in bed, seemed to have gained strength.
This interpretation is supported by an increase in the number of young
people between 17 and 24 years old who would consider an act of sexual
infidelity to be the end of a relationship; in a 1979 survey, 41 per cent held
that opinion and in 1989/1993 this had risen to 63 per cent. This very
trend was most spectacular for cohabiting youngsters (by then a 'normal'
way of life) from 30 to 65 per cent (CBS, 1994: 15). Research among a rep-
resentative sample of the Dutch population also suggests that, on the
whole, 'norms regarding sexual fidelity in marriage have become more
binding'; in 1970 and 1980, only 26 per cent totally rejected the proposition that one single sexual adventure on the side could not damage a good
marriage, but in the next decades this percentage kept rising: 35 per cent
in 1991, 45 in 1995, and 57 per cent in 1997 (SCR, 1998: 140). On the
other hand, however, these data on attitudes towards adultery are to be
understood within the framework of another trend on which there are no
research data available: the trend of ideals of openness, frankness and
always telling 'the truth' in these matters moving in the direction of: 'Might
keeping silent about unfaithful adventures range among the defensible
cowardices in a human life?' (Eijk, 2001: 42).

In the 1990s, the women's movement joined this trend under the new
name of 'power-feminism'. Women's solidarity was no longer axiomatic and
this attitude coincided with an attack increasingly mounted on those who
still emphasized oppression. This was branded 'victim feminism' and
denounced as 'victimism'. The attack was also aimed at romanticizing old
harmonious (as well as unequal) relationships and the traditional lust-balance
of predominantly 'sweet and soft'; by calling that 'vanilla-sex', a larger variety of tastes was indicated as acceptable.

In the homosexual world as well, pioneers in the cultivation of sex for its
own sake came to express an ambivalent if not critical attitude towards this
(tilted) lust-balance. Opposing the lust profit of 'the streamlined way in

which sex was organised, discarded from clumsy introductions and annoying questions', Stephan Sanders (1994: 47, 46, 13, 18) mentioned the loss of lust in having sex without passion: 'the continuous coupling ... of more or less perfunctory fucks – the waiting, the posing desirably, the taking down of the trousers, the panting, the hoisting up of the trousers'. Here 'the suspicion that, despite all his efforts, his grip on his desire had not gained strength, but had rather weakened' was gnawing at him. This outlook implies the view that, in the longer run, the absence of passion or emotional involvement limits the possibility of having a lustful orgasm. This was captured in the (1970s?) expression 'Fuck Romance!' that primarily relativizes romance to the point of sex, but in fact also sex to the point of romance.[3]

On the whole, the changes of the 1990s can be interpreted as a lust *and* love or relationship revival. On the basis of continued reinforcement of the principle of proceeding only by mutual consent, mutual trust became embedded in the prevalent relational or figurational ideal (Stolk and Wouters, 1987a, 1987b), to the extent that social interaction between the sexes has become more careful as well as more subtle. Because of the sensitivity and caution needed to proceed in such a way, erotic and sexual consciousness and tensions have expanded and intensified. Therefore, as 'No!' became more unswerving, latitude in sexual activity has enlarged and attempts at integrating sexual and relational desires have intensified. Together, these changes represent a shift in the ideal lust-balance towards 'diminishing contrasts and increasing varieties' (Elias, 2000: 382ff.), and they also represent a process of integration and 'civilization' of the sexes. This diagnosis is confirmed by other data showing that, 'on the whole, women feel like having sex more often, allow more sexual incentives more easily and have learned to discuss these matters more freely,' (for the USA: Hochschild, 1994), whereas 'on the whole, men have learned to connect relational satisfaction and sexual gratification' (Straver et al., 1994: 154-64).

The emancipation of female sexuality and its counterpart, the bonding of male sexuality, will have certainly been channelled by literature (such as feminist publications), by protest activities (such as those against sexual violence and harassment) and by changes in the law (such as making rape in marriage liable to penalty). But their significance in explaining these processes is strongly overvalued unless one also understands the pincer movement that has affected men: they have found themselves trapped between their longing for an enduring intimacy, on the one hand, which became subjected earlier and more strongly to more or less rigorous limitations such as desertion and divorce or the threat of them and, on the other, their increasing dependence upon their talent for arousing and stimulating a woman's sexual desires, (also) for satisfying their own sexuality. Further attempts at explanation follow in the next chapter.

8

International Comparisons, Theoretical Interpretations, and Regularities in Processes of Emancipation and Integration

8.1   From a Comparative Perspective: Developments in Europe and in the USA

By the end of the twentieth century, the monthly *Opzij* had become a popular and regular women's magazine, comparable to *Marie Claire* or the *Ladies' Home Journal*, only more feminist in the sense that women's rights and pleasures, sexual pleasures included, had become normal topics. This in itself already demonstrates a lust and love revival in the Netherlands, and this revival, in turn, implies that both longings of the lust-balance had been integrated on a higher level. Judging from the data presented above, in the USA this integration is stalled or lacking. The data indicate a strengthening of male-dominated sexuality and a revival of conservative ideals about the lust-balance, an attempt at restoring old-fashioned love relationships and, therefore, more a reactionary trend than a revival of love. And certainly not a revival of love *and* lust. My sources suggest that, by the end of the period covered in my research, the USA was lagging behind, that the dominant social definition of sexuality in that country was more male-dominated (and the social definition of love more female-dominated) than in the other countries under study. This was confirmed in the late 1990s by Peter N. Stearns, a prominent expert on American social history, who, upon reading my report on developments in the Netherlands answered that he could observe no signs of such a lust *and* love revival in the USA (see also Stearns, 1994).

Part of the explanation for this lagging behind is to be found in the initial head start of American youth in escaping from under the parental wing and developing the dating system: later, the codes of the dating system came to function as a barrier and slowed up the emancipation of women and (their) sexuality. The paying and petting codes of dating reflected the uneven balance of power between the sexes prevalent at the time when the dating regime was established. Due to the relatively early decline of control over youth by the older generation, young men have dominated the constitutive process of the new dating code. At the time, in retrospect, it was to a relatively large extent taken for granted that 'boys will be boys', that they would 'naturally' want some sexual activity, and would 'go for it', all the more because boys could blame the girl for all sexual acts, even if unsanctioned or uncalled for: either she had not set limits (in time) or she was not truly virtuous. This instrumental attitude to women was symbolized and materialized in the uniquely

American institution, typical of that era: the taxi-dance hall. These codes and ideals were formalized in the dating system and they largely kept their validity until the 1960s. Over the decades, they were incorporated as part of an American tradition, internalized, and as such, they became part of the American habitus. The persistence of this tradition demonstrates how firmly it is socially rooted, but also how strongly its underlying uneven balance of power between the sexes was internalized. This is how the initial lead in the emancipation of the young and their sexuality hardened and caused the traditional double morality to be and to remain stronger in the USA than in the other countries under study.

In this book, the rise of this double standard has been connected to the sociogenesis and further history of the dating system. My data suggest that, over the years, as the dating system became a firmly rooted social institution, a separate code for business situations developed, creating a gap between business manners – from which sex and sexuality were banned – and dating manners that centred on sex and sexuality. In the latter, old good-society sources of power and identity lingered on, which is apparent, for example, from the continued paying and petting attitude: women, by virtue of their sex, deserved to be 'treated' and should not pay for themselves. The two coexisting codes were solidified as another double standard, one that built upon the traditional double morality and also helped to preserve it: outside the world of business, women have had to confront the traditional double morality.

Living by both the youth code with its petting rituals – a convention of both forced and controlled erotic exploration – and by the adult code which dictated saving 'going all the way' for marriage, was in fact living by a double standard: one for moments of pleasure, and one for moments of responsibility. The double standard of an adult code and a youth code regarding sex – one for the college boy and his flame (sex) and one for the mature man and his sweetheart (love) – functioned like all double standards: they made it easier to lie and more difficult to be honest, in this case, about sex. Young women and men could enjoy their sexual energy and dedicate themselves to sexual experiments in the petting contest. As long as they did not go 'all the way', none of the sexual intimacies they experienced would count in an adult context. The gradual social acceptance of petting in the 1920s, but explicitly not of 'going all the way' (and condoms were illegal and hard to get), channelled sexual experimenting and sexual excitement equally gradually from breast fondling at first, towards masturbation and oral sex later. The popularity contest and its inherent boasting and bragging about these pleasures hardened into a cultural fashion, and subsequently into an enduring fascination with breasts and blow jobs, a reputedly 'American characteristic' (Duerr, 1997; Wouters, 1999a). The hardening also implied that both the youth code and the adult one came to be taken for granted, also by the older generations. This is implicitly acknowledged in the following statement: 'The tendency to equate "sex" with intercourse alone represents long-standing cultural norms of acceptable sexual behaviour and certainly applies to adults as well as to adolescents' (Remez, 2000). At some point in time, 'going all the way' became the main and then the only criterion among the young as to whether or not they lived up to the adult code. The bridge between the two codes became known by such names as 'technical virginity' and it was connected to 'technical fidelity'. At the turn of the twentieth century, these names were still used, the bridges were still in function, and so was the double standard: for several decades after the dissolution of the dating regime, more than half of a sample of American college youth did not regard oral sex (oral-genital contact), as having 'had sex' (Sanders and Machover Reinisch, 1999). However, as they were asked the question 'Would you say you "had sex" if ...' and this typically is an adult question raised in the adult context of a questionnaire, the respondents answered in terms of the adult code. It seems likely that, if asked by their friends what sex they had had, they would have answered in terms of the other code: blow job, French, tongue, 'third base' etc. As a rule, this double standard is overlooked in surveys.

By implication, the head start in the emancipation of sexuality was also related in explanatory ways to the reputed fascination of Americans with breasts and oral sex, that is, 'blow jobs', for 'eating pussy' is comparatively less celebrated (again signalling a rather male-dominated sexuality): 'Experts believe that the type of oral sex practiced by young teenagers is overwhelmingly fellatio, not cunnilingus' (Remez, 2000). In the same process, other all-American inventions originated, one of them being the taxi-dance, which is now extinct, but others such as the lap dance and the stripper collecting money from her audience in 'intimate' ways are alive and kicking. The competitive attitude that was institutionalized in the dating regime, expressed in the well-known words 'dating and rating', was extended to an instrumental and commercial attitude just as it was extended to 'paying and petting', and ever since the 1960s to an expanding massive consumption of sex bought on the market. Recent reports on 'hooking up' among college youth describe a code that allows for heavy petting and also sexual intercourse in casual relationships, no strings attached, in which no time is lost on the usual dating activities (see, for example, the article 'What's love got to do with it?' in *The Washington Post* (28 January 2003 by Laura Sessions Stepp). These 'buddysex' relationships with little commitment are reminiscent of: 'Don't go for happiness, just go for orgasm' (see Section 7.3b). In this sense, the young women and men who 'hook up' are the living extensions of that dating attitude: 'We smoke with more abandon and we kiss with more restraint' (see Section 6.7c).

The double standard regarding the lust-balance of love and sex, and the one regarding manners at work and on a date, relate to each other as thesis and antithesis, without many signs of a synthesis developing. Such a synthesis would mean an integration of both sides of the lust-balance and decreasing differences between manners in and outside the business world. My material suggests that the USA is lagging behind in both these types of integration. In all four societies under study, the 'dialectical' movement towards integrating the codes of good society and the codes of work clearly is far from complete; it it still an ongoing process. Taking the code of manners for relationships between women and men in good society as a thesis, that is, as point of departure, than its antithesis was a swing of the pendulum that went far in the opposite direction: in all countries under study women at work were initially expected to be impersonal, not feminine. From there, however, the contours of national differences loom larger. Around 1980, for example, men in all four countries came under attack for sexual harassment. Everywhere this implied that at work, making passes at someone in an inferior social position was taboo, but in the USA virtually all flirting at work was branded as harassment. In this country, the struggle for greater equality appears to be tougher. Hence Miss Manners' stance against using first names at the office (see Section 5.1a). The reputedly advanced greater freedom and independence of women in America seem to have been preserved at work, although at high costs, and to have vanished outside office hours. My material suggests that this can be understood as a social legacy of the dating regime, in which the taken-for-granted male dominance of the 1910s and 1920s was formalized, integrated and internalized in the dating codes and ideals, and more or less fossilized in subsequent years. This hardening explains why, in the second youth culture, when the emancipation from parental regimes was soon followed by a movement for female emancipation, the latter had harsher repercussions in the USA than in the other countries under study.

Considering the fact that the double standard implies that women at work are likely to be treated more on the basis of equality than they are at home, it is no surprise, therefore, that many, particularly married women with children, will tend to feel better (treated) at work than at home. This may explain why many of them experience their working hours as a comparative rest, as more leisurely than the hours when they have to put in their 'second' shift at home (see Hochschild, 1997).

Probably the perseverance of the practice and the word chaperonage in the USA is another social legacy of the dating system. From my study, it appears that the practice of chaperonage continued somewhat longer in the USA than in the other countries under study (in similar circumstances, comparing like with like, city with city, etc.). Up to the 1940s, the need for a chaperone was most frequently and most elaborately dealt with in relation to parties at fraternity houses and college dances, which suggests that for these and other occasions the chaperone was an integral part of the dating regime. This may partly explain why the chaperone lingered on longer in the USA: young people had won greater freedom but they had to keep up appearances in the face of the older generation by accepting the check-check ladies. However, they developed many ways of escaping from their supervision:

> Rules requiring chaperones and governing proper dancing form were usu-
> ally treated in cavalier fashion. Chaperones were invited but conveniently

seated in the parlor, superficially engaged in conversation (often the chore of the freshmen), and kept out of sight and hearing of the real activity on the dance floors, entertainment areas, and unlit grounds outside. (Fass, 1977: 196)

An additional part-explanation may be found in the continuation in the USA of a relatively greater confidence in external social controls and a correspondingly lesser confidence in self-controls than in the other countries. This seems to be a process-continuity that can be observed until at least the end of the twentieth century: parental generations demanding supervision, having little confidence in the capacity of the young to supervise themselves, and the young finding ways – and to some extent receiving the 'space' – to escape that supervision. An interesting initial report of a larger interview study, conducted in the 1990s by Amy Schalet among middle-class parents in the USA and the Netherlands, brings this out well (2000). The study compared parental regimes over the sexuality of adolescent children, at a time when 'slightly over half of American and slightly under half of Dutch 17-year-old girls had had sexual intercourse', and '59 percent of American versus 47 percent of Dutch 17-year-old boys had experienced sexual intercourse' (2000: 101). The most striking differences between the two countries, however, were differences in parental regimes and in sexual practices, particularly in contraceptive behaviour and teenage pregnancies. The study focused on the parental regimes; I will paraphrase and quote its main results.

Parents in the USA expressed little or no faith in their children being able to handle their 'raging hormones'. They tended to mention teenage sex in the same breath as alcohol and drugs. Without external constraints, they argued, their teenagers might become subject to 'wrong' peer influences, make the 'wrong' decisions, 'lose control' of themselves, and indulge. American parents did (want to) exercise the necessary authority and control, but without openly acknowledging or discussing their teenager's sexuality. This was seen as giving their children the 'space' they need; in a 'real family' only the husband and wife have sex.

Dutch parents had come to believe that their teenagers are capable of having a sexual relationship, that they are able to restrain themselves and to commit to others. In discussing drinking they expressed a similar trust. Dutch parents would permit a teenage child to sleep with a boy- or girl-friend, depending on the depth and stability of the relationship. They claimed their decision was a rational response to a reality they cannot control anyway, and helps to keep teenage sexuality from becoming a 'wedge' that could divide the family. Dutch parents seemed more at ease with situations where teenagers are left without adult supervision such as going on a vacation alone, and less at ease with the concept of parental authority as a justification for rules. They were neither fond of strict rules nor of hierarchical respect, that is, the respect of children for parents, but used the concept of horizontal respect or mutual consideration more often. Through conversation and family practices, Dutch parents addressed and negotiated, rather than prohibited, their teenage children's sexual involve-ment. Yet, the terms were decided by the parents, and the control they exerted over the sexual behaviour of teenagers did stem less from the negotiations that happen when a child becomes sexually involved than from the type of person, the ego-ideal which their family ideals and prac-tices sanctioned and helped to fashion. While American parents imposed clear rules and a rigid sexual morality, 'the Dutch parents endorse[d] a less blatant inequality but demand[ed] a more far-reaching orientation and adaptation to the social norms within the family'.

> The American parents expect sex to produce inevitable conflicts and sepa-ration not only within the adolescent but also in the relationship between parents and children. Assuming a greater continuity and harmony between parents and children, the Dutch parents expect to resolve conflicts through consultation and compromise, thus preventing separation between family members. (Schalet, 2000: 98)

Apparently, the more forbidding parental regime in the USA was and still is more strongly directed at exercising external social control of behaviour than at an internal control of impulses and emotions. This difference in the balance of controls corresponds to a higher level of fear and a higher level of trust and/or mutually expected self-restraints than in the other coun-tries. These differences of parental regime may also be understood as aris-ing from institutionalized inequality in the double standard and the dating regime, but only in part. To understand them demands a wider theoretical framework, a more encompassing perspective that also observes the dis-crepancy in social inequality and, correspondingly, in levels of social inte-gration between the two countries.

With the interruption of World War II, the Netherlands has remained a relatively crisis-free and highly integrated country. This has allowed for the development of a relatively generous welfare state, which is operated according to correspondingly strong principles and ideals of social equal-ity. Running in tandem with this development has been a corresponding decline in the level of mutual suspicion and a rise in the level of mutual trust or MES, and also a shift in emphasis from external social controls towards internal social controls, that is, self-controls. In contrast, social inequalities in the USA have remained far greater. Correspondingly, America's lower level of social integration, its class system of relatively open competition and of status insecurity have prevented a similar shift towards self-controls as in the Netherlands. In a country with so many sharp contrasts – between classes, ethnic groups, sexes, regions, etc. – it seems wiser to 'put your money' on external constraints, for there simply does not seem to be enough 'common ground' to put it anywhere else (Wouters, 1998a).

Another cross-national comparative study, reporting similar differ-ences as reported by Amy Schalet, may serve as a stepping-stone to illus-trate this point. It was conducted in an attempt to understand why teenage pregnancies in the USA were two to four times higher than in Canada, England and Wales, France and Sweden (Darroch et al, 2001). The comparison did not include the Netherlands where teenage pregnancies have, for several decades, remained seven to nine times lower than in the USA (Caldwell, 1999: 213). Just like parents in the Netherlands, adults in Canada, England and Wales, France and Sweden, were reported to be generally more accepting of teenagers having sex than American adults. For the latter, the fact that young people are having sex was more often considered to be the 'problem' *per se*. With regard to the younger generation they demanded abstinence from sex, that is, to live up to the adult code, also because they believed teenagers are incapable of using contraception effectively. For American teenagers it was more difficult and expensive to obtain contraceptives and they were less likely than their peers in the other countries to use any. Differences in the level of sexual activity or the age when teenagers become sexually active were small. Greater explanatory power was allocated to America's 'greater inequality and more widespread poverty, which are compounded by the country's history of slavery and racism', and, more specifically, to differences in social welfare systems. The latter in particular helps to understand why 'at all socio-economic levels' (read: not only among poor Hispanic and black teenagers), 'U.S. youth have lower levels of contraceptive use and higher levels of childbearing than their peers in the other study countries' (Darroch et al., 2001: 3–7; also Boonstra, 2002: www.agi-usa.org).

In the genre of manners books, as a rule, these social inequalities remain unnoticed, and with them, references to these groups of outsiders, excluded from good society. They remain virtually absent until a middle class develops from their midst, a 'bourgeoisie' with enough economic and social capital to claim and receive more respect. Thus, in the early 1970s, an inequality surfaced in American manners books that had been largely absent in Europe because European countries, at that time, still counted very few descendants of former slaves among their populations (nor, for that matter, many descendants of conquered indigenous peoples). Until the late 1960s, African Americans (as they are called today) had been American Negroes, and as such they had received little if any attention in these books. In the early 1970s, they surfaced as Blacks in the margin of the genre, in the form of special books with titles like *How to Get Along with Black People: A Handbook for White Folks* and *Sexual Life Between Blacks and Whites*. These books were pushed by celebrities: introductions were written by respectively Bill Cosby and Margaret Mead. Apparently, Black Americans were the first to surface in the field of vision of American good society; until then the authors of manners books had orientated themselves towards circles of White Anglo-Saxon Protestants – Wasps – to the extent that representatives of other groups were merely hinted at vaguely, never clearly enough to perceive ethnicity or hyphenated identity. At the time when Black Americans came in for attention, a large gap between Whites and Blacks was observed:

Black women who have worked from necessity since puberty are apt to view Women's Liberation as a white middle-class battle irrelevant to their own often-bitter struggle for survival. As Ida Lewis, former editor of *Essence*, commented, 'The Women's Liberation movement is basically a family quarrel between white women and white men.'

A movement designed to free comfortable middle-class white house-wives from the ennui of suburbia simply does not interest many hard-working black women, whose problems have and always will be much more basic than boredom. Ironically, they see some of the stated goals of Women's Liberation as things they already have, like it or not, even unto the poorest ghetto black mother: the right to work, families without men, and sexual freedom. (Day, 1972: 283–4)

Although these words disregard the rise and presence of a black bourgeoisie (see Dunning, 2003), from an international comparative perspective they are highly reminiscent of discussions in and about the Women's Movement in Europe at the turn of the nineteenth to the twentieth century. At that time, the chasm between working-class women and the middle-class women involved in the women's movement consisted of similar inequalities as those between black and white women in the USA in the early 1970s.

One of the first social settings in which these inequalities diminished was the college campus:

A tour of the major college campuses might lead one to the quick conclusion that interracial mixing these days is entirely one-sided, black man and white girl. The reverse situation, with the black coed and white male student, is occasionally seen, but not in comparable numbers. However, campus dating and marriage are two very separate things. (Day, 1972: 268)

I already mentioned the difference this author was referring to when I discussed the sociogenesis of the dating regime: the allegiance of young people at college, developing a separate social code and a subculture in which they could participate for only a limited number of years and, therefore, 'without significant long-term risk' (Bailey, 1988: 27). In the early 1970s, the college scene was reported to be a very open one with a lot of mixing and matching among whites, blacks and Asians: 'The protected atmosphere of the college campus or private school furnishes a hospitable milieu for racial mixing, but it is, as most students themselves seem to realize, an artificial security that does not correspond to the "real" world.' (Day, 1972: 268).

Indeed, the 'real' world of the USA was not as protected, not as socially integrated. Here, the tensions and conflicts between classes, ethnic groups, sexes, generations, and the relatively strong domination of European-Americans over other Americans, all these expressions of a comparatively lower level of social integration seem to be directly connected to a correspondingly lower level of mutual trust and a higher level of fear and mutual suspicion. In the words of Miss Manners: 'With an occasional truce for however long it takes to clean up after a natural or unnatural disaster, we have been living in a state of low-grade mutual suspicion, subject to sudden outbreaks of hostility' (Martin, 2003: 292). It is as if the maxim 'United we stand' needed and needs to be supplemented by a whispered sigh: 'Sitting we are divided'.

8.2 Balancing: The Lust-balance and the Balance of Power, the Balance of Controls, and the We–I Balance

In processes of social integration, people of different classes and groups have increasingly directed themselves to the same code of manners and emotion management. Particularly in the second half of the twentieth century, as networks of interdependency became more dense and expanded beyond the national and continental levels, all those involved came under an inherent pressure to widen their view, to develop more of a world-view, to widen their circles of identification, and to develop a stronger awareness of themselves and the relationships they were involved in. This awareness and the social and psychic knowledge that comes with it, soon became necessary requirements in status competition, that is, vital for both social survival and upward mobility. As the social and psychic distances between them decreased, people's openness and sensitivity increased, and this soon included the erotic and sexual tensions of their relationships, both pleasurable and unpleasurable. As they opened up to the erotic and sexual tensions in all encounters, 'approaches to sexual encounters' increasingly came to 'call for a particularly sensitive awareness of mood and timing'. This was partly because 'both parties seek assurance from each other about protection from possible risks' (Beyfus, 1992: 7), but mainly in order to maximize the pleasure and the pleasurable promises of these tensions.

Advice on such topics as courtship, dancing, dating, engagement and marriage, reveals the social emancipation of women and the accommodation of men, together with the inherent pressure to control feelings of inferiority and superiority. This trend towards decreasing (displays of) inequality can be observed not only in courting but also in the overall balance of power between women and men. The main breaking point came in the 1960s. Until then, most manners books (and marriage manuals, for that matter) stressed the subservence of women and thus recommended a resigned, forgiving and humble attitude towards male superiority. In the 1950s, women were still cautioned in an outright way about what would happen if they went too far or refused to back down and compromise: 'In every husband, a tiny tyrant lies dormant. Do not do anything to arouse that unpleasant dictator' (Bourg, 1950: 36). The female author of this book went on to advise her readers how to deal with this kind of situation, as for example: 'Learn the art of disarming him with a few sweet words, with a kiss, with a facial expression of almost comical defeat' (Bourg, 1950: 39). Until the 1960s, manners books served as manuals for relations of *harmonious inequality*, that is, for the type of female subservence that gave men the right to their care and sexuality in return for the protection from violence, poverty and status loss that men gave women.

In the 1960s, in widening circles of women and men it became increasingly difficult to imagine how a relationship of inequality could possibly be harmonious. It strengthened the ideal of sharing the tasks of providing care and earning an income, together with women's right to become and stay financially independent. And although harmonious inequality clearly regained some of its attractiveness in the 1980s and 1990s, individuals in all four countries, whether (potential) partners or not, were expected much more strongly than before the 1960s to be able to protect and take care of themselves, both financially and emotionally. Men and women were invited and compelled to negotiate the terms of their sexuality and their relationship, taking women's ability to protect themselves more or less for granted. On the whole, the expectation spread that intimate bonds should be kept as 'pure' as possible, unaffected by any appeal to traditional superiority or inferiority. Accordingly, men came under rising pressure to control their traditional superiority feelings and displays, while women pressured each other and themselves to control traditional inferiority feelings, for instance their inclination to be submissive and give in. As the demands to negotiate and to proceed through mutual consent increased, the demand to manage emotions in more flexible and subtle ways also increased, adding considerably to the importance of emotion management as a source of power and also as a source of respect and self-respect or identity.

Women's appreciation of the protection men traditionally offered them was also reduced as a result of the rise in prosperity and the distribution of this prosperity via the introduction of a range of welfare state arrangements, of which a major part was installed in the 1960s. In all four countries under study, simplification of the legal procedure for divorce (in combination with a sharp decline in the loss of status involved) and the installation of a safety net for women and children who fall from an oppressive (marriage) relationship, came to offer women a kind of protection for which they had previously been dependent on their husband or parents. So in relation to women, men were, to some extent, placed in a competitive position with the welfare state (Stolk and Wouters, 1987a). Because American welfare laws are few and ungenerous, American men will least of all, if at all, have experienced welfare arrangements as a competitor in their offering protection to women.

These shifts in the balance of power between the sexes help to explain the observed trends in the courting regimes and in the lust-balance, but not sufficiently. Two other developments, as necessary conditions connected to these trends in explanatory ways, were shifts in the balance of controls and in the We–I balance. According to Elias, shifts in these balances are important criteria for determining the direction of 'civilizing processes' (see also Fletcher, 1997: 82ff.). In this book, such shifts have been deduced from changes in manners in the direction of a decrease in the social and psychic distance between social superiors and inferiors, men and women included. They allowed me to conclude that a rise in the level of affect control and self-regulation as well as in the level of mutual identification occurred. Changes in manners books show how people have developed greater sensitivity and flexibility, qualities that have come to be more – and more clearly – required in all social interactions. It is mainly on this basis that the success of the moral appeal of women (directly and through the women's movements) to the conscience and behaviour of men can be explained.

Surveying the whole development from a lust-balance connected to 'calling' in the direction of a sexualization of love and an eroticization of sex connected to dating and 'going steady' as dominant ways of courting, it is obvious that this development would have been impossible if subsequent younger generations had not succeeded in removing their courting from under the authority of parents. It is also obvious that, in comparison to the seriousness of 'calling', dating involved dangerously playing with serious things. It was seen as a play-courtship. Accordingly, the expression 'playing with fire' was often used in this context (on 'playing with fire', see Elias and Dunning, 1986: 100, 119, 124). After World War II, particularly in the 1960s, the playing attitude expanded to include marriage. Young people in the USA and in Europe started to 'go steady' and to go steady was to play marriage. The powerful longing of women for more equal and trusting relationships allowing for a lust-balance with more sex, more playful sex and more equal play and pleasure, seems to have been a major driving force of these changes. On a broader social level, more equal balances of power and declining social and psychic distance between people from different classes, sexes and generations also appear to have been important driving forces. These forces and processes were and are interconnected: growing equality and intimacy in families of origin and in other relationships have extended to growing intensity of ideals about equality and a more intimate and gratifying lust-balance in one's own lifetime.

Of course, the 'usual suspects' of economic change (expanding wealth), technical innovation (improved birth control), cultural construction (in the USA: dating, paying and petting), and demographic shifts (in the USA: from less women to less men) have to be rounded up and convicted for their share. Indeed, as usual, they are partly responsible. But if changes in power and dependency relationships, in the network of interdependencies, are not rounded up and taken to court, the process as a whole will remain in the dark. Without them, the process of pacification – why conflicts tend to be resolved with words, not violence, cannot be accounted for. And that is not all: the same goes for connected changes in affect control and in the level and pattern of mutual identification. Without taking these into consideration, the rise in the level of mutually expected self-restraints – MES, particularly the 'moral incapacity' on the part of men to resist the higher demands women have been making of male–female relations – would otherwise remain largely incomprehensible.

With regard to the balance of controls, the erosion of the system of chaperonage is highly significant. This erosion surfaced at the end of the nineteenth century, accelerated powerfully in the 1920s, and chaperonage was washed away completely in the 1960s as part of the Sexual Revolution. Only with regard to children and teenagers did bits and pieces of the old system survive. Where once adults simply used to protect themselves and their offspring from the dangers of sexual 'falling' by severely restricting the possibilities for males and females to meet, communicate, and develop a relationship, they increasingly released these *outer* restrictions while at the same time becoming increasingly sensitive to the variety of ways in which they could make use of the widened spectrum of behavioural and emotional alternatives. Social controls directed at avoiding (dangerous) temptations by staying clear of situations and relations in which these temptations could arise, gave way to social controls directed at the individual strength of people's *inner* restrictions not to give in to temptations if that means to violate the social code.

In the process, the social code changed to become increasingly based upon the principle of mutual consent. In other words, the shift from a strict and external to a lenient and internal courting regime coincided with the change from hierarchical social controls directed at prevention from 'falling' via 'external avoidance' towards a less direct but more all-round (present in all relationships and situations) pattern of social controls directed at self-control, that is, at the results of a mutually expected 'internal avoidance' of 'falling'. Virtually everything done by mutual consent came to be socially accepted, with the exception of mutual consent in unequal power relationships such as those between adult and child, teacher and pupil, boss and subordinate. That the condition of mutual consent has come to prevail in these matters implies that external social controls, directed at preventing both socially unacceptable temptations and situations in which people could give in to such temptations, have been largely replaced by social controls based on mutually expected self-controls which demand proceeding only with mutual consent, that is, to stop in the absence of mutual consent. The rule that in sex and love 'NO!' gets priority implies an increase of social controls towards self-controls as well as a balance of controls tending in the direction of self-controls becoming both the *locus* and the *focus* of social controls. This allows for the conclusion that the emancipation of sexuality and the development of a lust-balance in the direction of a sexualization of love and an eroticization of sex have to a large extent depended upon these changes in the balance of controls.

These interconnected changes in the lust-balance and in the balance of controls have also been connected to changes in the We–I balance. A lust-balance emphasizing the wish to satisfy the longing for sexual gratification represents a We–I balance tilted towards the I, whereas emphasizing the longing for enduring intimacy represents a tilting of this balance towards the we-side. From this perspective, the reported changes in the lust-balance imply that both I-feelings *and* we-feelings have intensified. And to the extent that the wish to combine both longings has intensified, the tension level of the We–I balance has intensified likewise. The description of individualized dancing, as presented in the first chapter (1.1) can be used to illustrate my point, if only the word 'movements' is understood both literally and metaphorically, from movements in making love to movements in the relationship:

> The dancers follow less of a set pattern, their movements are more informal and more varied. It is less easy to see who is leading and who is following, and it is less predictable. Different shades and gradations of leading and following are possible. If the two partners are wellmatched, there can very well be moments when all the separate, loose movements nevertheless seem to flow together.

These partners, so to speak, dance the We–I balance to a higher level.

At the same time, these developments imply and coincide with a rediscovery and/or reappraisal of the 'animalic', first-nature side of human beings, including sexuality. It is an emancipation of emotions and more primary affects from under the wings of a largely automatically functioning 'second nature', exerting large but more or less blind power over 'first nature', transferring that power increasingly to the Ego, the I, thus enabling conscious decisions to be made. People became to a greater extent *able to think about* expressing or repressing urges and emotions. They became more conscious of both social and individual options and restrictions, and this heightened consciousness enabled them more than former generations had been able to, to opt for restraining or expressing impulses and emotions. For example, the biblical warning not to 'covet thy neighbour's wife' lost its moral ground. To covet is no longer perceived as sinful or dangerous, nor is acting upon this longing perceived as such, as long as the principle of mutual consent is respected.

The implicitly required type of self-regulation can only develop and become dominant in societies with a relatively high degree of integration of former outsider groups into the networks of interdependency. In other words, the further integration of lower classes into the social structure has allowed, and soon demanded, further integration of 'lower' or 'animalic' impulses and emotions into personality structures. This is characteristic of the process of informalization.

In so far as the processes of the sexualization of love and the eroticization of sex imply an emancipation of sexuality – allowing the more primary sexual drives and impulses into consciousness – and an integration of this emancipated sexuality into more equal (loving) relationships, they signify a 'third nature' type of personality emerging. The term 'second nature' refers to a conscience and self-regulation which functions automatically to a high degree. It refers to an authoritative conscience with a strong penchant for order and regularity, cleanliness and neatness, demonstrating a relatively strong fear of 'falling' on a 'slippery slope'. Without rigorous control, 'first nature' might run wild. Confronted with such a possibility, a typical reaction would be: 'If you allow it, it will grow, and, eventually, it will all get out of control', whereas a typical 'third-nature' type of reaction tends to go for 'controlled decontrolling': carefully restricted ways of allowing may result in more effective control *and* more pleasure, if only the pleasure of living a more reality-congruent life. The term 'third nature' draws attention to the development of a more reflexive and flexible form of self-regulation. Ideally, for this type of personality it has become 'natural' to perceive the pulls and pushes of both first and second nature as well as the dangers and chances, short-term and long-term, of any particular situation and relationship (Wouters, 1998b, 1999a, 1999d).

8.3   Regularities in Processes of Emancipation and Integration

In the processes of the emancipation (of women) and accommodation (by men) and in the interconnected changes in the dominant lust-balance, a few patterns can be discerned. These are regularities which occur in all processes of emancipation and integration, not only in those between women and men. To conclude this book, four of them will be presented.

8.3a   Lust anxiety: social and sexual fear of 'heights' and 'depths'

The first regularity is related to the mechanism of 'identification with the established': identifying with the uneven balance of power between the sexes (or between any other groups of established and outsiders) functions as a psychical impediment to developing a higher-level and more integrated lust-balance which involves more sex. It produces a lust anxiety that can be illustrated from a passage in a 1950s' Dutch advice booklet on 'becoming engaged':

> Look at this engaged couple sitting in the car of a roller coaster. The car is pulled up slowly and then descends with flying speed down the steep slope. Other couples in other cars laugh and scream while falling into each other's arms, the fair sex seeking protection, as it were, from the stronger sex. But both of the engaged couple, who have turned-into-themselves, do not have the courage to do likewise. They braced themselves in the corner of their seat. They clench their teeth and lips and do not want to admit that they too were terror-struck when screeching down the slope. When at the end the cars are stopped and the other couples go in search of the next amusement, arms dearly linked, the turned-into-themselves couple tell each other: 'There was actually nothing to it, it's a shame and a waste of money!' Well, a waste it certainly was, for they wasted an opportunity for people in love to let themselves go a little more on such an occasion than is possible when in serious company.

This lust anxiety is interpreted as follows: 'Quite often it is the result of a wrong kind of upbringing by dictatorial parents ... These dictatorially raised young people constantly ask themselves: "Is this permitted" or "Is it allowed?" ... They never really loosen up' (Mounier, n.d.: 13–15). Here, the explanation is found in the hierarchical relationship between the generations, but the same explanation can be applied to most expressions of lust anxiety in relations between the sexes: its inequality at least partly explains the greater difficulties of women in enjoying a lust-balance with more sex. They remain afraid of the 'shame' of becoming more of a sexual *subject*. This fear *and* these feelings of shame and embarrassment function as counter-impulses which invalidate more primary sexual impulses. They are manifestations of a more or less automatically functioning conscience or super-ego, moulded in processes of social shaming. The example of the roller coaster relates to forms of social shaming that were linked as sanctions to the pattern of supervision and control of sex-segregation, to the places and the manners of meeting. Before the Sexual Revolution little confidence existed in the capacity for self-regulation of either sex; the assumption prevailed that without social control and surveillance, sexual passions would be given free rein: 'if the bridle is removed, sexuality gallops' (Ritter, 1933: 152). This kind of opinion legitimated patterns of social control and self-control geared to sex-segregation, and both mirrored and confirmed the prevailing hierarchical sex (class and generation) relationships. The integration of this complex into the personality as a function of conscience largely explains lust anxiety among women: it is a fear of rising, a fear of raising themselves, of leaving the beaten tracks; they remained afraid of the consequences of repudiating, if only in fantasy, the attitude of (sexual) submissiveness. Because it was ingrained so strongly in the personality, an English author of a manners book, written in 1925, even called it an instinct, the 'limited outlook instinct', which 'seems to have been ground into women so thoroughly in the Ages, that they are unable to escape from it even in their new freedom' (see Chapter 3). Of course, it is not an instinct, it is an engrained fear, a 'fear of freedom'. From the fear of running wild through loosening up, they clam up. Their source of power and identity, the whole of their personality, is still strongly interwoven with the old balance of power between the sexes and also with the old lust-balance, the old ratio of relational and sexual desires.

In this respect, towards the end of the twentieth century, homosexual women had come to seem more like heterosexual women than homosexual (and heterosexual) men: 'Emotional involvement is the context within which most lesbian sexuality takes place. Lesbian couples indicate that closeness is more often a reason to have sex than arousal or orgasm. Monogamy is preferred by the majority of lesbians and most respondents act accordingly' (Schreurs, 1993a: 61). And many lesbian women reported having difficulties in taking sexual initiatives or in seducing their partners: 'In this context, their need to avoid even the slightest ring of dominance, power or male sexual behaviour, and to repudiate any behaviour that could possibly be experienced as an imitation of heterosexuality, is often mentioned as an impediment' (Schreurs, 1993b: 333).

From this outlook, the psychic repercussions of the uneven balance of power between the sexes are, at the moment of writing, still a substantial barrier for continued emancipation of sexual impulses and emotions. This barrier might be conceptualized as a fear of social and psychic (including sexual) heights. With regard to men's accommodation process, the counterpart of this barrier might be conceptualized as social and psychic (including sexual) fear of depths, a fear of losing traditional sources of power and identity and of the jealousy and desertion anxieties that are involved, which prevent men from imagining and enjoying the pleasures of a more restrained kind of relating to a woman – the more 'civilized' satisfaction which the ability 'to play just slightly more slowly than one's partner' may bring (quoted in Section 6.7g).

An example of a man struggling with this fear of depths comes from an interview with someone who reported that he sometimes watched pornographic videos with his wife and that he had been struck by a terrific stab of jealousy when his wife once said: 'It's odd, I'm 31 years old now and yet I only know your dick.' And he continued with an example of what he called the enormous gap between his emotions and his mind:

> For instance, the other day she asked me to lie on her side of the bed, so it would be pleasantly warm by the time she got in. That's what I did, and I don't see any reason why not, but I did feel like an idiot. I thought: 'Luckily my friends can't see me because they would laugh their heads off, Charlie impersonating a hot-water bottle.' (Stolk and Wouters, 1987a: 133, 249)

Lacking data, it must remain an open question how many and to what extent men have suffered from impotence or other forms of loss of lust through an 'accommodation cramp'. My study of the feminist monthly *Opzij* shows that, in the Netherlands, this issue was first raised in 1983. The tone was jeering: in a spoof interview with 'the last potent man', he is depicted as finally becoming violent (1983, [5]: 16). Four years later, the question was taken up somewhat more seriously: 'An equal relationship is pre-eminently an important support for sexual gratification, for only then can sexuality be liberated from ulterior motives like a display of power. Then you do what you do simply because you like it. And what can then fail?' (*Opzij*, 1987 [1]: 46-8). This stance overlooks the possibility of impotence as a transitory problem of accommodation. However, simply raising the question may suffice to suggest that the distinction between safe sex and emotionally safe sex (Orbach, 1994: 165) is significant for both sexes.

8.3b   *Three types: trend-followers, radicals and moderates*

Another important regularity follows from the fact that emancipation and accommodation are learning processes in which there are differences in tempo and emphasis, on which basis three different groups can be discerned: there are always trend-followers, radicals and moderates (Stolk,

1991: 59–60). With regard to the lust-balance, these three types correspond to the three possibilities or scenarios that are open after the first few preliminary moves on the road to love and sex have been made:

> At that point, the outlines of different possibilities become apparent: one resigns oneself to one's partner's limits and satisfies oneself with what has been accomplished [followers]. The second possibility consists of a continued transgression of boundaries, the path of lust [radicals]. The third solution consists of preserving or reviving sexual tension and challenge in contact with the present partner [moderates]. (Zeegers, 1994: 140)

The lust-balance of radicals is strongly orientated towards physical sex. They have become involved in the dynamics of lust as they continue to search for and to build up erotic and sexual tensions in situations or scenarios. In these dynamics, their sexual desire becomes specialized, while formerly lustful situations lose attraction:

> One thing I do occasionally regret ... If I compare myself to colleagues who, when looking at these girls in mini skirts, exclaim: 'Wow! What a delicious piece!', I can't help thinking: 'if you only knew what I've seen and done'. Do you understand? They still have that fantasy, that delightful 'Good God! What would she look like under her knickers?' In fact, I don't have that fantasy any more. Because I've experienced so much. (Zeegers, 1994: 119)

This development is reminiscent of the historical process in which bare ankles and loose hair lost most of their power to arouse sexual longing and fantasy.

The lust-balance of trend-followers is mainly characterized by the longing for a lasting and taken-for-granted intimacy. In that sense they are conservatives. Their sexual activity is directed at perpetuating their relationship: 'In the midst of social jostling and the ups and downs of personal positions and social identities, the family and, within that, sex, offer an *oasis of stability and predictability*, an area where one knows the do's and don'ts and who's who' (Zeegers, 1994: 131). Confronted with a widening range of socially acceptable behavioural and emotional alternatives, they clam up to some extent, from fear of jealousy, desertion, loneliness, and anxiety not to lose themselves or their relationship. The dangers traditionally connected with sex may have diminished since the Sexual Revolution, but for them the anxieties connected with those dangers persevered – an example of a cultural lag. Thus, they held on and remained conservative where moderates and radicals continued the emancipation of sexuality.

The lust-balance of moderates is relationship *and* sex-orientated. They combine attention for both person and body in intimate activity: 'In letting oneself go, in knowing that the partner does that too, in showing a certain "childlike" lack of inhibition and in getting rid of feelings of shame and embarrassment, the feeling of mutual contact and appreciation is actualised' (Zeegers, 1994: 138–9). In this way, moderates have 'learned' to combine their longing for an enduring intimacy with their carnal desires.

One might expect an unequal division of the sexes among the three types, if only because the dangers and anxieties surrounding sex (rape, unwanted pregnancies, etc.) have always been (and remain) greater for women than for men. In addition, for many women sex functioned as an important source of power (as a means of temptation, reward and punishment) and identity. On this basis it is also to be expected that their fear of giving up that traditional female pattern has been (and remains) stronger. However, research into these three types revealed that moderates consisted of just as many men as women. This can be understood from the kind of sex moderates are reported to have developed. For them, sex 'is not a personal feature but a characteristic of the interaction with the partner' – that is, of the relationship (Zeegers, 1994: 138–40). In their relationship, they succeed in connecting lust and proximity 'in intrinsic ways', and 'even indulging in lust has the denotation of frankness'. Thus the development of such a lust-balance of greater inhibition and candour in (sexual) behaviour and feeling was a relational as well as an individual process; in this double process they 'learned' to combine their longing for sexual gratification and for intimacy: it takes one to know one, and it takes two to tango. Both their I-feelings and their we-feelings expanded and intensified, taking the We–I balance to a higher level.

8.3c   *Phases in processes of emancipation, accommodation and integration*

Just as the accomplishments of one generation become habitually taken for granted by the next, so the feeling of liberation inherent in a successful emancipatory struggle, can topple over into its opposite when what was first an achievement becomes a taken-for-granted fact of life: when this happens, a feeling of oppression and of being burdened can become prevalent (apparently this may happen in the time span of only one generation).

In the period covered by my research, the feeling of liberation prevailed among large groups of *nouveaux riches* in the '*fin de siècle*' (around 1900), again among somewhat broader groups in the 'Roaring Twenties', and again, this time among virtually all groups, in the 1960s and 1970s. In those decades, entire groups were socially rising; there was a collective emancipation or, to put it differently, the most striking social pressure came from *below*. In such phases of emancipation and resistance, the *gains* in terms of we-feelings and I-feelings are usually emphasized and what prevails is the feeling of liberation from the straitjacket of old authoritarian relationships. In this phase, much of what had once been considered to be bad luck is then experienced as injustice.

When collective emancipation chances decrease and disappear, another phase of accommodation and resignation has begun. In this phase, the most striking social pressure comes (again) much more unequivocally from *above*. When this occurs, the gains of the emancipation phase have largely come to be taken for granted, and the pressures of having to comply with authority relations are thus emphasized and experienced more strongly. The same goes for increased demands such as enlarged knowledge, ability, reflexivity and flexibility in dealing with others and oneself. Complying with these demands had previously been a precondition for reaping the gains of emancipation, but only when the pressures from above clearly prevailed once again, did they also come to be experienced as demands. This opens a perspective in which the *loss* and the *oppression* of old we-feelings and I-feelings are emphasized. In this phase, in deliberations as to whether one is confronted with bad luck or injustice and whether it is befitting to react with resignation or resistance, bad luck and resignation will usually get the benefit of the doubt. In 1939, a Dutch author of an advice manual captured the emancipatory struggle of the past as well as the resignation prevalent at the time as follows:

> Women's yearning for freedom has been heard throughout the ages like a deep sigh, and even though the woman of today might have a degree of freedom that she hardly could have dreamt of fifty years ago, the acquisition of this freedom has only heightened the yearning for even greater freedom ... But ... if you cannot have freedom (not a little bit more freedom within the framework of your subservience, but a more complete freedom to do as you please), do not let it get you down, because in most cases the advantages of freedom do not counterbalance the worries and the heavy responsibility that go hand in hand with it. (Groskampten Have, 1939a: 114–15)

The following examples from the 1930s also illustrate an emphasis on the burden of liberation and on loss:

> By their equalization the sexes have certainly gained mutual understanding and conscious peacefulness in relating to each other, but they have lost happiness. (Haluschka, n.d. 1937: 178)

> If one only looks at photographs of life at the beach! Perfectly innocent if considered in themselves, but fatal in their effect, because, through lack of distance and deference, they continue to rob love of its poetry, its fine inner blossoming and spiritual contents. Love is in danger of becoming nothing but instinct or ambiguous friendship. (Haluschka, 1937: 26)

The lust anxiety that speaks through these words, as well as the romanticization of the relationships and the lust-balance of those 'happy days' of 'paradise lost' is expressed only in the margins of public debate in a phase of emancipation and resistance, when the feeling of liberation prevails.

In both phases, marriage was one of the institutions involved: while the old Victorian ideal of an elevated spiritual love lost vigour, the demand of always preserving one's marriage lost precedence. The married woman whose husband turned out to be a 'bad one' came to be defined as a victim of injustice rather than of bad luck. Particularly in phases of emancipation, the desires and interests of individuals gained importance – a shift in the We–I balance in the direction of the I. Moreover, by the 1970s, the social security provided by welfare arrangements in the more advanced welfare states had been transformed into an 'equanimity of the welfare state', on which material basis many women were able to liberate themselves from the shackles of their marriages (Stolk and Wouters, 1987a). In the 1980s and 1990s, as pressures from above gained precedence and collective emancipation chances disappeared, the longing for enduring intimacy strengthened and intensified – a shift in the We–I balance in the direction of the we. In this most recent phase of accommodation and resignation, this longing will also have gained importance by the trimming down of social security and welfare arrangements, corroding the 'equanimity of the welfare state'.

Seen from a longer-term perspective, these alternating phases appear to have been changing in a particular direction: in a spiral movement, both sides of the We–I balance, liberation as well as the burden of demands, have been raised. This is the third pattern or regularity in the connection between changes in prevailing power and dependency relationships and in the dominant lust-balance. On the one hand, the spectrum of accepted emotional and behavioural alternatives expanded. But on the other, an acceptable and respectable usage of these alternatives implied a continued increase of demands on self-regulation. Although sometimes one side is emphasized and sometimes the other, taken together, they are best understood as phases in the integration processes of the sexes and classes within states (for the classes, see my forthcoming book).

8.3d   Intensified tugs-of-war and ambivalence

Coinciding with the spread of less uneven balances of power and dependency and of stronger ideals of equality, was a change in the ideal of an intimate relationship towards one involving a couple of independent people, well matched, both sharing the tasks of providing care and earning an income. Attempts and expectations to live up to these ideals have made intimate relationships more strongly dependent on the style of emotion management of the partners involved: how are they to negotiate the terms of the relationship as two captains on the same ship without losing love and respect? At the same time, all kinds of conflicts or conflicting needs and interests, formerly a taboo non-topic, came out into the open and were subject to negotiation. According to traditional ideals, conflicts did not happen – female resignation would prevent them – and if they occurred, then they were seen only as a natural phenomenon, refreshing, like a thunderstorm. Since the 1960s, the art of 'conflict management' has developed, and marriage or living intimately together has become a conflict-prone balancing act (Mahlmann, 1991: 327). The same change and periodization is reported in a study of women's magazines in the USA:

> During the mid-1960s, most articles began to advise wives to express their anger and to permit their partners to do likewise. Readers were told that

disagreements were normal and sharing negative as well as positive feelings is a necessary part of intimate love ... In this period, the expression of anger came to signify the strength of a marriage, not its weakness ... The major change in norms about love was a shift from self-sacrifice to self-assertion. (Cancian and Gordon, 1988: 319–20)

As more egalitarian rules take time to 'sink in', both women and men have increasingly become subjected to a tug-of-war between old and new ideals (and power resources) and to related feelings of ambivalence. Most men and women seem to be egalitarian 'on the surface' and traditional 'underneath'. Most men react in accordance with the dynamics of established-outsider relationships: they do not want to accommodate and do not easily perceive the 'civilized' pleasures of a more egalitarian relationship. Therefore, they will use the 'gender strategy' of appealing to a woman's *old* identity underneath, trying to restore it, whereas most women will appeal to a man's *new* identity, trying to reinforce it and make it sink in. Therefore, 'sex and love are no longer given facts but talents to be exploited' (Schnabel, 1990: 16), and the art of obliging and being obliged as well as the art of escaping or sublimating these pressures have developed to increasingly higher degrees. As these demands increased, to lose oneself in making love was increasingly acknowledged as one of the ultimate forms of uncomplicated and unreflective existence. In the same process, the pursuit of a more stable and moderate lust-balance also intensified. Recent discussions of issues like sexual harassment, pornography, rape in marriage and date-rape, can be understood as a common search for ways of becoming intimate and of keeping at a distance that are acceptable to both women and men. Precisely because of the sensitivity and caution needed to proceed in such a way, erotic and sexual consciousness and tensions have expanded and intensified, stimulating a further sexualization of love and eroticization of sex. This quest for an exciting and satisfying lust-balance, avoiding the extremes of emotional wildness and emotional numbness, has also stimulated the emotional tug-of-war and ambivalence to a higher tension-level. That is so, if only because the increased demands on emotion management will have intensified both the fantasies and the longing for (romantic) relationships characterized by greater intimacy, as well as the longing for easier (sexual) relationships in which the pressure of these demands is absent or negligible, as in one-night stands. This ambivalence, together with an increasingly more conscious (reflexive) and calculating (flexible) emotion management as a source of power, respect and self-respect, is characteristic of processes of the decreasing segregation and increasing integration of the classes and the sexes. This forms another, fourth pattern or regularity in the connection between changes in figurations and in lust-balances: as long as such integration processes continue, these ambivalent emotions may be expected to accumulate and intensify, including both longings that make up the lust-balance. This is why the body, nudity and sex have become increasingly prominent in the media (for Germany, see König, 1990), and why this trend is likely to persist; they contain the promise of natural physicality and of a harmoniously combined attention for both person and body in intimate activity. It may be expected that, as the integration of the sexes continues to proceed, heightened sensitivity to this promise will accumulate as well, together with erotic consciousness and erotic tensions. However, because in the same process the ideal and the longing to be known and loved, body and soul, will increase as well, both longings will remain connected to each other in heightened ambivalence.[1] Overall, this boils down to intensified longings, more contradictory desires, and thus, on the whole, less satisfaction or gratification ... unless people (once again) manage to deal with these contradictions in playful ways.

Notes

1 Introduction

1 This can be understood from the fact that the authors of manners books took for granted that their female readers would only participate in non-bodily contact sports such as tennis.

2 Here lies a major difference between Foucault's views on 'expert knowledge' and 'discourse' and mine: changes in the regimes of manners and emotions include changes in discourse, not the other way round.

3 Revised editions were published in 1927, 1931, 1934, 1937, 1942, 1950, and 1960. Subsequent citations will specify the edition cited.

2 Confined to the Drawing Room

1 In 1940, as today, the 'cut direct' needed explanation; it was 'to look directly at another and not acknowledge the other's bow ... a direct stare of blank refusal' (Post, 1940: 30).

4 To Pay or Be Paid For?

1 This quotation is from a book written by an English author, Barbara Cartland, but it was written for and adapted to the American market, where millions were sold. When she discussed dancing, for example, she addressed the question 'can you ask someone to cut in and rescue you?' Cutting in was a very American custom, see Section 6.7a (Cartland 1984: 34).

6 Developments in Courting Regimes

1 The German words for 'lust-balance' and 'lust economy' have been translated into English as 'pleasure balance' and 'pleasure economy': 'The degree of anxiety, like the whole pleasure economy, is different in every society, in every class and historical phase' (Elias, 2000: 441).

2 In the last decades of the twentieth century holidays were still considered to be dangerous and worth a warning regarding the dangers of unsafe sex. For instance, in the summer of 1993 a (Dutch) government-subsidised leaflet, entitled 'Have Safe Sex, *Also* on Holidays', was distributed in a great number of public places. It contained, among others, sentences like 'Have you ever heard of AIDS?', 'Do you have a condom with you?' and 'I'll put on a condom, it's safer' in English, German, French and Spanish.

3 In the 1930s there was a turning inwards to motherhood and domesticity, 'partly caused by a decline in Society functions ... The woman is

now seen as guardian of her family's health and happiness rather than of its social place' (Davidoff, 1973: 99). This increased isolation of a more tightly drawn nuclear family and the strengthening of the mother's bond with her children, may also be interpreted as a 'civilizing offensive' of wives, consciously or unconsciously aimed at 'Bringing up Father', thus limiting double standards and his display of superiority feelings. ('Bringing Up Father' is the title of a series of popular drawings by the American George McManus, presenting 'father' as a captive of mother and of her longing for success in good society.)

4 To some extent the 'modern girl' was still the popular heroine that she had become when working on munitions in factories. She was known as 'the flapper', yet this was not a term of reproach. Flapper in the Nineties had meant a very young prostitute, scarcely past the age of consent, but the word had improved before the war to mean any girl in her teens with a boyish figure. The craze for the flapper ... reached England about 1912 ... 'Flapper' was now a term for a comradely, sporting, active young woman, who would ride pillion on the 'flapper-bracket' of a motor-cycle. It did not become a term of reproach again, with a connotation of complete irresponsibility, until 1927 ... The women who only a year or so earlier had been acclaimed as patriots, giving up easy lives at home to work for their Country in her hour of need, were now represented as vampires who deprived men of their rightful jobs. (Graves and Hodge, 1941: 43–4)
Thanks to Adrian Gregory for this.

5 Knigge wrote just as negatively about the female counterpart, the stagy type of favour-currying and coquettish women; he advised readers to shun them like the plague ([1788] 1977: 199).

6 Apparently, this author not only had introductions into sexuality in mind, but also books about social problems like alcoholism and prostitution, books containing sentences like: 'I will not tell you the number of servant girls that end as whores – but you clumsy, needy housewives, you should realize that it is from amongst their midst that prostitutes are recruited, and that it is your husbands and sons... but why relate this... it is common knowledge' (Alberts, 1918: 15–6).

7 Bailey did raise the question why these definitions of masculinity and femininity developed in the dating code, but as she lacked an international comparative perspective, she did not notice that none of the answers she came up with were specific to the USA.

8 The book was translated into Dutch by J.F. Kliphuis and appeared in 1964; the locally well-known physician-sexologist L.H Levie wrote a favourable introduction.

9 The social scientist Benthem van den Bergh (1990) suggested that political emancipation and the presence of nuclear weapons, creating a situation that has been summed up as Mutually Assured Destruction (MAD), have exerted pressure towards higher levels of caution and MAS, Mutually Assured Self-Restraints. His colleague Goudsblom (1998: 78)

deemed assurance in these matters to be out of the question and suggested that 'mutually expected self-restraint' (MES) is a more realistic phrase.

10 The use of the word 'intercourse' in this context shows how weak and/or repressed the sexual connotations of this word still were. From the Sexual Revolution onwards, along with the emancipation of women and their sexuality, these connotations have become stronger and also more openly acknowledged.

7 The Lust-Balance of Sex and Love since the Sexual Revolution

1 It was Bram van Stolk who initiated this study of *Opzij* and presented me with his notes and photocopies.

2 Nor can this difference be explained by a reference to the effect of prostitutes' organizations, for the Dutch one was only established in 1985, and the others either later or, if earlier, like the American organizations Coyote (1973) and the North American Task Force on Prostitution (1979), they were predominantly aimed at repealing the relatively harsh laws on prostitution in their country, on which basis relatively large numbers of prostitutes were arrested.

3 As a didactical aid, the feel for the lust-balance question can also be stimulated by trying to decide whether sex will help you through times of no love better than love will help you through times of no sex, or whether it is the other way round. Friends of Gilbert Shelton's *The Freak Brothers* will, of course, have recognized their famous sentence: 'Dope will help me through times of no money better than money will help me through times of no dope'.

8 International Comparisons, Theoretical Interpretations, and Regularities in Processes of Emancipation and Integration

1 The tension between these longings is likely also to be heightened by a relentless (and less religiously inspired) curiosity for what was placed behind social and psychic scenes in former centuries, for both sex and death. In this process, awareness of bodily attraction and erotic longings will increase together with awareness of transitoriness, and of death as the denial of all endurance, the durability of intimate relationships included.

References

Ang, Ien (1983) 'Mannen op zicht', *Tijdschrift voor Vrouwenstudies*, 15, 4 (3): 418–34.

Baltzell, E. Digby (1964,1987) *The Protestant Establishment: Aristocracy and Caste in America*, New Haven: Yale University Press.

Bailey, Beth L. (1988) *From Front Porch to Back Seat: Courtship in Twentieth-Century America*. Baltimore, MD and London: Johns Hopkins University Press.

Bailey, Beth L. (1994) 'Sexual Revolution(s)', in: David Farber (ed.s), *The Sixties: From Memory to History*. Chapel Hill, NC & London: University of North Carolina Press, pp.: 235–62.

Baltzell, E. Digby (1964, 1987) *The Protestant Establishment: Aristocracy and Caste in America*. New Haven, CT: Yale University Press.

Bellah, Robert N., Madsen, Richard, Swidler, William M., Sullivan, Madsen Ann and Tipton, Stephen M., (1985) *Habits of the Heart: Individualism and Commitment in American Life*. Berkeley, CA: University of California Press.

Benthem van den Bergh, Godfried van (1990) *The Taming of the Great Powers: Nuclear Weapons and Global Integration*. Aldershot: Gower.

Blom, J.C.H. (1993) 'Een harmonieus gezin en individuele ontplooiing', *BMGN*, 108 (1): 28–50.

Boonstra, Heather (2002) 'Teen Pregnancy: Trends And Lessons Learned', The Guttmacher Report 5 (1). See: http://www.agi-usa.org

Brinkgreve, Christien (1988) *De belasting van de bevrijding*. Nijmegen: SUN.

Brinkgreve, Christien (1995) *Droom en drift: Een onderzoek naar verborgen wensen van Nederlandse vrouwen*. Baarn: Anthos/Marie Claire.

Brugman, Emily, Goedhart, Hans Vogels, Ton and van Zessen, Gertjan (1995) *Jeugd en seks 95: Resultaten van het nationale scholierenonderzoek*. Utrecht: SWP.

Bruijn, Gerda de (1980) *Vrouw en seksualiteit: Tien jaar na een seksuele revolutie, literatuurrapport 13*. Zeist: Nisso.

Caldwell, Mark (1999) *A Short History of Rudeness: Manners, Morals, and Misbehaviours in Modern America*. New York: Picador.

Cancian, F.M. and Gordon, S.L. (1988), 'Changing Emotion Norms in Marriage: Love and Anger in U.S. Women's Magazines Since 1900', *Gender and Society*, 2: 308–42.

CBS (1994) *Sociaal-culturele berichten 1994: Trends in de leefsituatie van Nederlandse jongeren 1979-1989/1993*. Voorburg/Heerlen: Centraal Bureau voor de Statistiek.

Coleman, L. (1941) 'What is American– A Study of Alleged American Traits', *Social Forces*, 19: 492–99.

Cressey, Paul G. (1932) *The Taxi-Dance Hall.: A Sociological Study in Commercialized Recreation and City Life*, New York: Ams Press, 1971, reprint of 1932, Chicago.

Curtin, Michael (1985) 'A Question of Manners: Status and Gender in Etiquette and Courtesy', *Journal of Modern History*, 57: 395–423.

Curtin, Michael (1987) *Propriety and Position: A Study of Victorian Manners*. New York: Garland.

Daalen, Rineke van, and van Stolk, Bram (1991) 'Over revolutie en onwetendheid.

Seksuele ervaringen en klachten van jongeren', pp. 34–54 in Peter van Lieshout eand Denise de Ridder (eds), *Symptomen van de tijd: De dossiers van het Amsterdamse Instituut voor Medische Psychotherapie* (IMP), 1968–1977. Nijmegen: SUN. pp. 34–54.

Dahrendorf, R. (1969) *Society and Democracy in Germany*. Garden City, NY: Doubleday.

Dantzig, A. van (1994) '06', *Maandblad Geestelijke Volksgezondheid*, 11: 1276–8.

Darroch, Jacqueline E., Frost, Jennifer J., Singh, Susheela and The Study Team (2001) Teenage Sexual and Reproductive Behaviour in Developed Countries: Can More Progress Be Made– Occasional Report No. 3. New York/Washington: Alan Guttmacher Institute: www.agi-usa.org

Davidoff, Leonore (1973) *The Best Circles: Society, Etiquette and the Season*. London: Croom Helm.

Dekker, Joost (1987) 'Voluntary control of sexual arousal: experimental studies on sexual imagery and sexual history as determinants of the sexual response.', PhD dissertation, Utrecht University.

Derks, Marjet (1991) 'Steps, shimmies en de wulpse tango: Dansvermaak in het interbellum.', *Spiegel Historiael*, 26: 388–96.

Dowling, Colette (1981) *The Cinderella Complex: Women's Hidden Fear of Independence*. New York: Pocket Books.

Duerr, Hans Peter (1997) *Der erotische Leib*. Frankfurt am. Ma.in: Suhrkamp.

Dunning, Eric (1999) *Sport Matters: Sociological Studies of Sport, Violence, and Civilization*. London: Routledge.

Dunning, Eric (2003) 'Aspects of The figurational dynamics of racial stratification: a conceptual discussion and developmental analysis of black-white relations in the United States.', in Steven Loyal and Steve Quilley (eds), *The Sociology of Norbert Elias*. Cambridge: Cambridge University Press.

Eggermont, Patricia (1993) 'Van houwen, trouwen (en berouwen). Informalisering rondom verloving, huwelijk en echtscheiding in Nederland, aan de hand van etiquettevoorschriften, 1850–1990'. Doctoraalscriptie maatschappijgeschiedenis Erasmus Universiteit Rotterdam.

Ehrenreich, Barbara, and English, Deirdre (1978) *For Her Own Good: 150 Years of Experts' Advice to Women*. Garden City, NY: Doubleday.

Elias, Norbert (1991) *The Society of Individuals* (edited by Michael Schröter, trans. Edmund Jephcott). Oxford: Blackwell.

Elias, Norbert (1996) *The Germans: Power Struggles and the Development of Habitus in the Nineteenth and Twentieth Centuries* (edited by Michael Schröter; trans. Eric Dunning and Stephen Mennell). Cambridge: Polity Press.

Elias, Norbert (2000) *The Civilizing Process: Sociogenetic and Psychogenetic Investigations, rev. edn*. Oxford: Blackwell.

Elias, Norbert, and Dunning, Eric (1986) *Quest for Excitement: Sport and Leisure in the Civilizing Process*. Oxford: Blackwell.

Elias, Norbert, and Scotson, John L. (1994) *The Established and the Outsiders*, 2nd edn. London: Sage.

Elias, Norbert (1991) *The Society of Individuals* (edited by Michael Schröter, translated by Edmund Jephcott): Oxford: Blackwell.

Elias, Norbert (1996) *The Germans: Power Struggles and the Development of Habitus in the Nineteenth and Twenties Centuries*. (edited by Michael Schröter; translated by Eric Dunning and Stephen Mennell), Cambridge: Polity Press.

Elias, Norbert (2000) *The Civilizing Process: Sociogenetic and Psychogenetic Investigations*. Rev. ed. Oxford: Blackwell.

Ernst, Stefanie (1999) *Geschlechterverhältnisse und Führungspositionen: Eine*

Ffigurationssoziologische Analyse der Stereotypenkonstruktion. Opladen / Wiesbaden: Westdeutscher Verlag.

Fass, Paula S. (1977) *The Damned and the Beautiful: American Youth in the 1920s*, New York: Oxford University Press.

Fisher, W.A. and Byrne, D. (1978) 'Sex differences in response to erotica: Love versus Lust', *Journal of Personality and Social Psychology*, 36: 117–25.

Fletcher, Jonathan (1997) *Violence and Civilization: An Introduction to the Work of Norbert Elias*. Cambridge: Polity.

Fromm, Erich (1942) *The Fear of Freedom*. London: Routledge & Kegan Paul.

Garcia, L.T., Brennan, K., DeCarlo, M., McGlennon, R., and Tait, S. (1984) 'Sex differences in sexual arousal to different erotic stories', *Journal of Sex Research*, 20: 391–402.

Gorer, Geoffrey (1948) *The American People: A Study in National Character*. New York: W.W. Norton. (also published in 1959 as *The Americans: A Study in National Character*. London: Arrow Books).

Goudsblom, J. (1998) Reserves. Amsterdam: Meulenhoff86) 'Morele beesten. Notities over moraal', *De Gids*: .171–5.

Graves, Robert, and Hodge, Alan (1941) *The Long Weekend: A Social History of Great Britain, 1918–1939*. London: Readers Union Ltd. by arrangement with Faber and Faber.

Groenendijk, H. (1983) 'Vrouwelijke seksualiteit uit het kader van pornografie', *Tijdschrift voor Vrouwenstudies* 15, 4 (3): 352–71.

Halttunen, Karen (1982) *Confidence Men and Painted Women*. New Haven, CT: Yale University Press.

Hatfield, Elaine, and Rapson, Richard L. (1994) 'Historical and cross-cultural perspectives on passionate love and sexual desire', *Annual Review of Sex Research*, 4: 67–97.

Heiman, J.R. (1977) 'A psychophysiological exploration of sexual arousal patterns in females and males', *Psychophysiology*, 14: 266–74.

Hekma, Gert (1994) 'De klemmen van de lust: De ontwikkeling van het plezier sinds de seksuele revolutie', *Etnofoor*, 7 (2): 5–24. For a version in English: 'How Libertarian is the Netherlands – Exploring Contemporary Dutch Sexual Cultures', see: http://www2.fmg.uva.nl/gl/

Hemphill, C. Dallett (1996) 'Middle class rising in revolutionary America: the evidence from manners', *Journal of Social History*, 30: 317–44.

Hemphill, C. Dallett (1999) *Bowing to Necessities: A History of Manners in America 1620–1860*. New York: Oxford University Press.

Hinz, Michael (2002) *Der Zivilisationsprozess: Mythos oder Realität– Wissenschaftssoziologische Untersuchungen zur Elias-Duerr-Kontroverse*. Opladen: Leske + Budrich.

Hochschild, Arlie Russell (1983) *The Managed Heart: The Commercialization of Human Feeling*. Berkeley, CA: University of California Press.

Hochschild, Arlie Russell, with Anne Machung (1989) *The Second Shift: Working Parents and the Revolution*. New York: Viking Press.

Hochschild, Arlie Russell (1994) 'The commercial spirit of intimate life and the abduction of feminism', *Theory, Culture & Society*, 11 (2): 1–24.

Hochschild, Arlie Russell (1997) *The Time Bind: When Work Becomes Home and Home Becomes Work*. New York: Holt, Metropolitan Books

Hodges, Deborah Robertson (1989) *Etiquette: An Annotated Bibliography of Literature Published in English in the United States, 1900 through 1987*. Jefferson etc.: McFarland.

Jong, Erica (1973) *Fear of Flying*. New York: Signet Books.

Klein, Gabriele (1994) *Frauen, Körper, Tanz: Eine Zivilizationsgeschichte des Tanzes.* München: Heyne.

König, Oliver (1990) *Nacktheit: Soziale Normierung und Moral.* Opladen: Westdeutscher Verlag.

Kooy, G.A. (ed.) (1968) *Sex in Nederland.* Utrecht: Het Spectrum.

Kooy, G.A. (ed.) (1983) *Sex in Nederland.* Utrecht: Het Spectrum.

Krumrey, Horst-Volker (1984) *Entwicklungsstrukturen von Verhaltensstandarden: Eine soziologische Prozessanalyse auf der Grundlage deutscher Anstands- und Manierenbücher von 1870 bis 1970.* Frankfurt am Main: Suhrkamp.

Laan, Ellen (1994) *Determinants of Sexual Arousal in Women: Genital and Subjective Components of Sexual Response.* Amsterdam: University of Amsterdam, Faculty of Psychology.

Lasch, Christopher (1979) *The Culture of Narcissism.* New York: Warner Books.

Lasch-Quinn, Elisabeth (2001) *Race Experts: How Racial Etiquette, Sensitivity Training, and New Age Therapy Hijacked the Civil Rights Revolution.* New York: W.W. Norton.

Mahlmann, Regina (1991) *Psychologisierung des Alltagbewußtseins: Die Verwissenschaftlichung des Diskurses über Ehe.* Opladen: Westdeutsche Verlag.

McManus, George (1975) *Bringing Up Father.* Amsterdam: Real Free Press Int.

Mead, Margaret (1950) *Male and Female: A Study of the Sexes in a Changing World.* London: Gollancz; Part Four: The Two Sexes in Contemporary America.

Mooij, Annet (1993) *Geslachtsziekten en besmettingsangst: Een historisch-sociologische studie 1850–1990.* Amsterdam: Boom.

Mosher, D.L., and White, B.B. (1980) 'Effects of committed or casual erotic imagery on females' subjective sexual arousal and emotional response', *Journal of Sex Research,* 16: 273–99.

Nota met betrekking tot het beleid ter bestrijding van sexueel geweld tegen vrouwen en meisjes (1984), 's-Gravenhage: Ministerie van Sociale Zaken en Werkgelegenheid.

Orbach, Susie (1994) *What's Really Going on Here* – London: Virago Press.

Peabody, Dean (1985) *National Characteristics.* New York: Cambridge University Press.

Porter, Cecil (1972) *Not Without a Chaperone: Modes and Manners from 1897 to 1914.* London: New English Library.

Rapport der Regeerings-Commissie inzake het Dansvraagstuk (1931) 's-Gravenhage: Algemeene Landsdrukkerij.

Reiss, Ira L. (with Harriet M. Reiss) (1997) *Solving America's Sexual Crisis,* Buffalo, N.Y.: Prometheus (Revision of 1990 edition: *An End to Shame: Shaping our Next Sexual Revolution*).

Remez, Lisa (2000) 'Oral sex among adolescents: is it sex or is it abstinence?' *Family Planning Perspectives* 32 (6); www.agi-usa.org/pubs/journals

Ritter, P.H. Jr., (1933) *De drang der zinnen in onzen Tijd.* Amsterdam: Scheltema & Giltay.

Röling, H.Q. (1990) 'Samen of alleen. Initiatief en overgave in "Wij willen weten" (1938-1985)', *Amsterdams Sociologisch Tijdschrift,* 17 (2): 85-102.

Röling, H.Q. (1994) *Gevreesde vragen. Geschiedenis van de seksuele opvoeding in Nederland.* Amsterdam: Amsterdam University Press.

Rothman, Ellen K. (1984) *Hands and Hearts: A History of Courtship in America.* New York: Basic Books

Rubinstein, Renate (1983) *Liefst Verliefd.* Amsterdam: Meulenhoff.

Sanders, Stephan (1994) *De grote woede van M.* Amsterdam: Bezige Bij.

Sanders, Stephanie A. and Machover Reinisch, June Machover Reinisch (1999)

'Would you say you "had sex" if ..?', *Journal of the American Medical Association*, 291 (3): 275–7.

Schalet, Amy Townsend (1994) 'Dramatiseren of normaliseren. De culturele constructie van tienerseksualiteit in de Verenigde Staten en Nederland', *Amsterdams Sociologisch Tijdschrift*, 21 (2): 113–47.

Schalet, Amy Townsend. (2000) 'Raging hormones, regulated love: adolescent sexuality and the constitution of the modern individual in the United States and the Netherlands', *Body & Society*, 6 (1): 75–105.

Schlesinger, Arthur M. (1946) *Learning How to Behave: A Historical Study of American Etiquette Books*. New York: Macmillan.

Schnabel, Paul (1990) 'Het verlies van de seksuele onschuld', *Amsterdams Sociologisch Tijdschrift*, 17 (2): 11–50.

Schreurs, Karlein M.G. (1993a) 'Sexuality in lesbian couples: the importance of gender', *Annual Review of Sex Research*, 4: 49–66.

Schreurs, Karlein M.G.(1993b) 'Sexualität und Bedeutung der Geschlechtszugehörigkeit bei lesbischen und heterosexuellen Paaren: Ergebnisse einer empirischen Studie in den Niederlanden', *Zeitschrift für Sexualforschung*, 6 (4): 321–34.

SCR (1998), *Sociaal en Cultureel Rapport*, Rijswijk.: SCR.

Seidman, Stephen (1991) *Romantic Longings: Love in America, 1830–1980*. New York: Routledge.

Sigusch, V., and Schmidt, G. (1970) 'Psychosexuelle Stimulation durch Bilder und Filme: geschlechtsspezifische Unterschiede',; pp. 39–53 in G. Schmidt, V. Sigusch and E. Schorsch (eds), *Tendenzen der Sexualforschung.* Stuttgart: Enke., pp. 39–53.

Stearns, Peter N. (1993) 'Historical Causation in Emotions Research', *Amsterdams Sociologisch Tijdschrift*, 19 (3): 3–22.

Stearns, Peter N. (1994) *American Cool: Constructing a Twentieth-Century Emotional Style*. New York: New York University Press.

Stearns, Peter N., and Knapp, Mark (1992) 'Men and romantic love: pinpointing a twentieth-century change', *Journal of Social History*, 26 (4): 769–95.

Stolk, Bram van (1991) *Eigenwaarde als groepsbelang: Sociologische studies naar de dynamiek van zelfwaardering*. Houten: Bohn Stafleu Van Loghum.

Stolk, Bram van, and Wouters, Cas (1987a) *Frauen im Zwiespalt.: Beziehungsprobleme im Wohlfahrtsstaat. Eine Modellstudie. Mit einem Vorwort von Norbert Elias*. Frankfurt am Main: Suhrkamp.

Stolk, Bram van, and Wouters, Cas (1987b) 'Power changes and self-respect: a comparison of two cases of established-outsider relations', *Theory, Culture and Society*, 4 (2–3): 477–89.

Stolk, Bram van (1991) *Eigenwaarde als groepsbelang: Sociologische studies naar de dynamiek van zelfwaardering*. Houten: Bohn Stafleu Van Loghum.

Straver, Cees (1980) *Kijken naar seks*. Deventer: Van Loghum Slaterus.

Straver, Cees, Ab van der Heiden, Ab and van der Vliet, Ron (1994) *De huwelijkse logica: Huwelijksmodel en inrichting van het samenleven bij arbeiders en anderen*. Leiden: NISSO/DSWO Press.

Swidler, Ann (1980) 'Love and Adulthood in American Culture', in Neil J. Smelser and Eric H. Erikson (eds), *Themes of Work and Love in Adulthood*. London: Grant McIntyre. pp. 120–47.

Tarde, Gabriel ([[1890] 1903[1890]]) *The Laws of Imitation*. transl. E.C. Parsons., introd. F. Giddings, New York: Holt and Co. Reprint 1962: Gloucester, MA: Peter Smith.

Vennix, Paul, and Bullinga, Marcel (1991) *Sekserollen en emancipatie*. Houten/Antwerpen: Bohn Stafleu Van Loghum.

Vliet, Ron van der (1990) 'De opkomst van het seksuele moratorium', *Amsterdams Sociologisch Tijdschrift*, 17 (2): 51–68.

Vogels T. and van der Vliet, R. (1990), *Jeugd en seks*, Den Haag: SDU.

Waller, Willard (1937) 'The Rating and Dating Complex,', *American Sociological Review*, 2: 727–34.

Waller, Willard ([1938] 1951) [1938] *The Family: A Dynamic Interpretation*, Revised by Reuben Hill. New York: The Dryden Press.

Wander, B. (1976) 'Engelse en continentale etiquette in de negentiende eeuw: invloeden en ontwikkel literatuurrapport', *Volkskundig Bulletin*, 2 (2): 1–17.

Wattjes, Prof. J.G. (ca 1930) Wijsgerige gedachten over Het Huwelijk. Delft.

Wolfe, Tom (1976) *Move Gloves & Madmen, Clutter & Vine*. New York: Farrar, Straus & Giroux.

Wouters, Cas (1984) 'Vrouwen, porno en seksualiteit', *Tijdschrift voor Vrouwenstudies*, 5 (2): 246–50.

Wouters, Cas (1986) 'Formalization and informalization, changing tension balances in civilizing Processes', *Theory, Culture & Society*, 3 (2): 1–19.

Wouters, Cas (1987) 'Developments in behavioural codes between the sexes: formalization of informalization, The Netherlands 1930--1985', *Theory, Culture & Society*, 4 (2–3): 405–29.

Wouters, Cas (1992) 'On status competition and emotion management:; the study of emotions as a new field', in: Mike Featherstone (ed.), *Cultural Theory and Cultural Change*. London: Sage:, pp. 229–52.

Wouters, Cas (1995) 'Etiquette books and emotion management in the twentieth century; part two – the integration of the sexes.' *Journal of Social History*, 29 (2): 325–40.

Wouters, Cas (1998a) 'Etiquette books and emotion management in the twentieth century: Aamerican habitus in international comparison', in Peter N. Stearns and Jan Lewis (eds), *An Emotional History of the United States*. New York: New York University Press. pp. 283–304.

Wouters, Cas (1998b) 'How strange to ourselves are our feelings of superiority and inferiority', *Theory, Culture & Society*, 15 (1): 131–50.

Wouters, Cas (1998c) 'Changes in the "lust balance" of love and sex since the sexual revolution: the example of the Netherlands', in Gillian Bendelow and Simon J. Williams (eds), *Emotions in Social Life: Critical Themes and Contemporary Issues*, London: Routledge. pp. 228–49.

Wouters, Cas (1999a) 'Changing patterns of social controls and self-controls: on the rise of crime since the 1950s and the sociogenesis of a "third nature"'. *British Journal of Criminology*, 39 (3): 416–32.

Wouters, Cas (1999b) 'Die verlegte "Rue d'Amour": Über Hans Peter Duerrs Kritik and der Zivilizationstheorie von Norbert Elias', *Zeitschrift für Sexualforschung*. 12 (1): 50–7.

Wouters, Cas (1999c) 'Balancing Sex and Love since the 1960s Sexual Revolution', in Mike Featherstone (ed.), *Love and Eroticism*. London: Sage. pp. 187–214.

Wouters, Cas (1999d) *Informalisierung.: Norbert Elias' Zivilizationstheorie und Zivilizationsprozesse im 20. Jahrhundert*. Opladen: Westdeutscher Verlag.

Wouters, Cas (2001a) 'Manners', in *Encyclopedia of European Social History: From 1350 to 2000*, editor in chief: Peter N. Stearns, New York: Charles Scribner's Sons; Volume 4, Section 17, pp. : 371–82.

Wouters, Cas (2001b) 'The integration of classes and sexes in the twentieth century: etiquette books and emotion management', pp. 50–83 in Thomas Salumets, Thomas (ed.), *Norbert Elias and Human Interdependencies*. Montreal and Kingston: McGill-Queen's University Press, pp. 50–83. 2001.

Wouters, Cas (2002) 'The quest for new rituals in dying and mourning: changes in the we–I balance', *Body & Society*, 8 (1): 1–27.

Wouters, Cas (forthcoming) *A History of Manners: Informalization.*

Wouters, Kees C.A.T.M (1999) *Ongewenste Muziek.* Den Haag: SDU Uitgevers.

Zeegers, Wil (1994) *De zonnige zijde van seks: De nawerking van positief beleefde seksualiteit.* FSW, Rijksuniversiteit Leiden: DSWO Press.

Zessen, Gertjan van, and Sandfort, Theo (eds) (1991) *Seksualiteit in Nederland: seksueel gedrag, risico en preventie van aids.* Amsterdam: Swets & Zeitlinger.

Zwaan, Ton (ed.) (1993) *Familie, huwelijk en gezin in West-Europa.* Amsterdam/Heerlen: Boom/Open Universiteit.

Zwerin, Mike (2000[1985]) *Swing Under The Nazis: Jazz As A Metaphor For Freedom.* New York: Cooper Square Press.

Manners Books

A (1894) *Doodgewone Dingen.* Amsterdam: Centen.

Alberts, Joh. C. P. (1918) *De zegeningen van ons fatsoen (diagnose en prognose).* Baarn: Hollandia.

Alsen, Ola (1936) *Zoo zijn onze manieren. Een handleiding voor goede omgangsvormen.* Leiden: Leidsche Uitgeversmaatschappij. (translated from the German)

App, Austin J. (1947) *Courtesy, Courtship and Marriage.*, San Antonio, Texas: published by the author.

Armstrong, Lucie Heaton (1908) *Etiquette Up-to-Date.* London: Werner Laurie.

BakkerEngelsman, Netty (1983) *Etiquette in de jaren '80.* Utrecht: Luitingh.

Baldridge, Laetitia (1990) *Laetitia Baldridge's Complete Guide to the New Manners of the 90's.* New York: Rawson Associates.

Beyfus, Drusilla (1992) *Modern Manners: The Essential Guide to Living in the '90s.* London: Hamlyn.

Bolton, Mary (1955, 1961) *The New Etiquette Book.* London: Foulsham.

Bourg, Dominique Le (1950) *De Kunst van Beminnen en Beminnelijk te zijn. Een liefdesvademecum voor Eva's dochteren. (l'Art d'être aiméee).* Rotterdam: Donker. (reprint 1956, identical).

Bradley, Julia M. (1889) *Modern Manners and Social Forms.* Chicago: J.B. Smiley.

BreenEngelen, R.A. (1959) *Etiquette: Een Boekje voor Moderne Mensen (Etiquette: A Book for Modernem People).* Bussum (4th edition 1969).

Bremner, Moyra (1989) *Enquire within upon Modern Etiquette and Successful Behaviour for Today.* London: Century.

Brown, Helen Gurley (ed.) (1971) *The Cosmo Girl's Guide to The New Etiquette.* New York: Cosmopolitan.

Brown, Helen Gurley (1983) *Having It All.* New York: Pocket Books.

Bruck-Auffenberg, Natalie (1897) *De Vrouw 'Comme Il Faut'.* trans. from the German by Marie de Bock-Hardenberg. Leiden: Brill.

Brummell & Co. (1927) *De Man op z'n best. Een geestige Handleiding in Savoir-Vivre.* Den Haag: Moorman.

Bruyn, Klazien de (1957) *"Spiegel voor Eva" Goede manieren en het moderne meisje.* Maastricht: Schenk. [first half 1950s]

Burleigh (1925) *Etiquette Up To Date.* New York: Howard Watt.

Calcar, E. van (1886) *Gelukkig – ofschoon getrouwd. Een boek voor gehuwden en ongehuwden,* trans. from the English. Haarlem: Bohn.

Cassell's (1921) *Cassell's Book of Etiquette, by 'A Woman of the World',* London.

Caprio, Frank S. (1960) *Mijn man, mijn minnaar.* Amsterdam: Strengholt.

Cartland, Barbara (1984) *Barbara Cartland's Etiquette for Love and Romance.* Bath:

Chivers Press   (2nd edn. 1986).

Case, Carleton B (ed.) (1916) *The American Girl in Society: The Way to Social Success.* Chicago: Shrewesbury.

Courey, Anne de (1985) A *Guide to Modern Manners.* London: Thames and Hudson.

Day, Beth (1972) *Sexual Life Between Blacks and Whites: The Roots of Racism.* Introduction by Margaret Mead, New York: World Publishing Co.

Debrett (1981) *Debrett's Etiquette and Modern Manners,* edited by Elsie Burch Donald, 2nd edition: 1982; London: Pan Books.

Devereux, G.R.M. (1927) *Etiquette for Men: A Handbook of Modern Manners and Customs. New Edition. Entirely rewritten and brought up to date.* London: Pearson.

Dietrich, Heinz (1934) *Menschen miteinander.* Berlin und Darmstadt: Deutsche Buch-Gemeinschaft.

Duvall, Evelyn Millis, with Joy Duvall Johnson (1958 and 1968) *The Art of Dating.* New York: Association Press.

ECvdM (1911) *Het wetboek van Mevrouw Etiquette voor Heeren in zestien artikelen,* Utrecht: Honig.

ECvdM. (1912) *Het wetboek van mevrouw Etiquette in 32 artikelen.* Utrecht: Honig. 7th edition.

ECvdM. (1920) *Etiquette voor heeren.* Utrecht: Honig. 2nd enlarged printing; 1st edn: 1917.

Edwards, Anne, and Beyfus, Drusilla (1956) *Lady Behave: A Guide to Modern Manners.* London: Boswell & Co.; revised edition 1969.

Ehrhardt, Dr. Fritz (1905) *Das Buch der Lebensart: Ein Ratgeber für den guten Ton in jeder Lebenslage.* Berlin: Merkur.

Eichler, Lilian (1921) *The Book of Etiquette,* 2 vollumes. Gardean City, New York: Doubleday. Reprinted 1923.

Eichler Watson, Lilian   (1948) *The Standard Book of Etiquette.* New York: Gardean City Publishing..

Eijk, Inez van (1983) *Etiquette Vandaag.* Utrecht/Antwerpen: Spectrum.

Eijk, Inez van (1994) *Bij jou of bij mij – Erotische etiquette.* Amsterdam: Contact.

Eijk, Inez van (2000) *Etiquette: Over moderne omgansvormen.* Amsterdam: Contact: Amsterdam.

Eijk, Inez van (2001) *Hoog spel. Lexicon van de verleiding.* Amsterdam: HP/De Tijd.

Eldridge, Elisabeth (1936) *Co-Etiquette. Poise and Popularity for Every Girl.* New York: Dutton.

Eltz, J. von ([[1902] 1908) *Das goldene Anstandsbuch: Ein Wegweiser für die gute Lebensart zu Hhause, in Gesellschaft und im öffentlichen Leben.* Essen: Fredebeul & Koenen.

Engelberts, D.H. (1890) *De goede toon: Een wegwijzer etc.* Amsterdam/De Rijp: Van Raven.

Etiquette for Americans (1909) by a Woman of Fashion. New York: Duffield; new and revised edition; 1st edn: 1898.

Etiquette for Ladies: *A Complete Guide to the Rules and Observances of Good Society.* (1900) London: Ward, Lock & Co.

Etiquette for Ladies (1923, 1950) *A Guide to the Observances of Good Society.* London: Ward, Lock & Co.

Etiquette for Women (1902) *A Book of Modern Modes and Manners.* London: Pearson.

Etiquette for Ladies (1923; 1950) *A Guide to the Observances of Good Society.* London: Ward, Lock & Co.

Fein, Ellen and Schneider, Sherrie Schneider (1995) *The Rules: Time-tested Secrets for Capturing the Heart of Mr. Right.* New York: Warner Books.

Foerster, Dr. Fr. W. (1911) *Levenswandel. Een boek voor jonge menschen*. Zwolle: Ploegsma (2nd edn.; 1st edn: 1910) (translated from the German).

Franken, Konstanze von (1951/1957) *Der Ggute Ton: Ein Brevier für Takt und Benehmen in allen Lebenslagen*. Berlin: Hesse.

Frenken, Jos (1976) *Afkeer van seksualiteit*. Deventer: Van Loghum Slaterus.

Gillum, Lulu W. (1937) *Social Usage for High Schools*. Kansas City, MOissouri: Gillum Book.

Graham, Laurie (1989) *Getting It Right: A Survival Guide to Modern Manners*. London: Chatto & Windus.

Graudenz, Karlheinz and Pappritz, Erica Pappritz (1967) *Etikette neu*. München: Südwest.

Grosfeld, Frans (ed.) (1983) *Zo hoort het nu. Etiquette voor de jaren tachtig*. Amsterdam/Brussels, Elsevier (second and third editions 1984).

Groskampten Have, Amy (1939) *Hoe Hoort Het Eigenlijk? (What's the Right Way?)*. Amsterdam: Becht. (1-3 edns: 1939; 4-5 edns: 1940; 6th: 1941; 7th: 1942; 8th: 1947; 9th: 1948; 10th: 1953; 11th: 1954; 12th: 1957; 13th: 1966, revised by Ina van den Beugel).

Groskampten Have, Amy (1983) *Hoe hoort het eigenlijk?* Completely revised by Maja Krans and Wia Post, Amsterdam: Becht, (2ndsecond edition 1984).

Haeften, Olga van (1936) *Manieren. Wenken voor wie zich correct willen gedragen*. Amsterdam: Kosmos. (2nd edn. 1937, identical).

Haluschka, Helene (n.d./1937a) *Hoe vindt U het moderne jonge meisje?* Heemstede: De Toorts.

Haluschka, Helene (1939) *Wat is nu goede toon?* Heemstede: de Toorts. Translation: Alb. Schelfhout v.d. Meulen.

Handboek der Etiquette voor oud en jong (1905).

Hanson, John Wesley Jr. (1896): *Etiquette of To-Day: The Customs and Usages Required by Polite Society*. Chicago.

Hanstein (1971) *Ursula von Hanstein's Lexikon moderner Etikette*. München: Moderne Verlags GmbH.

Harland, Marion, and van de Water, Virginia (1905/1907) *Everyday Etiquette: A Practical Manual of Social Usages*. Indianapolis: Bobbs-Merrill.

Hennenhofer/Jaensch (1974) *KNIGGE 2000. Befreiter Umgang mit dem Anderen. Ein Teambuch des Schönberger Institut für Programmierte Instruktion*. Cologne Köln: Kiepenheuer & Witsch.,

Holt, Emily (1901; revised editions: 1904 and 1920) *The Secret of Popularity: How to Achieve Social Success*. New York: McClure, Phillips. revised editions: 1904 and 1920.

Houghton, Walter R. et al., (1882) *American Etiquette and Rules of Politeness*, 6th edition, Chicago: Rand McNally.

Hout, H.P.M. van den, M.A. (1982) *Omgangsvormen (Etiquette).*, Rijswijk: Schoevers.

Humphry, Mrs. C. E. (1897) *Etiquette for Every Day*. London: Richards.

Humphry, Mrs. C.E. (1902) *Etiquette for Every Day*. London: Richards.

Jonathan, Norton Hughes (1938) *Gentlemen Aren't Sissies (A Modern Guide Book for the Young Man About Town)*. Chicago: Winston.

Kandaouroff, Princess Beris (1972) *The Art of Living: Etiquette for the Permissive Age*. London: Allan.

Kasson, John F. (1990) *Rudeness and Civility: Manners in Nineteenth-Century Urban America*. New York: Hill and Wang.

Keulaerds P.L. and v. Tienen, P.M. (1950s) *'"Savoir Vivre"': Omgangvormen en etiquette voor jonge mensen*. Maastricht: Schenk.

Klickmann, Flora (1902) *The Etiquette of To-day*. London. 2nd edition: 1915; 3rd edn: 1916.

Kloos-Reyneke van Stuwe, Jeanne (1927) *Gevoelsbeschaving. Handboek voor huis en gezelschapsleven*. Rotterdam: Nijgh & Van Ditmar.

Knap, Henri (1961) *Zo zijn onze manieren*. Amsterdam: Bezige Bij.

Knigge, Adolph Freiherr von ([1788/] 1977) *Über den Umgang mit Menschen*. Herausgegeben von ed. Gert Ueding., Frankfurt/M: Insel Verlag.

Koebner F.W. (1919) *Der Man von Welt: Ein Herrenbrevier*. Berlin: Eysler (new improved edn., 46-40 thousand. 1stst edn. 1913).

Krampen, Hans Joachim von (between 1910 and 1915) *Was ist Vornehm– Vom Herzens- und gesellschaftlichen Takt*. Berlin: Langenscheid.

Kuitenbrouwer, Jan (1990) *Lijfstijl: De manieren van nu*. Amsterdam: Prometheus.

Landers, Olive Richards (1936) *Modern Etiquette for Young People*. New York: Greenberg.

Lansbury, Angela (1985) *Etiquette for Every Occasion: A Guide to Good Manners*. London: Batsford.

Latouche, Anette (1946) *Etiquette of de sierlijkheid des levens*. Tilburg: Bergmans. (From the Swiss, adapted by Clara Eggink).

Löwenbpirg. Sylvia Lichem von (1987) *Das neue Buch der Etikette*. Munich: Droemer Knaur.

Ludden, Allen (1956) *Plain Talk for Women Under 21!* New York: Dodd & Mead 1956.

Manners and Rules of Good Society (1879), [by] A Member of the Aristocracy. London: F. Warne. (32rd edn: 1910, 32rd edition; 1921; 42nd edition 1921). Published in 1940 as:

Manners and Rule of Good Society (1946). London and New York: Warne. Revised by Joan Storey (reprints in 1946,1947, 1950, 1955).

Margaretha, Anthonia (1921) *Vormen en manieren: De eischen der Wellevendheid toegelicht voor onze Christelijke Kringen*. Kampen: Kok.

Marschner, Osw. (1901) *Takt und Ton: Plaudereien über den feinen Takt und guten Ton im geselligen Verkehr*. Leipzig: Maier.

Martin, Judith (1979) *Miss Manners' Guide to Excruciatingly Correct Behaviour*. New York: Warner Books/Atheneum Publishers. (reprinted: 1980/1981/1982/1983).

Martin, Judith (1983) *Miss Manners' Guide for the Turn-of-the-Millennium*. NewYork: PharosBooks/Fireside.(reprinted:1984/1985/1986/1987/1988/1989/1990).

Martin, Judith (2003) *Star-Spangled Manners. In Which Miss Manners Defends American Etiquette (For A Change)*. New York: Norton.

McGinnis, Dr. Tom (1968) *A Girl's Guide to Dating and Going Steady*. Garden City, NY: Doubleday.

Meissner, Hans-Otto (1951) *Man benimmt sich wieder*. Giessen: Brühlscher.

Meister, Ilse (1933) *Vom Backfisch zur Dame: Vom Jüngling zum vollendeten Herrn. Ein neues Anstandsbuch*. Stuttgart: Union. (7th reprint).

Miller, Llewellyn (1967) *The Encyclopedia of Etiquette: A Guide to Good Manners in Today's World*. New York: Crown.

Mounier, P.J.J. (n.d.), *Gestroomlijnd leven voor de verloving*. Kanarie-boekje No. 212. Den Haag/Antwerpen: Succes.

Naber, Johanna (1923) *Na XXV Jaren 1898–1923. Het feminisme in zijnen bloei en in zijne voleinding*. Haarlem: Tjeenk Willink.

Oheim, Gertrud (1955) *Einmaleins des guten Tons*. Gütersloh: Bertelsmann.

Ostrander, Sheila (1967) *Etiquette Etc: A Concise Guide with a Fresh Look*. New York: Sterling Publishing, New York.

Paeuw, L. de (1934) *Nette manieren: Een handboek der wellevendheid voor jong en oud.* Baarle-Hertog: De Belgische Boekhandel (2nd edn).

Palts-de Ridder, Yvonne and Eikhof, Vera (1960) Hoe het '"hoort':". Van kennismaking tot huwelijk. *Regina Goede Raad* Serie Nr. 3, Haarlem: de Spaarnestad.

Penelope, Lady (1982) *Etiquette Today.* Kingswood, Surrey: Paperfronts, Elliot Right Way Books. (reprinted 1989).

Pierce, Beatrice (1937) *Etiquette for Young Moderns.* Home Service Booklets.

Polak, J.H., and Polak, Maurits Polak (1903) De Ceremoniemeester in de Balzaal, de Cotilloneur, Danse et Maintien. Alkmaar: Kluitman.

Post, Emily (1922), *Etiquette in Society, in Business, in Politics and at Home.* New York: Funk and Wagnalls. (revised editions: 1923; 1927; 1931; 1934; 1937; 1942; 1950; 1960; Replica Editon of first edition: 1969).

Post, Elisabeth L. (1965) *Emily Post's Etiquette.* Revised by Elisabeth L. Post. New York: Funk & Wagnalls. [next edition: 1968]; 1975 edition: *The New Emily Post's Etiquette.* New editions in 1984 and 1992.

Post, Elisabeth L. (1992) *Emily Post's Etiquette.* 15th edn, New York: HarperCollins.

Post, Toos (1938) *Zoo Hoort Het. Wellevendheid als uiting van innerlijke beschaving en liefde tot den evenmensch.* Utrecht: Urbi et Orbi (3erd edn.).

Rappard, Jonkvr. H.A. (1912) *Goede manieren. Wat men doen en laten moet in het dagelijksch leven.* Haarlem: Visser, 3rd improved and enlarged edition. (1st: 1909, 2nd: 1910, 4th: 1920).

Rees, Nigel (1992) *Best Behaviour: A Complete Guide to Manners in the 1990s.* London: Bloomsbury.

Richardson, Anna Steese (1927), *Etiquette At a Glance.* New York: Appleton.

Schidlof, Dr. B. (1926) *Lebenskunst und Lebenstakt: Winke und Ratschläge.* Berlin: Oestergaard.

Schliff, Sebastian (1977), *Gutes Benehmen – Kein Problem!* München: Humboldt-Taschenbuchverlag; 1981 Taschenbuchausgabe ('leicht gekürzt').

Schönfeldt, Sybil Gräfin (1987) *1 x 1 des guten Tons.* München: Mosaik Verlag: Hamburg, 1991.

Schramm, H. (1893) *Der Ggute Ton oder das richtige Benehmen: Ein Ratgeber für den Verkehr in der Familie, in der Gesellschaft und im öffentlichen Leben.* Berlin: Schulke (4th edn.).

Schrijver, Elka (1954) *Kleine gids voor goede manieren.* Assen: Born. (reprints 1959 and 1962)

Scott, H. (1930) *Good Manners and Bad.* London: Ernest Benn.

Segaloff, Nat (1997) *The 'Everything' Etiquette Book.* Holbrook, Mass.: Adams Media Corporation.

Seidler, Dr. H.J. [1911-15] *Hoe men zich bij de heeren het best bemind kan maken.* Rotterdam: Bolle (trans. from the German).

Sherwood, Mary E.W. (1907) *Manners and Social Usages.* New York: Harper.

Staffe, Baronesse (1900s) *Bestemming. Dochter, Echtgenoote, Moeder. vrij bewerkt naar het fransch door G.J Bakker Korff-Hoogeboom.* Amsterdam: C.L.G. Veldt.

Stratenus, Louise (1909) *Vormen. Handboek voor de samenleving in en buiten huis.* Gouda: Van Goor.

Swartz, Oretha D. (1988) *Service Etiquette.* Annapolis, Maryland: Naval Institute Press (4th edition).

Sweeney, Ester Emerson (1948), *Dates and Dating.* New York: The Women's Press. New York.

Terry, Eileen (1925), *Etiquette for All, Man, Woman or Child.* London: Foulsham.

Troubridge, Lady L. (1926), *The Book of Etiquette.* Kingswood: Windmill Press. (reprinted 1927, 1928, 1931).

Troubridge, Lady L. (1939), *Etiquette and Entertaining*. London: Amalgamated Press.
Umgangsformen Heute (1970), *Die Empfehlungen des Fachausschusses für Umgangsformen*. Niedernhausen: Falken (revised edns: 1988, 1990).
Unger, Art (ed.) (1960), *Datebook's Complete Guide to Dating*. Englewood Cliffs, N.J: Prentice Hall.
Vanderbilt, Amy (1952) *Amy Vanderbilt's Complete Book of Etiquette: A Guide to Gracious Living*. New York: Doubleday 1952 (reprints 1958, 1963, 1972).
Vanderbilt, Amy (1956) *Everyday Etiquette: Answers to Today's Etiquette Questions*. New York: Hanover House (other editions: 1952, 1954, 1967).
Vanderbilt, Amy (1978) *The Amy Vanderbilt Complete Book of Etiquette, revised and expanded by Letitia Baldrige*. Garden City, NY: Doubleday.
Veen-Wijers, Olga van (1936–/40) *Etiquette: Encyclopedie der correcte omgangsvormen*. 's-Gravenhage: Succes. Universiteit voor zelfstudie. (1936-1940, also 1946-50).
Velde, Th. H. van de (1933/1928) *Ideal Marriage: Its Physiogomy and Technique*. London: Heinemann.
Viroflay, Marguérite de (1916 /1919), *Plichten en Vormen voor Beschaafde Menschen*. Amsterdam: Cohen Zonen.
Viroflay-Montrecourt, Marguérite de (H.W. van Tienhoven-Mulder) [(192–]) *Goede Manieren. Een Etikettenboek voor dames en heeren*. 2 volumes; I for Ladies, II for Gentlemen. Amsterdam: Cohen.
Vogue (1948) *Vogue's Book of Etiquette: A Complete Guide to Traditional Forms and Modern Usage*. by Millicent Fenwick, Associate Editor of Vogue. New York: Simon and Schuster.
Wachtel, Joachim (1973), *1 x 1 des guten Tons heute*. München etc: Bertelsmann Ratgeberverlag.
Wade, Margaret (1924) *Social Usage in America*. New York: Thomas Crowell.
Wallace, Lily Haxworth (1941) *The NEW American Etiquette*. New York: Books.
Weber, Annemarie (1956) *Hausbuch des guten Tons: Ein Knigge von Heute*. Berlin: Falken.
Weißenfeld, Kurt von (1941) *Der moderne Knigge: Über den Umgang mit Menschen*. Berlin: Möller (1st edn: 1919; many new improved editions until 1960).
Whitcomb, Helen and Lang, Rosalind (1971) *Charm: The Career Girl's Guide to Business and Personal Success* (2nd edn; 1st edn: 1964). New York: Gregg Division McGraw-Hill.
Wilson, Margery (1942) *The Woman You Want To Be: Margery Wilson's Complete Book of Charm*. Lippincott, Philadelphia and New York (eleventh impression; copyright 1928, 1933).
Wolter, Irmgard (1990) *Der Ggute Ton im Privatleben*. Niederhausen/Ts: Falken Bücherei. Überarbeitet von Wolf Stenzel.
Woman's Life (1895) Published by George Neurnes Ltd. First issue 14 December 1895.
Wrede-Grischkat, Rosemarie (1992) *Manieren und Karriere: Verhaltensnormen für Führungskräfte*. 2nd edn. Wiesbaden: Frankfurter Allgemeine, Gabler. 2nd ed.
Zitzewitz, Rosemarie von (1986) *Wenn Sie mich SO fragen: Rosemarie von Zitzewitz gibt Antworten auf Benimmfragen*. München: Mosaik Verlag.
Zutphen van Dedem, Mevr. van (1928) *Goede Manieren*. Amersfoort: Logon.

Name Index

A 33, 44, 68, 121
Alberts, Joh. C.P.141n
Alsen, Ola 28, 67, 71,
Andreae 63
Ang, Ien 130
App, Austin J. 105, 106
Armstrong, Lucie Heaton 52

Bailey, Beth L. viii, 30, 85–95, 105,
    108, 109, 111, 125, 147, 141n
BakkerEngelsman, N74
Baldridge, Laetitia 32, 116
Baltzell, E. Digby 86–88
Batenburg, H.L 121
Beatrix, Queen 12
Bellah, Robert N. et al. 88
Benthem van den Bergh, Godfried van
    141n
Beyfus, Drusilla 26, 41, 42, 53–57, 148
Blom, J.C.H. 124, 127
Bodanius 63
Bolton, Mary 50, 54
Boonstra, Heather 146
Bourg, Dominique le 148
Bradley, Julia M. 33, 75–77
Bremner, Moyra 27, 42, 56
Brinkgreve, Christien 135
Brown, Helen Gurley 112, 113, 115
Brugman, Emily et al. 138
Bruijn, Gerda de 129
Brummell & Co 69, 70
Bruyn, Klazien de 21, 74
Bullinga, Marcel
    see Vennix
Burleigh 23, 52

Calcar, E. van 48
Caldwell, Mark 87, 94, 146
Cancian, F.M. and S.L. Gordon 4, 127,
    160
Caprio, Frank S. 125
Cartland, Barbara 31, 115, 140n
Case, Carleton B. 86
Cassell's 33
CBS 138
Chesterfield, Lord 14
Coleman, L. 97
Coronel, S. Sr. 121

Cosby, Bill 146
Courey, Anne de 55
Cressey, Paul G.92
Curtin, Michaelviii, 9, 10, 11, 14, 18,
    24, 51, 53

Daalen, Rineke van ix,
Daalen, Rineke van, and Bram van
Stolk 129
Dahrendorf, R. 84,
Dantzig, A. van 125
Darroch, Jacqueline E. et al. 146
Davidoff, Leonore 15, 17, 18, 51, 53,
    141n
Day, Beth 97, 147
Debrett 26, 41, 42, 55
Dekker, Joost 131, 132
Derks, Marjet 21
Deutscher, Irwin ix
Deutscher, Verda ix
Devereux, G.R.M. 53
Dietrich, Heinz 57
Dowling, C. 134
Driver-Davidson, Lisa ix
Duerr, Hans Peter 141
Dunning, Eric ix, 5, 147, 150
Duvall, Evelyn Millis 30, 104, 107,
    109–111,

ECvdM 19, 28, 64–69, 121, 122,
Ebhardt, Fritz 58, 60,
Edwards, Anne, and D. Beyfus 26, 41,
    42, 53–55, 57,
Eggermont, Patricia 120
Ehrenreich, Barbara, and Deirdre
English 127
Ehrhardt, F. 57, 59,
Eichler, Lilian 21,
Eichler Watson, Lilian 37, 95, 103,
Eijk, Inez van 46, 75, 138,
Eldridge, Elisabeth 30, 91, 92, 96, 99,
    100
Elias, Norbert ix, 2, 3, 5, 10, 47, 57, 84,
    139, 149, 140n
Elias, Norbert, and Eric Dunning 5, 72,
    150
Elias, N. and J.L. Scotson 10, 16, 135,
Ellis, Albert 109,

Eltz, J. von 59
Engelberts, D.H. 121
Ernst, Stefanie 44
Etiquette for Americans 78
Etiquette for Ladies 24, 51, 52
Etiquette for Women 25

Fass, Paula S. viii, 87–90, 94–96, 144
Fein, Ellen and Sherrie Schneider 32, 117
Fisher, W.A., and D. Byrne 131
Fletcher, Jonathan ix, 149
Foerster, Fr.W. 45
Foucault, Michel ix, 140n
Franken, Konstanze von 13, 27, 28, 58
Frenken, Jos 126
Fromm, Erich 133

Garcia, L.T. et al. 131
Gillum, Lulu W. 88
Gordon S.L.
    see Cancian
Gorer, Geoffrey viii, 30, 89, 92, 96, 97
Görz 46
Goudsblom, J. 141n
Graham, Laurie 56
Graudenz, Karlheinz, and E. Pappritz 63, 131
Graves, Robert, and Alan Hodge 51
Greene, Gael 112, 113
Gregory, Adrian 141n
Groenendijk, H. 134
Grosfeld, Frans 29, 46, 74
Groskamp-ten Have, Amy 29, 45, 73, 74, 158

Haeften, Olga van 29, 71
Haluschka, Helene 29, 45, 71, 72, 158
Halttunen, Karen viii
Handboek 64
Hanson, John Wesley Jr. 16, 34
Hanstein, U von 61, 63
Harland, Marion, and Virginia van de Water 33, 34, 35, 77, 87
Hatfield, Elaine, and R.L. Rapson 124
Heiman, J.R. 131
Hekma, Gert 48
Hemphill, C.Dallett viii, 16, 89
Hendin 133
Hennenhofer/Jaensch 63
Hinz, Michael 4
Hochschild, Arlie R. 34, 139, 143
Holt, Emily 21, 78
Houghton, Walter R. et al. 11
Hout, H.P.M. vd 46, 74
Humphry, Mrs. C.E. 16

Iley, Chrissy 117
Inglis, Tom ix

Jonathan, Norton Hughes 92, 96, 100–102
Jong, Erica 127
Juliana, Queen 12

Kandaouroff, Princess Beris 55
Kasson, John F. viii
Keulaerds, P.L. and P.M. v. Tienen 74
Kilminster, Richard ix
Klein, Gabriele 23
Klickmann, Flora 15, 16
Kliphuis, J.F. 141n
Kloos-Reyneke van Stuwe, Jeanne 20, 70
Knap, Henri 46
Knapp, Mark
    see Stearns and Knigge, Adolph Freiherr von14, 59, 61
Koebner, F.W. 23
König, Oliver 160
Kool-Smit, Joke 128
Kooy, G.A. 124
Krampen, Hans Joachim von 59, 60
Krumrey, Horst-Volker viii, 27, 60, 63
Kuitenbrouwer, Jan 138

Laan, Ellen 131, 132, 135
Ladies' Home Journal 91, 127
Landers, Olive Richards 37, 80, 95, 98
Lang, Rosalind
    see Whitcomb
Lansbury, Angela 25
Lasch, Christopher 133
Lasch-Quinn, Elisabeth 127
Latouche, Anette 45
Levie, L.H 141n
Lewis, Ida 147
Ludden, Allen 104, 107–109, 111

Machover Reinisch J. see Sanders
Mahlmann, Regina 159
Manners and Rule 16, 51
Manners and Social Usages 77
Margaretha, Anthonia 28, 69, 70, 122
Marschner, Osw. 58
Martin, Judith viii, 32, 39, 98, 117,118, 148
McGinnis, Tom 97, 104, 112
McManus, George 141n
Mead, Margaret viii, 89, 92, 94
Mennell, Stephen viii, ix
Meulenbelt, Anja 128
Meissner, Hans-Otto 24, 27, 43, 44, 61

Meister, Ilse 27, 60
Miller, Llewellyn 38, 82
Miss Manners viii, 39, 98, 118, 119, 143, 147
Mooij, Annet 123
Mosher, D.L. and B.B. White 131
Mounier, P.J.J. 154

Naber, Johanna 45
Nota 131

Oheim, Gertrud 28, 44, 61, 62
Orbach, Susie 155
Ostrander, Sheila 30, 37, 108

Paeuw, L. de 23, 73
Palts-de Ridder, Yvonne, and Vera Eikhof 74
Pappritz, E.
    see Graudenz
Pastoetter, Jakob ix
Peabody, Dean 84
Penelope, Lady 26, 56
Pierce, Beatrice 80, 99
Pola Negri 20
Polak, J.H. and M. Polak, 19
Porter, Cecil viii, 18, 50, 51
Porter, Cole 97
Post, Emily 11, 15, 23, 30, 31, 35, 36, 37, 38, 78–81, 90, 98, 103, 104, 107
Post, Elizabeth L. 37, 79, 82, 83, 105, 107, 114, 115, 116
Post, Toos 73

Rappard, H.A. Jonkvr. 66
Rapport 21
Rees, Nigel 42, 56
Reiss, Ira L. 132
Remez, Lisa 142
Ritter, P.H.Jr. 154
Röling, H.Q. 127, 135
Rothman, Ellen K. viii, 86
Rubinstein, Renate 134
Richardson, Anna Steese 79
Robertson Hodges, Deborah viii

Saal 123
Sanders, Stephan 139
Sanders, Stephanie A. and J. Machover Reinisch 142
Sandfort, Theo zie Zessen
Schalet, Amy Townsend 138, 144, 145
Schary, Jill 112
Schidlof, B. 43
Schlesinger, Arthur M viii, 91

Schliff, Sebastian 63
G. Schmidt
    see Sigusch
Schnabel, Paul 160
Schneider, Sherrie see Fein
Schönfelt, Sybil Gräfin 44
Schramm, H. 58
Schreurs, Karlein M.G. 124
Schrijver, Elka 122
Schröter, Michael ix
Scott, H. 40
SCR 138
Segaloff, Nat 83
Seidman, Stephen 48
Seidler, H.J. 68, 121
Shelton, Gilbert 142n
Sherwood, Mary E.W. 77, 78
Sigusch, V. and G. Schmidt 131
Simpson, G. 122
Staffe, Baronesse 68, 121
Stearns, Peter N. 86, 87, 140
Stearns, Peter N. and Mark Knapp 91, 95
Stepp, Laura Sessions 142
Stolk, Bram van ix, 129, 155, 142n
Stolk, Bram van, and Cas Wouters 69, 127, 128, 137, 139, 149, 155, 159
Stratenus, Louise 68
Straver, Cees 131
Straver, Cees, et al. 139
Swartz, Oretha D. 115
Sweeney, Ester Emerson 24, 104
Swidler, Ann 127

Tarde, Gabriel 11, 12
Terry, Eileen 22
Tienen, P.M. v. see Keulards
Troubridge, Lady L. 25, 33, 41, 52, 53

Umgangsformen Heute 64
Unger, Art 31, 105, 107–110

Valentino, Rudolf 20
Vanderbilt, Amy 31, 32, 35, 37, 39, 40, 81, 82, 106, 108, 114
Veen-Wijers, Olga van 72
Velde, Th.H. vd 125
Vennix, Paul, 136
Vennix, Paul, and Marcel Bullinga 127
Viroflay, M. de 20, 65, 69
Viroflay-Montrecourt 3, 20, 69
Vliet, Ron van der 138
Vogels, T. and R vd Vliet 138
Voerman, Sam ix
Vogue's Book of Etiquette 81

Wachtel, Joachim 63
Wade, Margaret 17
Wade Farrer, Eliza 36
Wallace, Lily Haxworth 103
Waller, Willard viii, 87, 89, 94, 96
Water, Virginia van de *see* Harland
Wattjes, J.G. 125
Weber, Annemarie 61, 62, 63
Weißenfelt, Kurt von 43
Whitcomb, Helen, and Rosalind Lang
    38, 40, 114
White B.B.
    see Mosher
Wilson, Margery 35, 37
Wolter, Irmgard 64

Woman's Life 50
Wrede-Grischkat, Rosemarie 44
Wolfe, Tom 132
Wouters, Cas viii, 3, 22, 57, 84, 98,
    133, 141, 145, 153
    see also Stolk and Wouters, Kees 23
    Wouters, Luuk viii

Zeegers, Wil 48, 156
Zessen, Gertjan van, and Theo Sandfort
    124
Zitzewitz, Rosemarie von 63, 64
Zutphen van Dedem, Mevr. van 71
Zwaan, Ton 124
Zwerin, Mike 23

Subject Index

accommodation 2, 4, 44, 124, 148
  cramp 155
  phase of 157, 159
  process 113, 153, 155, 157
acquaintance, acquaintances 1, 10, 15,
  16, 25, 36, 46, 50, 52, 53, 69, 74, 77
adultery 63, 135, 138
advances 5, 91, 100, 109
  welcome 74
  unwelcome 38, 74, 119,
affects 110, 152
affect control 135, 150
African Americans 146
  see also Black Americans and
  American Negroes
AIDS 135, 137, 140n
alert, alertness 37, 56
alternatives
  socially accepted 2, 3, 56, 127
  behavioural and emotional 1, 9, 26,
  47, 75, 112, 133, 151, 156, 159
amatrice 123, 125
ambivalence 22, 26, 34, 35, 55, 77, 81,
  83, 99, 134, 159, 160, 161
American Negroes 92, 146
Anstandsdame, Anstandswauwau
  57, 60
anti-pornography movement 130,
  133–135
anxiety 4, 23
  see also lust anxiety and status
  anxiety
apartheid 127
ascent, social ascent
  individual 12,
  of whole groups 4, 12
attitude 34, 36, 101, 140, 142,
  150
avoidance, external and internal 151
aware, awareness 6, 41, 56, 59, 88, 94,
  148

ballroom 3, 19, 22, 60, 65, 66
balance of controls
  of social controls and self–controls
  3, 4, 8, 83, 85, 145, 148, 149, 151
balance of love and sex:
  see lust-balance

balance of power 1, 8, 91, 93, 124, 140,
  141,148, 149, 153, 154, 155
bachelor 26, 50, 52, 61, 73, 81, 119
bed-sitting room, bed-sitter 54, 61
bicycle, bicycling 18, 50, 51, 60, 66, 70,
  74
Black Americans 146, 147
blow job 141, 142
boarding school 52, 76, 86
bobbed hair 89
boundaries of decency 70, 71, 75, 120,
  127, 156
bourgeoisie 14,15, 49, 84,
  black 146, 147
breasts 112, 141, 142
business woman 35, 36, 37, 45, 52
business manners 39, 42, 44, 141

camaraderie 52, 53
campus, campuses 84, 86, 87, 88, 90,
  94, 106, 147
  campus mores 87, 88
carrot and stick mechanism 102
centres of power 1, 11, 12, 14, 84,
chaperone, chaperonage 1, 5, 6, 7, 18,
  21, 22, 24, 33, 47, 49–54, 57, 58, 60,
  64, 65, 75–86, 95, 99, 111, 116,
  120, 151
Chippendales 136, 137
Christian name 53, 66
civilizing offensive 110
class, classes 9, 12, 15, 19, 22, 40, 41,
  51, 58, 64, 75, 84, 85, 126, 145, 146,
  148, 150, 154, 159, 160, 140n
  higher, upper 11, 15, 16, 36, 51, 76,
  83, 86, 88
  lower 9, 11, 12, 20, 53, 97, 123, 147,
  152
  middle 11, 15, 18, 36, 50, 51, 53, 76,
  87, 95, 144, 147
club, clubs 16, 28, 52, 53, 66–68, 79,
  87, 100, 103, 119
  country club 77, 88
code, codes, social code 4, 12, 25, 26,
  34, 36, 42, 46, 47, 57, 61, 65, 87, 91,
  99, 100, 102–104, 112, 120, 125,
  133–135, 143, 146, 147, 151
  and ideals vii, 4, 7, 12, 47, 126

business 37, 42, 141
dating 49, 91, 93, 98, 140, 141n
double, co-existing 34, 36, 37, 39,
    41, 42, 46, 47, 91, 98, 110, 117,
    141, 142
dominant 12, 61, 124
of manners 12, 40, 41, 47, 77, 126,
    143
and emotion management viii, 41,
    148
paying and petting 93, 140
co-education, coeducation 65, 66,
    73, 76, 93
coeducational colleges 80, 87,
college 80, 84, 86, 87, 88, 90, 92, 93,
    95, 96, 99, 101, 102, 106, 107, 114,
    122, 141, 142
competition 5, 9, 15, 66, 94, 95, 96, 97,
    101, 102, 105, 108, 132, 145, 148
commercial 16, 40, 49, 86, 135
concert 51, 58, 61, 65,
confidence 44, 54, 67, 144
conflict, conflicts vii, 2, 12, 42, 83, 91,
    127, 128, 131, 145, 147, 150, 159
conflict management 114, 159
conscience 9, 61, 62, 105, 133, 137
contraception, contraceptives, contra-
    ceptive behaviour 82, 123, 126, 144,
    146
contracts 14, 15, 49
control vii, 2, 3, 4, 15, 25, 30, 48, 49,
    53, 70, 91, 92, 94, 144, 149, 150,
    153, 154
    parental control   5, 6, 7, 19, 64, 72,
    74, 84, 85, 87, 90, 91, 120, 140,
    145
    see social control   see also balance of
    controls
controlled decontrolling 9, 22, 85, 135,
    153
counter-impulses 8, 154
courtesy, courtesies 11, 27, 35, 42,
    44–46, 55, 67, 69, 75, 116, 119
courtship 4, 50, 56, 57, 60, 70, 74, 84,
    89, 96, 104, 106, 118, 119, 120, 148,
    150
courting 1, 6, 7, 17, 24, 39, 49, 50, 56,
    57, 59, 60– 62, 64, 67, 70, 71, 73,
    75, 86–88, 91, 94, 97, 105, 114,
    120, 148, 150
    courting regime1, 6, 7, 17, 47–50,
    57, 65, 85, 95, 119, 120, 125, 149,
    151
courtesy book, courtesy-book genre 14
cunnilingus 142
cultural lag 156

cut direct 17, 140n
cutting in 93, 95, 108, 140n
dance, dances, dancing 1, 2, 3, 5, 6, 18,
    20–23, 36, 51–54, 62, 64, 66, 73, 78,
    79, 82, 95, 96, 99, 103, 107, 148,
    152
    ballroom dance 19, 22
    college dance 80, 87, 143, 144
    lap dance 142
    private dance 19, 78, 79, 119
    public dance 1, 5, 19, 20, 66, 69, 78,
    taxi-dance 92, 140, 142
dancing shapes 105, 106, 110
date, dates, dating vii, 1, 3, 4, 6, 7, 24,
    30, 31, 49, 53, 56, 75, 83, 86–106,
    108–113,115–120, 122, 123, 140,
    142, 147, 148, 150
    blind date, double date, group date
    104
    date rape 160
dating manners, dating codes 39, 49,
    91, 93, 98, 110, 140, 141, 143, 141n
dating contest 109
    dating and rating contest 94, 96, 98,
    102, 106, 142
dating system, dating regime 6–8, 30,
    47, 49, 75, 84, 85, 86, 88, 91, 92,
    102, 106,108, 120, 122, 140–143,
    145, 147
    rise of, sociogenesis of 49, 50, 141,
    147
debutante 51, 88
deference, deferential distance 24, 49,
    53, 66, 67, 158
differentiation of social functions 2
dinner, dinner party 1, 16, 17, 31, 51,
    53, 56, 61, 66, 81, 113, 120
discipline, disciplining (of people) 9, 56
displays of inferiority and superiority
    10, 97, 149, 141n
    of distinction 2, 41
distance, social and psychic distance
    vii, 2, 5, 19, 39, 41, 47, 52, 65, 126,
    148, 150, 158, 160
distrust 84
divorce 54, 90, 128, 139, 149
double standard, code, morality 7, 39,
    44, 47, 61, 110, 117, 133, 141n
drawing room 5, 14, 15, 17, 18, 37
Dutch date, Dutch treat, going/go
dutch 30–32, 39, 92, 117

emancipation
    see also processes, emancipation
    chances 157, 159
    cramp 133

emancipation cont'd

demands 128, 130, 135, 153, 158

of women, female 5, 6, 7, 18, 41, 47, 69, 72, 74, 79, 93, 110, 120, 124, 126, 129, 135, 136, 140, 143, 148, 142n

of female sexuality 8, 110, 124, 126, 136, 139, 140

of emotions vii, 20, 21, 133, 135, 152

of sexuality 6, 55, 112, 126, 130, 133, 135, 137, 142, 151, 152, 155, 156

of younger generation 7, 47, 49, 53, 57, 89, 93, 120, 141, 143

emancipation-via-segregation 127, 129

embarrassment 9, 31, 32, 41, 42, 62, 71, 78, 95, 154, 156

emotion, emotions 1, 2, 8, 9, 22, 47, 48, 55, 68, 75, 108, 112, 126, 131, 160

emotion management 1, 2, 4, 9, 22, 41, 114, 159, 160

engaged (getting), engagement 4, 7, 17, 120, 121, 122, 123, 148

breaking off an 121, 122

eroticization 6, 48, 131, 133, 150–152

escort, escorts 24, 28, 29, 52, 54, 58, 60, 65, 79, 84, 95, 104.105, 107

etiquette 9, 10, 15, 15, 18, 25, 38, 42, 51, 52, 55, 69, 75–78, 81, 90, 98, 112, 116

Madame Etiquette 60, 65, 69, 122,

etiquette book vii, viii, 11, 12, 14, 22–25, 27, 35, 81, 90, 95

equal 6, 8, 40, 46

rights 44, 45, 63

equality, equalization 2, 26, 27, 29, 32, 34, 55, 74, 75, 113, 115, 117, 132, 143, 145

equanimity of the welfare state 159

facts of life 68, 72, 119

fast girls 53, 110

fear, social and sexual fears 133, 157

fear of social and psychic heights,

fear of rising 153, 154, 155

fear of social and psychic depths, fear of falling 152, 153, 155

fear of freedom 133, 134, 14

level of 145, 147

fellatio 142

female

emancipation 18, 41, 47, 120, 124, 129, 143

functions 45

female cont'd

leadership 44

lust 136, 137

sexuality 8, 89, 110, 123, 124–126, 136, 139, 140

sexual pleasure 125, 131, 136

solidarity 130

sources of power and identity 1, 5, 34, 35, 41, 69, 141

–submissiveness, subservience, resig nation 93, 149, 159

feminists, feminism 2, 45, 115, 117, 128–130, 134, 135, 138

femininity 26, 34, 37, 38, 55, 114, 115, 136

definitions/models of 18, 36, 50, 141n

feminization 136

fidelity, technical fidelity 138, 142

figuration, figurational ideal 5, 15, 139, 160

Fin de Siècle 2, 157

first nature 152, 153

flapper 53, 141n

flirt, flirting, flirtation 38, 42–44, 50, 51, 53, 56, 59–61, 67, 68, 70, 71, 84, 118

formal 16, 41, 43, 112

engagement 71, 108,

introductions 25, 51, 104

formality 2, 19, 39, 53, 71, 112

formalize, (re)formalization 2, 8, 9, 15, 116, 141

frankness 48, 72, 138, 157

fraternity, fraternity house 80, 87, 88, 91, 107, 143

Freak Brothers 142n

freedom 7, 8, 19, 21, 22, 26, 45, 52, 53, 58, 63, 65, 68, 70, 71, 73, 76–78, 83, 87, 93, 103, 111, 113, 122, 135, 143, 147, 154, 158

friends, friendship 50–54, 57, 58, 60–62, 71, 73, 74, 77, 83, 84, 88, 95, 101, 107, 110, 123, 126, 142, 155, 158

frigid, frigidity 62, 125

generation, generations 9, 10, 20, 49, 53, 64, 70, 72, 74, 85, 87–91, 93, 97, 109, 114, 120, 124, 125, 128–130, 140, 141, 143, 144, 146, 147, 150, 152, 154, 157

getting stuck 6, 95

girl

fast girl 53, 110

girl-epidemic 72

girl cont'd
good–bad girl 89, 95, 99
good society 1, 4, 5, 10, 11, 12, 14, 15,
    16, 17, 34, 36, 37, 40, 41, 51, 75, 84,
    88, 97, 141, 146, 141n
    modelling function of 10, 11
    good-society roles, attitudes, codes
    34, 36, 37, 143
gossip, gossiping 8, 14, 16, 49, 65, 75,
    80, 81, 118
going all the way 111, 141, 142
going out/going somewhere 5, 6, 19,
    24, 29, 58, 73, 86, 91,
going steady 6, 7, 94, 101, 102,
    105–111, 113, 116, 119, 120, 123
guilt 113, 117, 127, 128, 131

habitus, social habitus 4, 9, 11, 37, 85,
    141
Hollywood 13
homosexuals, homosexuality 2,
    126–128, 130, 138, 154
honour 49, 54, 101
hooking up 142
host, hostess 22, 23, 46, 51, 52, 78, 79,
    91
hotel 16, 63, 69, 80

ideal, ideals, 3, 6, 10, 12, 36, 37, 41–43,
    48, 49, 72, 77, 91, 105, 108,
    115,120, 123, 127, 130, 131,
        137–139, 149, 150, 153, 158–161
identification 4, 148
    mutual identification vii, 2, 150
    with the established 2, 11, 69, 135,
    137, 153
identity 21, 128, 130, 146, 156, 160
    I–identity, personal identity 3, 11, 47
    sources of 1, 5, 15, 17, 22, 34, 35,
    41, 69, 141, 149, 154, 155, 157
    we–identity, group identity 3, 11, 47
ideology 83
    –national ideology 77, 83, 85
ideological lip service 77
ideological resistance 84
impersonal, impersonal machine,
impersonality 35–38, 99, 143
impotence, impotent 155
impulses 8, 48, 89, 105, 108, 152
    sexual 126, 130, 133, 135, 145, 154,
    155
    see also counter–impulses
independence, independent 14, 65, 77,
    92, 115, 159, 143, 159
    financial 26–30, 33, 34, 46, 55, 60,
    93, 133, 149

individualizing, individualization 3,
    130, 136
inequality 2, 49, 145, 146, 148, 149,
    154
    harmonious 3, 138, 149
inferiority, inferiority feelings 3, 5, 10,
    148, 149
    gestures of, displays of 2, 5, 10
informal 3, 43, 50, 61, 78, 87, 105,
    116, 152
informality 67, 116
informalization vii, 1–4, 9, 22, 26, 41,
    46, 48, 126, 133, 152
integration, social integration, integration
    processes vii, 1, 2, 3, 4, 7, 8, 10, 41, 93,
    120, 121, 139, 140, 142, 143, 145,
    147, 148, 152–154,157, 159–161
interdependency networks, networks of
    interdependence 2, 5, 148, 150, 152
internalize, internalization 4, 82, 83, 85,
    141, 143
intimacy 6, 47, 50, 52, 86, 90, 94, 104,
    108, 110, 113, 116, 120, 125, 128,
    133–136, 139, 150, 151, 156, 157,
    159, 160
introduce, introduction viii, ix, 6, 10,
    14, 25, 39, 52, 55, 61, 62, 64, 69, 74,
    90, 104,119, 132, 139, 146 141n
invite, invitation 14, 16, 17, 19, 20,
    23–25, 30, 31, 36, 40, 43, 46, 51, 52,
    54, 55, 59, 61, 65, 66, 72, 73, 77,
    80, 81, 102, 113, 119, 149

jazz 20, 23, 51, 91, 100
jealousy 36, 126, 128, 155, 156

kiss, kissing viii, 7, 24, 64, 70, 71, 86,
    89, 92, 98, 99–101, 104, 105, 111,
    112, 120, 121, 142, 148
knowledge 11, 17, 68, 148, 158

living together 64, 115, 119
leg, legs 44, 71, 72, 74,
lesbian 128, 129, 134
line 6, 49, 95–97, 99, 100
love 6, 7, 31, 41, 43, 46–48, 55–57, 59,
    60, 62, 68, 71, 72, 84–87, 97, 101,
    103–107, 113–117, 119, 121, 123,
    124, 126–128, 130, 131, 133, 134,
        137–142, 150, 151,153, 156,
            158–160, 142n
    make love 81, 82, 103, 114, 129,
    135, 136, 152, 160
    puppy love 101, 106, 107
lust 48, 55, 113, 114, 124, 128,
    134–136, 139, 157

lust cont'd
    anxiety 153, 154, 156 158
    economy 47, 140n
    path of 94, 156
    revival 126, 135, 137, 140
lust balance, lust-balance 6, 7, 8, 47, 48,
    55, 89, 93, 105, 113, 115, 118,
        120, 123–126, 128, 130, 133, 134,
           136–140, 142, 148–151, 153, 154,
           156–160, 140n
lust-balance question 6, 105, 120, 124,
    142n

male courtesies 42, 97,
male dominance 93, 143, 148
male double standard 110
male mysticism 128
male nudity 135, 136
male oppression 93, 130
male pride 25, 39, 92,
male sexuality 125, 129, 139, 140
manners
    see also code/regime of 1–3, 5, 6,
        8–13,15–17, 25–27, 34, 38–42, 44,
        47, 49, 55, 57, 58, 61, 66, 73, 74,
        77, 121, 138, 154
    business/office manners 5, 7, 39, 42,
        44, 141, 142, 149
    courting / dating manners 39, 49, 56,
        73, 106, 141, 142
    drawing-room/good-society manners
        5, 47
    manners books 1, 2, 4–6, 8, 10, 11, 15,
        16, 19, 23, 30, 32, 34, 43, 45, 49, 50,
        52, 57–61, 66, 67, 70, 71, 74, 75, 79,
        80, 84, 89, 98, 99, 107, 115, 119,
        120, 121, 124, 125, 146, 148,
        150, 140n
    genre of 35, 146
masculinity, masculinization 114, 115,
    136
masturbate, masturbation 55, 115, 131,
    132, 136, 141
marital duty 48
marriage 4, 17, 34, 45, 48, 49, 57, 58, 60,
    61, 63, 64, 67, 68, 88–90, 102, 106,
    110, 111, 113, 119–122, 127, 133,
    138, 139, 141, 147–150, 158–160
mobility, upward 12, 15, 16, 148
moral indignation 39, 72, 130, 132,
    133, 135
mutual consent 112–114, 120, 149,
    151, 152
mutual identification vii, 4, 150
mutual suspicion 4, 145, 147, 148,
mutual trust 4, 111, 139, 145, 147

money 16, 24, 27, 28, 30, 32, 39, 40, 59,
    73, 91–94, 100, 102, 108, 115, 117,
    142, 145, 142n
    paying, pay 5, 7, 8, 22, 24–32, 39,
        40, 46, 47, 55, 80, 92, 93, 100,
        116, 117, 141
Mrs Grundy 22, 54, 63, 79, 80, 81, 120
music 3, 23,
    unwanted 23
    wild 6,19,
mutually expected self–restraint, MES
    4, 111, 126, 145, 150, 151

national
    code 4,
    differences/varieties vii, 5, 7, 8, 47,
        83, 85, 119, 143
    habitus 85
    ideology 77
    pattern 37
nationalist, nationalism 59, 65, 67, 83
necking 6, 49, 88–91, 98, 100,
    102–104, 108–111
nostalgia, nostalgic 55, 67, 76
nouveaux riches 9, 157
nude, nudity 109, 135, 136

office 37, 40, 41, 43, 143
    machine 37, 45
    party, parties 42, 43
    romance 38, 46
    wolf, wolves 39, 42
    see also manners, office
one-night stand 56, 118, 120, 134
one-partner craze 22, 23
openness 129, 138, 148

parents17, 19, 23, 31, 32, 53, 54, 57, 61,
    62, 64, 65, 69, 70, 72–74, 76, 82–85,
    87, 88, 90, 92, 93, 98, 103–106, 108,
    114, 116, 119, 120, 138, 144–146,
    149, 150, 153
park, parking 92, 98, 101, 104, 106
party, parties 17, 51, 53–55, 61, 77, 80,
    84, 116,
    bachelor 52
    children's 57
    petting 90
    teen/teenage 57, 82,
    see also dinner party, office party
parvenu 77
passion, passionate 48, 57, 59, 61, 68,
    106, 113, 136, 139, 154
peers, peer group 87, 90, 94, 103, 144,
    146
    peer-group pressure 90, 94, 95

peers, peer group cont'd
  peer-group code 91, 98–100
permissive, permissiveness 2, 55, 56, 107, 114
personality 9, 11, 94, 126, 137, 153, 154
  structure ix, 9, 135, 152
pet, petting 6, 49, 88, 89–91, 95, 96, 98–100, 102–104, 110, 111, 141, 142
  as a demonstration of conformity 94
  as a ritual/convention 90, 94, 141
  paying and petting 93, 102, 140–142, 150
  contest 96
phase, phases 5, 41, 70, 114, 126
  in integration processes 159
  of accommodation and resignation 157, 159
  of emancipation and resistance 157, 158
  of informalisation 2
  of sexual emancipation 113
  of transition, transitional phases 61
pick up, pick–up girl 31, 50, 104, 116
play, playing 32, 57, 60, 68, 89, 97, 102, 107, 114, 118, 150, 155, 161
  around 109
  marriage/courtship 111, 150
  with fire, with danger 59, 72, 150
Playgirl 130, 135, 137
pleasure, sexual/erotic 27, 103, 106, 112, 115, 118, 119, 125, 127, 130, 133, 138, 148, 150, 155
  female (sexual) pleasure 89, 110, 111, 132, 133, 135–137
  male (sexual) pleasure 132
  pleasure economy 153, 160, 140n
political correctness 4, 116
popularity 90, 94, 95, 96, 102, 103, 108
  contest, competition 94, 95, 98, 100, 141
  promiscuous 102, 105
pornography, pornographization 126, 129–135, 137
pornoviolence 132
power 4, 5, 30, 46, 48, 87, 93, 110, 114, 128, 134, 135
  centres 1, 4, 11, 12, 14, 84
  inequalities 2, 151
  power-feminism 138
  power and dependency relationships 150, 159
  sources 1, 5, 15, 17, 22, 34, 35, 41, 69, 84, 141, 149, 154, 155, 157, 160

power cont'd
  transfer 24, 25, 30, 31, 33, 34, 92
  see also balance; balance of power
private vii, 15, 43, 66, 82, 84, 147
  ball, ballroom 19, 66, 87
  club 66, 119
  dance 19, 78, 79, 119
  life, occassions, sphere 12, 26, 35, 37, 41, 44, 84, 114, 134
process, processes viii, ix, 2, 3, 5, 10, 12, 29, 48, 67, 85–87, 91, 95, 96, 106, 112, 114, 131, 150, 152, 154, 157
  accommodation 4, 113, 125, 153, 155
  'civilization', 'civilizing' 139, 149
  collective 126, 157
  emancipation 4, 12, 18, 47, 49, 72, 113, 120, 153, 155, 157, 158
  emancipation and integration 1, 3, 8, 140, 153
  formalizing/formalization 9
  see formalize, (re)formalization
  informalization (*see*) 1–4, 9, 22, 26, 126, 133, 152,
  integration (*see*) 2, 4, 41, 93, 120, 139, 148, 159, 160
  learning 34, 126, 135, 155
  overall, general vii, 4, 150
  part-process 1, 47, 93
  process-continuity 84, 97, 144
promiscuity, promiscuous 89, 90, 98–100, 102, 105, 114, 119, 120
prostitute, prostitution 53, 141n, 142n
protection 24, 31, 35, 39, 42, 44, 49, 55, 56, 58, 61, 64, 78–81, 83, 85, 94, 104, 114, 116, 137, 147, 148, 149, 151, 153
pub, pubs 29, 55, 62–64, 127
public viii, 1, 18, 26, 30, 35, 43, 51, 58, 66, 71, 76, 84–86, 91, 92, 134, 136, 140n
  agenda 113, 124
  attention, eye, interest, concern, opinion 10, 65, 122, 125, 130, 132
  dance, dance halls1, 5, 19, 20, 69, 78
  debates, discussion 2, 7, 123, 124, 126, 130, 133, 158
  publication gap (of manners books) 46, 74
puritan, puritanical 21, 89, 100, 135
puppy love, *see* love

raging hormones 111, 119, 144
rank, ranking vii, viii, 2, 4, 8, 11, 33, 48, 97, 129
rating 6

rating cont'd
and dating 94, 102, 142
reality-congruent 153
regime, regimes
courting 1, 6–8, 47, 48, 64, 65, 85,
95, 119, 120, 125, 149, 151
dating, *see* dating system / regime
escort 58,
parental 7, 47, 57, 93, 143–145
of manners and emotions 8, 9, 140n
of emotion management 9
reflexive, reflexivity, (level of) 9, 73,
75, 85, 135, 153, 158, 160
regularities
in processes of emancipation and
integration 8, 153, 155, 159, 160
reputation 1, 14, 16, 17, 49, 54, 63, 65,
85, 99, 110, 121, 125
respect 1, 2, 4, 5, 8, 12, 14, 27, 28, 35,
38, 43, 49, 69, 79, 82, 92, 109, 110,
127, 144, 146, 149, 159, 160
respectable, respectability 1, 4, 14, 17,
18, 50, 53, 54, 76, 85, 118, 125, 159
restaurant 16, 20, 27, 41, 56, 63, 69,
81, 103
rite de passage 43
rights 12, 34, 140
equal rights 44, 45, 63
right to courtesy 46
right to earn, work 5, 33, 46, 147,
149
right to pay 5, 7, 8, 25, 28, 29, 31,
33, 47
rink, skating rink, ice rink 58, 60, 66,
100
Roaring Twenties 2, 53, 99, 157
romance 27, 67, 85, 86, 101, 102, 106,
112, 116, 119, 139
novels 135, 137
see also office romance
romantic 48, 53, 100, 101, 103, 106,
107, 112, 117–119, 124, 130, 131, 160
romanticize, romanticization 48, 72,
76, 130, 138, 158

second nature 9, 152, 153
second shift 34, 143
secretary 36, 41, 43, 45, 75
segregation 5, 20, 49, 68, 69, 71, 76, 93
see self-segregation
self-control, -command, -possession
3, 4, 8, 37, 47, 49, 54, 75, 76, 80, 81,
83, 85, 95, 101, 144, 145, 151, 154
self-discipline 14
self-protection 80, 83, 85, 149
self-regulation vii, 8, 9, 12, 22, 47, 56,

self-regulation cont'd 75, 130, 152–154,
159
self-restraints vii, 2, 8, 111, 126
see mutually expected
self-respect 104, 149, 160
self-segregation 127
sensitive, sensitivity 9, 41, 43, 56, 75,
85, 114, 128, 133, 137, 139, 148,
150, 151, 160, 161
sex, sexy 26, 27, 33, 34, 36, 38, 39,
41–43, 47, 48, 55, 56, 75, 87, 90, 93,
96, 97, 104–107, 109–118, 120,
122, 124–129, 131–142,
144–146, 150, 151, 153, 154,
156, 157, 160, 142n
see also eroticization of sex
equality 34, 55
instant, anonymous 127, 155
soft sex 129, 130
sexual 15, 31, 38, 43, 48, 56, 91, 92, 93,
95, 96, 104–107, 110, 113, 116, 120,
126, 127, 129–132, 134, 138–141,
145, 146, 148, 151, 154–156, 160,
161
activity, behaviour, practices 6, 87,
89, 91, 94, 104, 109, 110, 129,
135, 139, 140, 144–146, 148,
154, 156, 157
advances 91, 109
advice books 7, 124, 125
attraction, sex–appeal 34, 39, 41,
112, 113
conquest 31, 131
consciousness 89, 126, 139, 152,
160, 161
experiments, exploration 17, 63, 89,
114, 120, 121, 127, 141
fantasies 127, 134
freedom, licence, leniency 51, 63,
113, 122, 123, 127
generosity, generous 112, 113
gratification, fulfilment 6, 47, 48, 56,
106, 117, 126, 129, 139, 151, 155,
157
harassment 38, 39, 42, 43, 75, 129,
143, 160
intercourse, consummation 48, 62,
89, 111, 125, 131, 142, 144
impulses, emotions 126, 130, 133,
134, 152, 154, 155
intimacy 110, 121, 133, 141
liberation 126–129
longing, desire, feelings 54, 69, 106,
110–112, 125–127, 130, 133, 139,
154, 156
object 6, 110, 116, 133, 134

sexual cont'd
oppression, dominance 9, 126, 129
pleasure, *see* pleasure
relation, partner 6, 82, 95, 96, 144,
160
restraint 89, 91
Revolution 7, 38, 55, 111, 112, 114,
115, 120, 123–126, 128, 129, 134,
138, 151, 154, 156, 142n
subject 6, 111, 116, 133, 154
sphere, area 14, 110
violence 93, 129, 130, 131, 139
sexuality 34, 41, 48–50, 55, 72, 75, 89,
105, 112, 120–127, 129, 131, 136,
137, 139–141, 144, 145, 149, 152,
154, 155
of younger generation 7, 49, 89, 104
male-dominated 140, 142
lust-dominated 6, 48, 124, 128
relationship-dominated 6, 48, 124, 128
see emancipation of
see female
sexualization of love 6, 48, 150–152,
160
shame, shameful, shaming 10, 72, 103,
115, 121, 128, 131, 133, 153, 154,
156
fear 10, 154
single woman, female, girl, man 54, 55,
61, 67, 81, 109, 116
slippery slope 68, 99, 103
snubbing, snub 16, 17, 99
art of 16, 17,
spiral movement, spiral process, 2–4,
159
sociability 14, 39, 40
social contraints towards self–restraints
vii, 2
social controls 4, 9, 49, 76, 85, 151, 154
external 3, 8, 49, 54, 81, 83, 85, 95,
97, 144, 145, 151
internal, *see also* self-controls 8, 83,
85, 145, 151
social legacy 7, 143
sociogenesis 50, 141, 147
sport, sports 5, 18, 19, 58–61, 66, 68,
73, 95, 103, 118, 119, 140n, 141n
stag line 6, 93, 95, 107, 108
status 2, 4, 8–10, 33, 39, 54, 62, 88, 123
competition 5, 9, 96, 102, 132, 148,
defeats, decline, loss 10, 49, 149,
fears, anxieties, insecurity 9, 10, 49,
79, 145

steady, *see* going steady
stripper 136, 142
supervise, supervision 69, 75, 82, 83,
85, 90, 97, 143, 144, 154
superiority feelings, gestures, displays
2, 4, 5, 10, 97, 148, 149, 141n
suspicion 4, 49, 61, 63, 73, 84, 139,
145, 147, 148
synthesis 5, 37, 39, 42, 46, 142

taxi-dance hall 92, 140
teenage pregnancies 144, 146
third nature 152, 153
theatre 29, 51, 52, 58, 61, 72
thrill, thrill-seeking, quest/pursuit of
thrill 89, 94, 98, 118
treat, treats 24, 28, 40, 91, 116
see also dutch treat 30–32, 92, 117
trust 14, 49, 60, 78, 81, 83, 106,
109–111, 144, 145, 150
see also mutual trust
tours 73, 147
cycle or bicycle, skating 60, 62, 66,

virgin, technical verginity 72, 142,
verkering 70, 123
victim feminism, victimism 138,
vice–epidemic 72
visit, visiting, visiting hours viii, 1, 16,
17, 50, 52, 54, 58, 61–63, 65, 69, 71,
73,

wasp 146
we–identity, *see* identity
We–I balance 3, 4, 8, 11, 148, 151
welfare state, arrangements, systems
145, 146, 149, 159,
equanimity of the 159
wife, wives 14–16, 43, 49, 50, 57, 63,
67, 99, 133, 144, 147, 152, 155, 159,
141n
women's movement 7, 93, 124, 125,
128–130, 132, 135, 138, 147, 150,
work, workplace 5, 7, 12, 17, 24, 26,
30, 33–36, 38–47, 61, 62, 66, 97,
115, 117, 135, 142, 143, 147, 141n
sex-is-work view 133

youth culture 6, 13, 49, 50, 74, 86, 91,
93, 94, 120, 124, 125, 143

zigzag spiral movement 3
zipless fuck 127, 128, 133